MAYOTTE:
THE MUSINGS OF A NARCISSIST
A SURVIVOR'S STORY
BY DOUG PROBST

Mayotte: The Musings of a Narcissist.

A Survivor's Story.

Book Editor: Yasmin Gruss
Book Cover Design: Anthony Coombs

ISBN: 978-1-7363629-3-8

Acknowledgements

This book is dedicated to all of the children in the world who have suffered physical and sexual abuse. I know what it's like to cry out in pain and no one hears you. I listened. I heard you. There will be no more suffering.

I also dedicate this book to everyone who died of AIDS and are now suffering and dying from COVID-19. But I especially want to remember my friends who died on the streets of Long Beach from a virus that had no name yet. I'll never let the world forget you. Many people have made significant contributions to this work:

My wife, Marie Probst has been invaluable to me not only for her dedication and commitment to providing her knowledge and talents, but also for pushing me to finish this book when I was worried and felt depleted. She's truly my heroine and I could not have completed my life's story without her help. I love you honey.

For my son Joshua Probst, I thank you for being my biggest supporter, an honorable and trustworthy man, and loving me unconditionally even when I made my mistakes. I'm honored to call you son. I love you.

To a true partner, Neal Eglash. I thank you for your expertise, your generosity and being the most loyal friend one could ever have.

To Ritch Esra, for your insightful, sensitive understanding of who I am, I cherish our friendship.

My dear friend, John Michael Cox, for loving me, advising me and protecting me even when I didn't know it.

To Yasmin Sara, my editor. Your guidance, expertise and willingness to work on my oddball terms were an invaluable asset. Thank you for everything!

Matthew Rettenmund, no words can express how grateful I am for being my biggest champion. Your honesty has made me a better writer and I'm eternally grateful for your availabilty and belief in me.

To Anthony Coombs, my book cover deigner, thank you for saving my butt at the last minute!

To Tony Trujillo, and incredible artist and a lifelong friend who drew the amazing likeless of me that graces the backcover. I love you Tony. Thank you

To Michael Heintz, your love and willingness to contribute time and resources to this project are immensely appreciated. I treasure our friendship.

To Meyer Persow, my Iron Man. You're a brother and a soul mate in one. Your support has been invaluable from the very beginning. I love you.

My gratitude is endless to Sandra Meadows, Dr. Douglas Davies, Stephen Michael Shearer, Darrel Larson, The Rev. Maria Wilson, The Rev. Ken Goodban, Johnnie Millan, Michael Michaud, Duane Abner and Jon McCool, in addition to the many other teachers I've had throughout my life; helping me with the process of growing up.

And many thanks to Dr. Adi Jaffe for your belief in my music talents.

To all of my fans, I cherish all of you and I'm eternally grateful for your love and support.

And for all the musicians, singers and bands famous and unknown, that I've worked with in my life; I've learned many lessons from all of you. Thank you for putting up with my dictatorial style of music leadership.

I want to thank all of my counseling clients and AA comrades who taught me that I can preach a better sermon with my life than with my lips.

To Mindy, the mother of my son: Thank you for being a mother our son could always count on.

And of course to Archie, our Boston Terrier, your boundless energy, farting and unconditonal love have made both Marie and I better furbaby parents. To anyone I've not mentioned here, I'm grateful for all of you too.

I think it's a mistake to ever look for hope outside of one's self. One day the house smells of fresh bread, the next of smoke and blood. One day you faint because the gardener cuts his finger off, within a week you're climbing over corpses of children bombed in a subway. What hope can there be if that is so?
– Arthur Miller

1

A Room With a View

Hollywood California, Roosevelt Hotel, Top Floor, 1985

"Oh! Oh! Show me your male genitalia!"
"Oh God! You're so manly. You're so virile!"

The mystical orange glow of a sunset is illuminating the sky over Hollywood on this late afternoon, the fifth day of October, 1985. Into the night, the skies bestow colors that flood crystalline beauty into this hot, thirsty, desert world.

Two men have scheduled a rendezvous. One man is an investor, the other an entrepreneur. Neither one knows the other by his real name. Concealing identities is essential. Secrecy bonds the men.

There's a lot of truth that shouldn't be passed around.

They meet in the Hollywood Roosevelt Hotel, on the top floor. The investor always rents the most expensive suite. He spends handsomely for his pleasure.

The suite is actually two large rooms — they adjoin, but there's a divide. A king-size bed sits undisturbed in the suite. It will not be touched. It has no relevance for their meeting. All the action today will be done on the floor.

I'm the entrepreneur. It's what I like to call myself, but it's not what my clients call me. You could say there's confusion over who and what I am.

When I knock on the door, I hear a barrage of frustrated barking from my friend inside. As he opens the door and sees me, he becomes overwhelmed with giddy, childlike excitement. The two of us have respect for each other, and when we meet, it's a sincerely warm occasion. I believe he's expressing more than just sexual craving for me. We care for one another in our own unique way. Of course, I'm impressed by the room, a rich man's suite. I've seen many of these lavish rooms before, and it feels like home.

As I enter, right on schedule, the investor goes back to toying with his camera, voicing his frustration with the machinery he's purchased. He wants to film this event to relive it in the future, but even his best efforts at operating the camera are ineffectual. He simply can't figure out how to get his equipment to work and gives up.

The investor starts the show, getting naked and lying on the floor, lowering his bloated belly on top of a towel. He's short, maybe 5' 5", but his magnanimous personality makes him seem much larger.

Though he's a wealthy and very powerful man in New York, he exudes an innocent, trusting charm that's genuinely uncomplicated. I'm wearing my favorite tight white t-shirt with "Beverly Hills University" emblazoned on the front. I'm also wearing tight 1985 stone-washed jeans, so I feel like a stud.

He's getting excited as I take my clothes off, and I stand in front of him so he can receive the maximum visual pleasure he's paying for. In the middle of this, I make sure I'm positioned near the mirror on the wall. I need to visually confirm that my hair stays perfect throughout our activity.

I've never met a reflective surface I didn't like.

I see in the mirror a smooth, tanned, blonde-mulleted twink with a big dick that gets hard in seconds. I have the exact right look at the exact right time, which is why I got this job.As he moves, he begins shrieking with animalistic passion. Every sentence he shouts engulfs the room with furious pleasure. The odd quirk? His pornographic outbursts are punctuated with unsexy words describing sex.

"Oh! Oh! Show me your male genitalia! Oh my God! You're so manly — so virile! Tell me about performing coitus!!"

Performing coitus? I guess this would sound hot if you get off on encyclopedias. Princeton meets porno.

I'm the only witness to the glorious howling of an articulate beast with impeccable syntax.

The rich, fat man exclaims his pleasure as he grinds his corpulent, fleshy pelvis further into the hotel carpet.

"You like to fuck pussy, don't you?!"

Now I know his enjoyment is reaching a fevered pitch. He stares at my erection as I stand directly in his view, bored but boned and making my usual valiant effort to keep him happy.

"Tell me how much you like to fuck pussy," he rasps. "Don't hold back now. Your sexuality is so manly and robust!"

"I love to fuck pussy!" I say in a deep voice. "It feels so wet and warm around my dick!"

That's true. I do love to fuck pussy.

"I'm getting horny thinking about fucking, my dick is getting harder," I tease him. "Do you see how hard my dick is?"

"C'mon, tell me about fucking pussy!" he shouts. "I know you fuck a lot of pussy — I want to hear!"

2

While stroking my cock to help keep it hard and firm, I shout, "I fucked Angie last night. My God, her pussy was tight and wet, so fucking warm. and I'm gonna cum if I keep stroking my dick!"

True again.

"Oh! Oh, God! That's so exciting!" he wails. "I bet you thrust into her with manly force! You're so masculine, so male!"

I better be male, since I work very hard at it. I have a boyish face, but my body looks like it's chiseled from stone. What's interesting to me is how much my weight lifting is paying off. I guess my workouts are like investments. I've also noticed I do better financially the tanner I am. It's simple, really. The better I look, the more money I make.

My mind wanders, but I go back to work. After all, I do like working for him.

"Tell me about how you achieved climax while performing coitus!" he demands.

It's easy for me to give him what he wants. "I rammed her creamy pussy harder and harder!" I say. "Fuck! My eight and a half inch cock is straining to shoot my load now... I mean now!"

The longer I keep my penis erect, the more generous he'll be. This is an honorable man. He's honest and kind to me. I admire him and I've learned a lot from him. After all, I'm a cocky, manipulative twenty-one-year-old without any accomplishments to speak of, and he is a distinguished, prominent person on Wall Street. He's certainly distinguishing himself on the floor of the Hollywood Roosevelt Hotel right now, albeit in a way his colleagues would find impossible to believe.

He must like women also, because he has a wife and daughter and he doesn't want to hear about men having sex with each other, he only wants to hear about how my erection has been inserted into as many vaginas as possible. He rolls around on the towel with rabid carnality, staring up at my hard-on, howling questions at me.

He never requests any physical interaction between us. He's never once asked to touch me. This is good, because I don't think he has enough money to entice me to fulfill that request. Then again, I know he's got more money than God, and I probably would let God have his or her way with me for enough cash. Deep inside, I know money is my master.

I've heard it said that there's only one class in the community that thinks more about money than the rich, and that's the poor. The poor can think of nothing else. I know which class I'm in, I'm a poor street whore. I'm the asphalt of society. At least I can be proud that I'm the hottest street whore around. I'm a lonely vagabond scavenging for table scraps, pretending I fit into a world that's never wanted me from birth, but at least I'm the best-looking one.

I'm the top of the bottom, which is funny because I'm also a top who looks like a bottom.

I advertise my services in the escorts section of "The Advocate," the national gay magazine, but I don't even know if I'm gay. Call me gay for pay, I don't really give a fuck.

I like to portray to the rest of the world that I have deeper values than what's between my legs, but I need to make money. So fuck the rest of the world. I need to play the role I'm required to play to survive. The biggest spenders like Shawn Mayotte, and they fantasize that I'm some rich white boy from Orange County, so that's how I behave and that's how I look. I've learned how to act.

"C'mon, Shawn! I need to hear you tell me how you filled her vagina with your full blood engorged erection!"

His shrieking jolts me out of my temporary self-analytical state. I've gotta get back to work. I've gotta make him happy. I'll keep my dick hard no matter how strange the scene before me is.

He thrusts his torso into the carpet as if he's making love to it. The room is filled with his guttural groans. He barks at me loudly. Changing things up, I grab my heavy balls.

"Yes!" he shouts. "Show me those testicles. They're so round and full." I lift my erection up so my balls dangle directly in front of his face, showing them off just like he requests. I'm trying so hard to please my mentor, even if the only thing that matters to him is my body, which is what seems to matter the most to everyone I've ever met. I don't know if that's bad or good. I only know that since I was a boy, my body parts get me the attention I crave. I'm beginning to feel aggravated, but his voice is so unique and peculiar in his fantasy state that my aggravation quickly changes back to listening and learning — I'm trying to understand him.

"Oh! Oh God! This is so sexual!" he says, stating the obvious. "Oh, Shawn, keep your erection full and hard!"

I'm fascinated, but I'm also tired and I want to lie down. This is not good — I've gotta keep it up, in both senses of the phrase, and keep the fat man happy.

Plus, I can't lie down because I'll ruin my hair.

I've seen repulsive and deviant sexuality in my short life. I feel like I've already lived a thousand perverted lifetimes. Sex was a family affair when I was growing up. Nothing he's doing bothers me. This is how he enjoys himself, and I'm being paid to perform, not to judge. Still, it's not easy to keep an erection while watching a massive heap of flesh undulate before me.

His wailing is so primeval, it sounds like he's suffering. A sweaty, balding, obese old man grinding his dick into the floor in front of me (isn't that painful?) is not very arousing. At least his genitals are out of my sight. He keeps them on the towel, pleasing himself in his own unique and personal way. For me, it's not personal — it's business, so I stay hard.

He's so far into sexual heaven the floor is shaking. His sexual obsession with me has a singleness of purpose about it. It's who I am, and that's what he pays for. He's even paid to watch me perform with girls, which is my favorite way to get paid. It's not hard work to fuck a gorgeous girl in front of a nice, rich man, and then get paid two or three thousand dollars for it.

And though I care about my girls, when our fucking is over, I'm in charge of the distribution of wealth. She's lucky I've found this guy for her to make easy money. They're usually grateful — especially Angie. She knows she wouldn't be able to make this kind of money if I didn't call her. While I'm pumping her hard, he gets right down there, where even I'd love to be, and watches my cock thrust in and out of the lucky pussy I have chosen. It's a living.

I don't feel revulsion for any person's fantasy, especially any fantasy involving me. That's society's problem, the affliction of judgment. They used to say, "If the judge gets a hard-on, it must be obscene." Just last week I gave a judge a hard-on, I remember with a smile.

To me, true revulsion is sitting through a badly acted, poorly scripted Hollywood movie, the kind for which famous directors are praised for steamrolling over a character's head to get laughs and millions of dollars from millions of twelve-year olds. I'm revolted by dishonest hypocrites. Cruelty is revolting. Lying is revolting. Doing nothing while someone is crying out for help is revolting.

My father's terrifying rage was revolting. I get angry myself, and when I get angry, I, too, sometimes react explosively. I hate that part of me. I believe I'm kind and compassionate, and these are values I admire when I see them in other men. I think differently than other guys my age. Or I think I think differently.

My mind is racing with a million thoughts. My head sometimes feels like a popcorn machine, with thoughts popping like kernels, falling back into the machine, landing aimlessly, pointlessly, directionless. Although I'm still standing here, my penis pointing straight out, my mind is twisted, and I'm trying to convince myself I'm not doing anything to be ashamed of.

I think about all of this while keeping an erection. I've become an expert at mentally distancing myself during these activities. My dick comes first.

"Motherfucker!" I growl. "I'm about to explode all over the place!"

He should be appreciative of my improvised sex talk. I never know which lines could translate into a couple of thousand more bucks. Every syllable, every bead of sweat uniting his crown of perspiration, represents another $100 bill. This fucking guy is sweating $100 bills in front of me.

Get it over with already, rich, fat man!

And yet, it's not just about the money. I want his approval. I realize he's the father I never had. I don't care if my dad's getting off looking at my cock thrusting in and out of a girlfriend's vagina, I need his praise. Oh, how I crave a father's admiration. I'll keep my dick hard, and Dad will be proud! But his needs are fucking endless. I really shouldn't complain. I know that once the ritual is over we'll have a magnificent conversation, and I'll ask a ton of questions regarding topics and people to which only he is privy.

It doesn't matter that he's sexually aroused by young, blonde men and their rock-hard cocks — he converses with the President of the United States, Ronald Reagan. He has respect for ol' Ronnie. He sees Mr. Reagan as a real person, not a typical Washington political phony. He admires him because he feels that Ronnie toiled among the working class, came from the Heartland, giving him a perspective on the American people not shared by the Washington establishment.

I like hearing about his other pals, too, like Donald T. and Jay Rockefeller. He went to a West Virginia College football game with Jay just this week. He refers to Mr. T. as "Donny." He calls him brash, a natural born thief and a liar, but he likes his determination. I don't know my client's exact vocation, but it entails mergers and acquisitions. The most he'll reveal is that after he's through putting a deal together, he and his friends split the proceeds, which run into seven figures at times.

His animated personality and sincerity of heart while answering my inquiries fascinate me. He's a moral man. He speaks with conviction and authority. After our conversation, he'll need to attend to business (wanting me to return to the hotel for another round), and then he'll pluck at least $2,000 out of his coat pocket hanging in the closet. I'll be two thousand times happier this weekend. I'm learning while earning.

5

Who is he? He claims his name is Travis, but I know that's a lie. He's very protective of his true identity, probably because his friends on Wall Street wouldn't understand (nor would his wife, I suppose). He's no name-dropper, only someone who is genuinely on a first-name basis with presidents and titans of industry.

I wonder if he really cares about me, or if he's only here to get off. I like to think he has seen something special in me, some inner quality he admires. Someday I'll find out exactly who he is and what he does that makes him so important and powerful.

But today's not that day. Today, my erection and I are what's important and powerful. I'll play whatever game he wants to play.

Without warning, a vague uneasiness travels through my mind. It moves into my body, and soon, a palpable feeling of dread manifests within me. It's physical as well as mental. It starts talking to me. I call it the voice in my head. It's attempting to cast its usual gloom over everything.

But look at how you're earning this money. You're doing something disgusting. You're sick. You're really fucking sick, just like your father. You're a fucking prostitute. With men. You know what your friends would say? They'd say you're a faggot.

The battle with the voice in my head is on. I argue with the voice, but I'll control it because I want the money. I don't think I'm gay. I know a lot of guys who were definitely born gay, but I'm not one of them.

I argue back.

What's shameful and disgusting is that I'm only getting a paltry 2,000 bucks. Who the fuck is hurt by this? Besides, I bet you wouldn't turn down $2,000 to stand naked in front of a rich fat man for a couple hours, would you? But no one would pay you, you crazy, hypocritical bitch.

The voice's position is less tenable after that comeback.

You're a pervert just like your father.

Yeah, but I'm a pervert with $2,000 in his pocket. I think someone in my head is jealous. My philosophy is that if I'm not making money at it or fucking it, then it's not worth wasting my time with it.

Deep down, I'm shallow.

I've had "real" jobs, but they don't pay as well as this one. Besides, I always have to fill out applications and answer questions about my past occupations. Why does it matter what I've done or haven't done? Does beauty need a resume?

"Shawn, Dammit! I need to hear about how much you've been fucking lately! Have you been fucking lately, like a good boy should be?"

Shawn is a moniker given to me by a successful photographer of nude models who thought I looked like a "Shawn." He says I have the face that's launched a thousand hard-ons.

I arrive at my higher self for a moment. This non-judgmental location in my heart feels good. Why is it bad to be gay in so many minds? Why does the fat man feel compelled to hide his interest in gazing at handsome young men? Why is he ashamed of his own hard-on? I've always felt flattered being admired by any gender, albeit male, female, or those with genitals in transition.

In my experience, I've met gay priests, probation officers, counselors, politicians and CEOs. Some of the pillars of society are gay. They've given me more attention than anyone in my family ever has. I've even met some of them in the L.A. County probation system, and they sucked my dick better than most of the girls who've given me head. My dick wasn't complaining, although I knew out there in the world there were people who would disapprove.

I love everybody, but most of all, I love myself. But who am I really? Shawn? Doug? Someone else? Or am I just a human hard on?

2

Rancho San Antonio

I entered Rancho San Antonio Boys Home at age 13 in February of 1979. My mother and father were separated and neither one wanted to be parents, especially with me in their presence. My sister was already living on the streets with a guy who committed armed robberies for a living. I became a ward of the court after both of my parents refused to pick me up from the Lakewood Sherriff's after I was picked up for truancy, because my mother and her gangster heroin addicted boyfriend failed to understand the importance  of education. In other words, I got into trouble on the streets because they didn't enroll me in school.

Rancho San Antonio was run by the Catholic Jesuits who advertised it as if it was a place where boys would be loved, cared for and nurtured until we became fine, honorable young men. But I soon found out how bogus and fake that image was.

Rancho was run by unrestrained adults who gave themselves permission to fulfill their most perverted sexual desires with young boys who had no parents. It was an atmosphere where I could exploit and be exploited. Rancho San Antonio wasn't the only Boys Home with this problem during these years, but it was the first and the worst.

As a boy, I dreamed of being in a band. I loved the Beatles, and I could play any musical instrument extremely well at a very early age.

Although my musical abilities were evident to everyone, and that gave me confidence, it wasn't enough to overcome my internal fears.

I latched onto something else: My exterior outer shell.

As a young child, I realized I had something people were willing to pay for. I know it

8

had something to do with my parents, but I'm not exactly sure what the event was. Something caused me to define myself by an ability to attract people sexually. It seemed to be more important than any talent or intelligence I possessed.

I always knew I was cute. I was prettier than Shaun Cassidy in the 70's. From when I was very small, I can remember being fawned over because of my looks. But my entrepreneurial nature didn't declare itself until I was in Rancho San Antonio Boys Home in Chatsworth, California, when I was thirteen years old.

Men wanted sex with me. Women wanted sex with me. Boys and girls wanted sex with me. My father, mother, sister and an aunt and uncle all wanted sex with me.

But at Rancho, I felt it everywhere, and the priests, brothers and counselors knew they could get away with it.

I hated the dormitory setting and I also hated being housed with guys much more violent than I could ever be. I cried and cried until I realized it would never change anything, especially my parents.

I cried until I shut that mechanism off. Anger started to feel better. Tears weren't an acceptable coping mechanism in my environment. Being angry was.

Rancho San Antonio was also populated by gangbanging teenagers. I slept next to killers.

I remember some guy from the Varrio San Fernando who slept in the bed next to mine. He was a frightening asshole who threatened to kill me every hour of the day. He punched me all the time. I never told the staff because I'd be labeled a snitch and my life expectancy would lower exponentially. He hated white people, and I was his white punching bag.

One night I awoke to a strange smell coming from the San Fernando "vato" sleeping next to me. He was bleeding from his nose. It looked like gallons of blood, but he was still sleeping.

I realized he was bleeding to death in his sleep because he had sniffed so much glue that the inside of his nose was shredded. My bed was right next to his in the dormitory, and I awoke that night to gurgling sounds coming from his cot.

I could see a consistent flow of blood soaking his blanket, and a pool of it had formed on the floor. I nearly didn't say anything because this fucker was always threatening me.

Still, I couldn't let him die. It was instinctual for me once I saw how much of his life's blood was coming out of his nose. I yelled and screamed for the night counselor to come.

Pablo raced down the middle of the dormitory and we grabbed a towel to press his nostrils together. I heard he lived, but he never returned to Rancho San Antonio. I was grateful he never came back, and I was grateful he lived.

It was here that I met Brother Robert.

The rules at Rancho San Antonio Boys Home were simple. No minor was to ever be off grounds. Period.

This night, Brother Robert, the head counselor of my cottage, had plans for me. He was a Brother of the Holy Cross, a Catholic organization in charge of this institution. He was also extremely interested in a particularly cute new thirteen-year-old blonde boy named Doug.

I could feel it from the way he had been eyeing me. I was thirteen and a virgin. I had been masturbating furiously for two years, but I hadn't actually penetrated anything yet.

Brother Robert entered the dorm at about 7:00 p.m. after dinner and asked me if I

9

would accompany him to the store.

I knew it was against the rules, but since he was in charge, I figured I'm not the one who would get in trouble.

So, I leapt at the chance to get off the grounds even if only for a few minutes. I could instinctively tell there's something other than groceries on Brother Robert's mind.

"If you'd like to go with me, Doug, I could use your help picking up a few items."

I answered yes.

Brother Robert explained, "I know it's unusual for a minor to go with us to the store, but since you're with me, it's ok."

We got into his car. I sensed I had power, and I expected that I should get something in return for this. So much for proms and first dates and innocent petting with girls and boys. That shit ain't a part of my world (although deep down I wish it could be). I knew other teenagers out there in the real world were doing these things, but I wasn't.

Fuck you and your world.

I had to make the best of my situation. I didn't relate to your world. Brother Robert was not the vision I had in my head of a man I'd want to give me head. Fucking fat asshole dining on my pre-teen penis as if he'd ordered up a meal, and I was just there for him to gobble it down for free. I wondered, what the fuck was I here for? I started to understand that my purpose was to satisfy everyone's lust. Which was okay, at least I had a purpose.

And Brother Robert sure could suck a cock.

My dick was extremely hard, throbbing intensely in his mouth as he sucked. I felt a surge of sensations throughout my body that curled my pre-teen toes. I wasn't sure what was happening to me, but I realized there was some kind of climax about to happen. Suddenly, my penis throbbed, blood filling it up, hardening, and I reeled back and shot my thirteen-year-old cum down his throat. God must have surely been pleased

I grew tired of being around gangbangers who told me what to do during the day and then wanted to suck my dick at night. They demanded I obey them in the daylight, and then bent over for me to fuck them in their asses at night. I met a lot of these kinds of guys at Rancho.

3

A Playboy, an Escort, and a Realtor

Huntington Beach, 1986

I'm gonna party with my favorite young GOP buddy, Boz. Boz (short for Bosley) is twenty-two, blonde, muscular, good-looking and a real energetic party friend. This guy loves to refer to himself as a Republican, World-Class Skier, native Minnesotan, financial planner, etc. He even looked like he reeked of wealth.

We look good together, and girls come very easy for the two of us. Sometimes though, I wonder about his supposed "morality" and Republicanism. I really wonder about it when he starts advising me on the best spots by his beach apartment to peep on couples having sex.

I've got nothing against Republicans. They're some of my best customers. Tonight, Boz and I are in a Huntington Beach nightclub filled with yuppies and a few gorgeous girls.

"That latin girl over there is staring at you big time buddy," Boz exclaims to me.

"I know, I know. I noticed her earlier, but right now I need to kick back for a while before I make any moves."

Boz wants me to make a move. He always wants me to make a move.

"Go get her, man. She's got your name written all over her chest, dude."

Her ample breasts do seem to be calling for my personal attention. But within seconds, I'm angry. She probably isn't really looking at me. If she is, it's because I look stupid or like a little boy. I hate my boyish looks.

I know this shirt I'm wearing isn't cool either. I'm muscular, but this club requires "collared button-down shirts," so my muscularity is not apparent. I feel inadequate. I don't even know this chick and she's already making me feel inadequate! It becomes much easier just to hate her.

One thing I love about Boz is that he sincerely appreciates my musical talent and supports my artistic endeavors to the fullest. Anyone who encourages me artistically is endeared forever in my soul.

"Have you finished that last song you played for me a couple days ago, man? That was seriously a killer tune." Boz is building my confidence back up.

I know I write good songs, but I rarely ever complete a song. I'm a dynamic beginner, but awful at completion. I get bored.

"Still working on it, dude," I answer him somewhat half-heartedly. "I'll be working on it for a while."

If I keep drinking this Long Island Iced Tea, tomorrow I'll be working on a serious hangover. Fuck it, I'll keep drinking. Consequences resulting from my choices are never a concern of mine. That's an issue for tomorrow.

Boz breaks through my momentary reflection.

"Your music is just as good as what they're playing right now. You've got to get that shit out there. Then I'll manage you and be your financial planner. But…look at that blonde chick. Oh man, she reminds me of Jennifer, my ex-girlfriend. Probably a bitch just like her too."

Uh oh, he's started on his ex-girlfriend. I try some amateur counseling. "Boz, man you need to forget about her. So she fucked around on you. It's over, dude. Let it go."

"Yeah I know, man. It's over. But at least I've learned from the experience."

"What have you learned?" I sincerely want to know.

"I've learned you can't trust anything that bleeds for a week every month and doesn't die."

This fucking guy. My head is reeling from his hypocrisy, but I love him anyway. I don't know whether to laugh or to be appalled. For his sake, I laugh.

In my head, I'm fascinated at his denial. This is Mr. God-fearing, mom-loving, yuppie-yearning, moral-preaching Boz, saying this shit about women. Didn't his God create women? Then there must be something inherently good about them, right?

I like to think of myself as having some principles.

I struggle with countering his "lower" opinion with a higher one, or simply lowering myself by agreeing with it. It depends upon my need for approval at the moment. Right now, another factor is weighing in, tipping the scales in favor of the lower road. It's this fucking booze. I feel belligerent, obnoxious, and I want approval now. My "lower" self-wins out thoroughly.

"Boz, women simply aren't worth the mental effort. There's only one part of a woman

12

that matters to me."

I gesture with my hands, bringing my right hand level with his throat, and my left level with his upper thighs, emphasizing the "part" including breasts and vagina. He loves it.

"Fuck yeah!"

Boz is such a geek at times. He's attempting a high five in full view of several girls. And even though I might hate them, I know that I won't be able to fuck them if they see us geeking out. So I downplay his actions. Now he claims he's got to go. This is typical of Boz. We go out, talk about the girls we see, he makes an early exit. That's cool, I feel more comfortable talking to females on my own.

Boz makes his official exit. For a second, I imagine serenity. But I realize there's never serenity in my head.

I'm more cognizant of my drunken state of mind. I feel slightly out of control, with less of a concern for consequences. My self-judgments are turning into self-pity.

So fucking what? No girls seem to be noticing me. How in the fucking world could they not be? I'm the best-looking guy in this place…and yet…I know! I've got gayness written all over me. The voice appears in prime form.

'Thought you could get away with being a fag for the money in the day, and transforming into Mr. Straight Macho Man tonight, huh? Sorry, loser. It doesn't work that way.

Fuck you! I'm now at war with the voice. Nobody here has a clue what the fuck I did this afternoon, and I certainly am not the least bit gay, so fuck off.

You are what you do.

Not as long as no one knows. It's no one's business what I do, and I don't give a fuck what anyone thinks. My life and body are mine to use any way I want to.'

The voice is temporarily interrupted by a more pressing matter at hand. The latin girl is staring right at me.

Holy shit! She's ready for my move. She's looked at me and looked away. It's "the sign." Girls don't want you to know they've looked at you, but they can't help themselves. It's me, for Christ's sake. But God, she is gorgeous.

Now that she's obviously interested, my brain starts planning the future faster than a microprocessor reads information.

She's mine now. She wants to be all mine, especially after we've made love. She realizes I'm the best.

I have a big dick, and she can't get enough of it. She loves to do it with another girl. She loves to do it with another guy, girl and me. She's try-sexual. I won't fuck around on her unless she's involved.

But she doesn't want any other guy, she only wants me to be happy, and she has fantasies of her own that need to be fulfilled. She's never met a guy like me: Good-looking, sensitive, caring, honest, trustworthy and trusting of her, artistic, athletic, intelligent, and courageous.

When we're married, she wants to raise kids just like me. Then she falls even more in love with me because she sees how devoted I am to our children. How will she handle my fame?

She's impressed by my musical talents, loves for me to play for her, and appreciates all that my music can bring to our lives.

All this and I haven't even met the fucking girl yet.

But this is how my head works. I'll meet you, and have the rest of your life planned out for you in seconds. To avoid unnecessary conversation that could lead to unintentional awkwardness, this is my Modus Operandi:

"Hi, I hope I'm not being too forward, but you're gorgeous. I wish I had more time to talk, but I'm on my way out. Do you have a phone number where I could reach you?"

"You've got to leave? That's too bad. Well, I guess there's no harm in giving you my number. The best time to reach me is in the early evenings. My name is Christine. Call me."

She passes a hastily scrawled number on a napkin to me.

"I sure will. I just gotta get outta here. I will call you."

And I make my exit. I really don't have any place I have to be, it just works out, acting as if I'm in some kind of a hurry. It's all bullshit. But everything is bullshit. So now I've got to make an exit to nowhere, and as I scramble out the front door of the club half-drunk, some guy brushes up against me pretty harshly.

Big mistake.

The amount of anger I can summon up in seconds is astounding. Plus, the booze adds to that feeling of invincibility. I look back at the guy, to see if he's looking back at me, and guess what? He is. Now I'm ready for combat.

Partly because I'm an asshole when I want to be, and partly because there's enough people around to break it up after I punch him. I always assess these situations beforehand.

I really don't have the stamina to continue a protracted fight, so I like to punch and then have it broken up. That way I win without getting hurt. Some guys love the battle. I like to shock, stun, and get out. I also love it when guys underestimate me. Of course, in my mind, everybody underestimates me. I'm fast and I'll punch you before you've gotten your last threat out of your big mouth.

I can't make my mind up because I'm too angry. Anyway, he asks me what the fuck I'm looking at, we do our Neanderthal man dance, and I punch him hard enough in the mouth to cause blood to flow immediately.

It's a nice crimson deluge. The sight of your own blood pouring out of your face always gets your attention.

After all, cute guys with boyish faces aren't expected to explode into street fighting maniacs. My look of innocence is my best weapon. The club's bouncers rush in to break it up, and before this guy can get back at me, it's over.

But then I notice Christine watching the whole thing. She has a real disgusted look on her face. She apparently disapproves of the he-man role. Oh well, I probably blew that one. I blow them all.

Then the voice chimes in, *Nice one asshole. That's what you are; an asshole.*

I'm walking away from the scene to my car very much alone. But I'm never really alone with the voice in my head.

No girl in her right mind would ever want to be with you, and you'd probably punch her if she pissed you off. Why don't you just realize you'll never have friends because you can't get along with anybody?

Now the panic is setting in. The panic is worse than the voice. The voice I can fight with, but the panic is paralyzing. The panic takes over my whole being, literally consuming my body. I feel absolutely worthless, without any ability to function mentally or physically.

I'm paralyzed. I'm bad. Bad, bad, bad. I get into my car realizing I made a fool of myself trying to be tough, only the voice and the panic gang up to make it worse.

Luckily tonight I've got just enough booze in my system to disconnect my frontal lobe from the inner brain, so the alcohol has saved me from totally panicking. I can't really think straight enough to panic so I drive home alone looking more forward to a good night's sleep than anything else.

I've got a lunch date with one of my surrogate dads, so I'll need a good night's sleep. Still, I've managed to check my hair at least five times in the rear-view mirror before I get home.

I love this game. I get up, shower, shave, put on my favorite business suit, then head to the real estate office so I can sit at my desk for a while and pretend to work.

Then, after a total of four phone calls (three personal), and maybe a title search on the one deal I have in escrow, I'll call it a day.

Only thing is, today I have a lunch meeting with Mr. John Thompson, oil producer, a true American Rothschild. I met this man through an advertisement I placed in the Advocate, a national Gay Men's magazine:

LONG BEACH FOX
19, 5'10", blonde, muscular, gorgeous face
surfer type, 8 ½ inches, cut, (XXX-XXXX)

I was seventeen (or eighteen, to whom it concerned at the time) and the advertisement was an idea offered to me by two friends, Alan Belanger and John Movido, better known as Robbie Leonetti in the Adult Film Business.

It turned out to be lucrative beyond my wildest dreams.

At the time, I had no cognizance of the "Advocate," let alone the power it wielded in the gay community. I made a ton of money off that three-line ad, not to mention meeting men who would influence my life profoundly. But not one man that I met from that advertisement did I have more rapport with or was more influenced by during my early adulthood than Mr. John Thompson.

Mr. Thompson was extremely generous (which is always the best way to get my attention) and he took a genuine fatherly interest in me. However, his world and upbringing were very different than mine. This man inherited a huge oil and gas entity from his father and uncle at age sixteen, providing an income for the rest of his life that most of us could not fathom.

The man has been insulated from the real world his whole life. And yet, he's the most down to earth wealthy person I've ever met.

For reasons I never understood, the man also married and had three kids, although he's gay. Some men are bisexual, but John is 100% gay. Still, he married a woman and fathered children. Accomplishing that must have been tough for him.

John thought he made a lot parenting mistakes. It occurred to me that having money doesn't make you a good parent. John complimented me on my ability to converse on many worldly subjects. He always made me feel good when we were together. I wasn't a loser in his eyes. I was a winner! I had come through adversity and here I am, an example of how a young man can educate and support himself with no help from his family. Two things John did for me that I'll never forget: He taught me how to dress and he taught me how to eat.

"My boy, dogs go to their plates for food, we bring our food to our mouths."

I didn't know what to think. I was enjoying a steak dinner with John at Bob Burns, an expensive Newport Beach continental restaurant, while at my plate, lifting a fork full of food to my lips. Or so I thought.

At least he was somewhat nice about it. Right then and there, I realized I was moving my face towards my plate, more than bringing my fork up to my mouth. And I didn't get mad at him for pointing this out to me. It took a few weeks for me to change this eating habit permanently, but I did change.

He also taught me how some expensive clothing is expensive for a reason. I grew up worshipping rock stars. In the 70's that meant tight jeans, bell bottoms, and tank tops.

I told him I had just received my California Real Estate license, and John said I'd need a suit and tie for that job. He added that he'd enjoy seeing me at dinner in more refined clothing. Ok, fine with me. He took me to a store called Neiman Marcus. I think it was in Beverly Hills. Everyone knew John, and he brought me over to a tailor, and he measured my waist, leg length, and shoulder size. It was all new and exciting to me.

I never thought about this style of clothing, but with my new short haircut, I thought this would work for me. John picks out a blue blazer from "Brooks Brothers" and a shirt by Perry Ellis. The tailor loved them, and when I tried them on with the slacks and shoes, I was stunned! Looking in the mirror, I fell in love with myself all over again. I looked fantastic.

Fuck the rock star look, I thought. I'm a young entrepreneur now. Behold, my people, I've arrived. There ain't no way anyone, male or female, will be able to turn me down now with me in these clothes. I want to wear them everywhere. I'm sold. I walked out excited, delighted, and more confident than ever. Nothing thrills me more than myself.

I'll never forget one thing Joe said to me. I told him about my father and his rage, my mother's alcoholism, and the years I spent in Boys' Homes. He listened and said this: "My boy, you have quite a story to tell. I know a psychiatrist who could be of help. Most people don't care to hear about someone else's problems. When you're telling someone your life story, do you know what they're usually thinking?"

"No, what?" I ask.

"I've got a plane to catch in fifteen minutes; I wish he'd hurry up so I can go."

I've never forgotten. Most people don't care; they've got troubles of their own.

Today I drive to Newport Beach and my weekly luncheon with Mr. Thompson.

Arriving at his offices in Newport Beach is always intimidating. Before entering, the first thing you notice is the designation on the door: John Thompson, Oil Operations.

Impressive bullshit to me. Daddy handed it to him. But he still had to hold on to it. And everybody was trying to steal his fortune.

I want one of those monikers for my office: Doug Probst, P.D.S: Pleasure Delivery Service.

On entering, you'll notice his stodgy but kind secretary, Ellen. Every week, for three fucking years, it's been the same damn thing. I arrive at 12:25, greet Ellen, and head back to Joe's main office.

It's enormous, with twelve leather chairs perfectly placed around a long oval table. The room has global maps on the wall, with red markings distinguishing where the Thomas Oil Operations are located. It's very similar in style to the Geneva summit room. There must be many powerful men who meet here. I wonder if they actually discuss urgent matters or if they just gather and gloat about being richer than everyone else.

He has lunch booked for two at Bob Burns' restaurant. I think he must have stock in the place. We have our lunch, he lectures me on my eating etiquette, we share similar perspectives on the state of sexual hypocrisy in America, and he hands me a $500 check. Sometimes it's $1000, sometimes $1500. It depends on how the Dow Jones is performing that day.

We used to have sex, though it never amounted to much. I'd let him suck me off or we'd just converse together in the nude. Sometimes I'd fuck him. Lately he's been telling me his wife, Jill, not only wants to see my cock, but wants me to fuck her with it. Apparently, thanks to their unique marital status (him being gay), she doesn't have sex with anyone, and now it's time for her to get what he's been getting for years.

"I really think Jill could use a little livening up. My boy, you've got the goods, and you say you like women. I think this just might work out."

I'm not so sure. Naked wrinkly old ladies are about as erotic as a trip to the dentist.

"How does $1500 sound, Douglas?"

Suddenly, she's the sexiest old lady I've ever laid eyes on.

"Sure, I'm up for it. Jill's attractive, and we do have quite a rapport."

This much is true.

John is now the matchmaker for his wife. Interesting marriage we have here. A little different than those fairy tales I remember as a child.

I do like Jill. She's a class act. Of course, being married to Mr. Oil & Gas as opposed to Mr. Beer & Belly guarantees a course in refinement.

Still, my rendezvous with Mrs. Thomas is scheduled for a week away. I've got other issues to ponder at the moment. I've got $500 in my pocket, but do I want to spend it or save it?

When I used to fuck John in the ass and afterward, he cleaned everything up, placing with elegant etiquette, every used condom in the Four Seasons hotel room trash can. He reminded me of Winston Howell the 3rd, the wealthy man played by Jim Backus on Gilligan's Island with Jill being "Lovie." The difference was that John was much better looking, and both he and Jill were more refined. Of course, Gilligan's Island was a comedy sitcom, and I was performing with real people who weren't acting.

For a sixty-year-old woman, Jill's very attractive. She's got very sexy breasts that don't sag, and she has the body of a much younger woman. I meet her at the Beverly Hilton on Wilshire Blvd. She greets me in a gorgeous, expensive bathrobe that exposes her breasts. I'm immediately aroused. I love meeting women who have no sexual hang ups. She's got two scotch and sodas prepared for us, and I see she has a straight adult film playing in the VCR and I can see the male actor and actress's sexual intensity.

Jill's done her research and is ready for me to perform my duty on her. And so, I do.

We watch the film as we drink our scotch, slowly becoming aroused together. She reaches for my zipper and pulls out my erect penis Joe's told her about. When she remarks "It's true, you're very well endowed", it reminded me of the scene in Blazing Saddles when Madeline Khan unzips Clevon Little's pants and shouts while stroking her first black penis "It's twooo, it's twoo what they say about you people. You are gifted."

We don't waste time. Soon we're kissing and I move to her large breasts, taking the nipples into my mouth, caressing the rest of her body. As she squeals and moans, I realize she's probably never been eaten out. So, I stay down there a while and give her a couple of orgasms with my tongue before she begs to feel my erection inside her. Afterwards, we lounge together in bed conversing like long lost friends. She's intelligent, well read, soft spoken and genuinely interested in me. And before I leave, she points to a $2,000 check with my name on it, ensuring I'm not to leave without it. She put in $500 more dollars than John and I agreed to. She captured my heart that night. I was grateful as I left, entered the elevator and got into my car after the valet had retrieved it and brought it to my feet. It's great work, and I'm the lucky worker with benefits.

Money can't buy happiness, but it sure rents a lot of fun. I can buy a year's worth of tanning.

Or I can put it under the mattress and save it for an emergency. I save it because I'm not willing to go back to sleeping on bus benches, and I don't know how long this fascination with me is gonna last. Also, I have no family offering me a safety net.

Jill asked me to drive to Newport Beach so I could stay in one of their luxurious guest rooms. She and John wanted me to dine with them the following evening with their three grown children who were home from college.

Though John was gay, he and Jill were married in the 1950s, and they had three children: John, Jody and Jill. Joe had given me his address to their home on Lido Isle in Newport Beach before, and although I hadn't been there before, I was honored to be invited to spend the night and enjoy the next day and night with the Thomas family. It was an hour drive from Beverly Hills to Newport Beach. I left one massive wealthy city and drove directly to another. I didn't know what to expect, but when I drove the strip to Lido Isle, I entered a land of wealthy homes that made Beverly Hills look more like a city of middle-class people to me.

They had an oceanfront property with a 300-foot yacht stationed in front with a yacht boy who called it home to take good care of it.

I was greeted by a walkway led to the yacht. I'd never seen wealth like this before. The butler and John greeted me simultaneously at the front door. Their house had nine bathrooms and seven bedrooms with an indoor pool that adjoined with the "guest room," where I was to sleep for the night.

I was awakened at 7 a.m. to have breakfast with the family. I showered, put on clothes that were left for me in the guest dresser, and attempted to navigate my way through the house to find the dining room. I was very nervous as I'd never seen anything like this before. I'm more accustomed to a cell with a bar of soap, a mother passed out on the floor, guns to my head or robberies committed in broad daylight.

I was greeted first by their personal chef inquiring how I'd like my eggs. Not knowing if it was white trash to order mine over easy, I took the easy way out and said: Scrambled. He looked at me with disdain but kindly informed me I could choose from eggs Benedict with Hollandaise sauce, eggs hardboiled with grapefruit, or my scrambled eggs with bacon.

Looking at the eggs Benedict made me want to throw up, so I stuck with my first choice. I don't like the taste of bacon, but I didn't argue with him. John called everyone to the table, and breakfast was served.

I heard footsteps arriving and I looked up to see John and Jill's three young adult children enter. John and Jill walked in normally and greeted me with handshakes and smiles. The older son, Jerry, entered wearing a vested suit, and smoking out of a pipe. He was twenty-three years old, and it looked very odd to me. As he approached me, I stood up and Jerry took his pipe out of his mouth, exhaling the putrid stench of "Trust fund baby tobacco" and extended his hand to me with, "So you must be Doug. Mom and Dad have told us all about you. Welcome to the family."

Jerry was arrogant and strange. But he was the eldest son, home from a private school in Switzerland, so I kept my thoughts about him to myself. I knew my place. And I knew my paychecks were sitting at opposite ends of the dining table. I was torn between feeling like I was finally part of a real family and knowing my place was just to fuck Mom and Dad. I guess I didn't worry about it too much. I preferred paychecks over family.

After breakfast, John and I went out and sat on the deck chairs sitting on his yacht. It was nice to view the Orange Coast College Men's Skulling team Joe's money supported. They were skulling by through the Lido channel and waved at Joe. John was paying for his privilege to watch the boys paddle hard past his yacht. The amount he contributed to Orange Coast College was enormous.

John also took me to the Orange County Symphony to see many renditions of his favorite classical pieces. He loved Bach and Mozart and complained that everything Straus ever wrote sounded the same. After sitting through the 4th Straus waltz, I felt the same way.

I saw a flyer at the OC Theater, and it listed the "Platinum Level Donors" and what they donated to be in that circle. Joe and Jill Thomas were in the first five, contributing $50,000 a year to keep the Symphony alive. I thought that was great, although one night sitting at the table with Joan Irvine and Bill Gillespie (the heirs to the Irvine fortune), I gently brought up the subject that there were too few rock clubs in Orange County and though they listened, my words fell on deaf ears. Especially Bill's. He kept trying to grab my bulge underneath the table. I wanted to charge him, but decided it was best to just let him cop a feel.

John Thompson influenced me greatly. He was a father figure to me. We spent more time at the dinner table conversing about every subject under the sun than having sex. I learned about refinement, etiquette, classical music, and table manners from him. I fucked him in the ass once in a while, and he sometimes sucked my cock. He and I got together for years. He always made sure I was compensated well for my companionship.

John was my first introduction to massive wealth. He dressed in clothes that were obviously expensive. He didn't brag about his wealth or who he was. I'd never seen or paid attention to what a rich person looked like until I started living and hustling on the streets. After meeting John and a few other rich men, I learned to spot wealth faster than a clergyman could spot a boy scout. I stayed the night reading and watching a movie with John and Jill, fell asleep and hugged them both as I left the next morning.

I exit Newport Beach and head back to my home in Long Beach. I feel pretty good. The voice hasn't reared its ugly audio head yet, and I've paid my bills for the week. Sustaining contentment has never been easy for me. As I drive, I become cognizant of my inability to focus on a particular thought.

But I also feel captive to my desires. I want a relationship with someone.

I know I should work harder at my musical career, and forgo relationships until I'm successful, but maybe I'm just too fucking codependent. I wonder why I'm so intent on having a partner in my life.

I keep my phone book at hand so I can reach any one of a number of potential partners at any time I want. In my phone book, it's first names first, because I don't even know most of their last names. Everywhere I go, I'm convinced my soulmate is around the corner. Or in the next lane on the freeway, or in the supermarket checkout line. Or at the health club or walking in the mall. I've got to keep my eyes open and my hair perfect, because I don't want my future soulmate to miss me. I must see myself staring back at myself so I know whether or not I have to fix my hair.

See how my mind works?

I don't spend my waking hours just scouting prospective soulmates. No, no, no! There's a strategy at work here. I walk the malls, venturing into stores, feigning interest in items where my future soulmate is at work. Then, I deposit myself there, so she'll have no choice but to notice me. Same as the Missing Persons song playing in my cassette deck right now — I am one of the noticeable ones... NOTICE ME!

Tonight, however, I think I'll just kick back at my place and head to bed. I've worked hard and I'm exhausted.

4

Opening Old Wounds

I awake… On an early cold January morning in 1983, I wake up with terrible pain on my shoulder.

I reach around to see what's causing this, and it's a frightening red rash. It's a horrific, piercing, stinging sensation that is relentless. I naively touch it, and OH My fucking God! It stings so bad, I scream! It's not stopping. Fuck! I scream loudly, rolling onto the floor. It's like a red rash with scabs, but the pain is unbearable. I called my friend Chris and he said it sounded like I had shingles. I've never heard of shingles.

He says it's a chicken pox virus, but it's also brought on by stress. Everyone says they're stressed. It's an overused meaningless term to me. But this pain is overtaking thoughts of analyzing the word "stress." I need a doctor. I need this shit to go away. The only doctors I know are clients, and I'm not bugging them at work right now. I also don't want to jeopardize the money I make from my doctor clients by showing up with shingles. They'd probably never want to see me naked again. I look up shingles in the Encyclopedia I have, and it confirms what Chris had said. It also states there's no treatment. It's just got to run its course, which could mean serious unfathomable pain for up to two weeks. I decide to call John Thompson. He's my version of a father, and I respect his advice. I tell him I have shingles, and he sounds surprised.

"My boy that usually happens to older people, not someone your age."

Now I feel like the worthless piece of shit I intrinsically know I am. Of course, I'm the only young person to get something that old people get.

"So, what do I do?"

"There's not much you can do, Douglas. But I think it's also due to your childhood trauma. I'm going to give you the number to my Psychiatrist in Newport Beach. I want you to go and see him. Set up a schedule to see him regularly. He's one of the best, and he can really help you if you tell him about your childhood. You've got to be honest and really open up. Please call him and set up an appointment with him. Most importantly, go to the appointment. Tell him to bill me for his services. Let me know how it goes."

I call the psychiatrist and tell him "John Thompson sent me." He says Joe told him about me, and we set an appointment to meet at his Balboa Island, Newport Beach Office. He says he's known Joe for years, and he respects him very much. And of course, that's where he sends the bill. Joe really cares about me. I'm happy to speak to a Psychiatrist about me. I love to talk about me. And there are many people who want to hear about me, but most of those people also want to suck my dick. There's nothing wrong with that, but with a Psychiatrist, it's all about me, all the time. And hopefully, there won't be any sexuality involved. Although, I won't know until I go.

I arrive at our scheduled time. He's got a beautiful office. He's got a firm handshake, and I can tell he's not after me sexually. He offers me a seat, and I sit down. Not knowing this guy or his agenda, I'm tentative but hopeful. I've had sessions with Psychologists during my years in the LA County Probation System, and I enjoyed being able to talk openly with them. It's funny how I don't remember what I talked about, but I remember that I liked being paid attention to. This Psychiatrist's name is Norman. He notices something right off the bat.

"You're picking your skin, Douglas."

"Yep. I do it sometimes."

He tells me that he only sees that habit with the most devastatingly abused clients he has. (Those were his exact words: "devastatingly abused.") My exact thoughts at the exact moment after he said those words were: "Yeah, but you don't know how bad of a kid I was." I didn't express them out loud, but that's what my head told me.

He asks me how I'm feeling right now. I tell him I'm glad I'm here, but I'm not sure what we can accomplish. He says that we can set goals if I'd like, but he'd like to get to know me first. Of course, that immediately strikes me as an invitation to have sex. I brush it off because he truly seems interested in doing his job. He asks me how I feel about being here. I say I'm happy to be here, and I know I've got to stop picking my skin. I've got a bigger problem and that's my shingles.

. He doesn't start asking me questions. Rather, he stares at me and I stare back. Don't stare at me too long, or I'll get up and punch you. You don't know me. He seemed to sense anger welling up in me, and changed the subject, asking me about my parents. I'm already getting angry, and now he wants me to describe my relationship with my parents.

Surprisingly, I feel nothing as I describe my parents. I'm detached from emotion as I describe the two people, I despise more than any other human beings on earth.

I tell him my dad hit me in the face almost daily, and he raped my sister almost daily for most of our lives when we lived with him. I can't remember when he didn't do either of these things to us.

"How did your mother respond?"

"She didn't do shit. She approved of his beatings, and denied that he did anything sexual to Jamie, until she walked in on them. Jamie had my dad's penis in her mouth."

"How old was Jamie?"

"Jamie was thirteen."

"So, your mom allowed your father to rape Jamie for years under her roof?"

"Yep. She ignored it, and she also put me in a mental hospital because my dad was complaining that I was crazy. He said both my mother and I needed help, but of course my mother never thought she needed any help for anything, so I was admitted to a crazy hospital when I was eleven. I think it was just a way for my father to continue to have sex with Jamie without me getting in the way by being there."

The doctor has an intent look on his face. He's pondering what I've told him.
He asks me about the mental hospital I was in at eleven years old.

"It was La Habra Community Hospital. I was there for three weeks. I made some friends. I really liked a guy named Paul Liddycoat. He was twelve. There was one counselor I liked, but he was a bit weird. He used to sit in a chair and have me put my hand on his hard on. I didn't mind. He told me to squeeze it. I could see the outline of his hard dick in his white "nurse" pants. I just squeezed it. He told me to do that to him. No big deal. My mother is a bigger freak than Joey. That was his name; Joey Hernandez."

"What do you mean "my mother is a bigger freak than Joey?"

"My mother sucked my dick and tried to get me to fuck her more than once. "

The Psychiatrist looks startled. I don't think that's good. I want a cure for these fucking shingles. This other shit is just history. I don't mind talking about it, because at least I'm being paid attention to. And I get to talk about things that matter. But I'm in pain too. Maybe it's more than physical pain.
He looks stuck, and I cut through it.

"My parents weren't great — I didn't even live with them half of my life. The mental hospital was only the first facility I called home. I was in Boys' Homes, Juvenile Halls, and Probation Camps for all of my teenage years. I only saw the outside world a couple of times my whole teenage life. I had more life education in those places than I did in the outside world. They released me to the streets when I was seventeen."

"Could you explain what you mean by life education, Douglas?"

"It's a different world man. I lived with criminals, animals who would kill me for my shoes. I didn't have a lot of love. I didn't have fun, but there were a few people who cared about me."

"Who were these people who cared about you?"

"One of them called me last week. His name is Dan Dobbins . He was a counselor at a Catholic Boys' Home I was in for almost a year. I was fourteen. I cried for my mom the whole time I was there, and I was sure she'd come and get me, but she never did. I made sure no one ever saw me cry, or the gangbangers would fuck me up. I couldn't be a pussy, even though I had sex with some of the hard-core dudes. Eddie from Pacoima liked me to fuck him in his ass at night, and he was a shot caller for the Pacas gang. Fifteen years old and the baddest dude you'll ever meet. I think he stabbed someone later and went to the California State Youth Authority for five years." Y.A. is prison for murderers under eighteen.

"Tell me about Dan Dobbins."

"I like Dan. He cared about me. That's why he called me. He's a piano player like me, and he wanted to get together. I don't know how he found me after all these years. I haven't seen him since I was kicked out of Rancho San Antonio Boys' Home in 1980."

"Dan Dobbins called you last week. What did he say?"

"He said he missed me and had been thinking about me. When I was in Rancho San Antonio, he let me play the piano once in a great while, when he could. Just because we had sex didn't mean he didn't care. He treated me better than my parents. They left me there, and never visited me once."

"You had sex with Dan Dobbins, a counselor at Rancho San Antonio Boys' Home?"

"Yes. I had sex with Father Francis, Brother Robert, and Dan Dobbins."

"Tell me when sex with Dan first happened."

Uh oh, now I'm wondering if I have a pervert psychiatrist who just wants to get off hearing details of man boy sex. My instincts tell me no. He seems to genuinely be interested in exploring this issue for reasons other than sexual gratification.
I start telling him, although I'm embarrassed to reveal everything to him. That's not going to happen here.

Rancho San Antonio Boys' Home, July 1979
The Laundry Room.

I had a pile of my dirty laundry in my hands, and I was ready to stick them into the washing machine. In this compact room, there were eight washing machines and four dryers. This was laundry day for me. Here at Rancho San Antonio Boys' Home, they had certain days set aside for four residents from each dorm to wash their clothes. I didn't like to be near anyone else when I washed my clothes, and luckily, today, I was alone in here.

There was also an adjoining room. It was a musty, foul smelling cramped storage room with an old rusty sink and a faucet that sometimes offers water. As I was stuffing my pants and shorts into a washing machine, I heard my favorite counselor, Dan Dobbins, ask me if I was alone. Before my skinny fourteen-year-old self could answer, I looked over and saw his large bulky frame walk inside and shut the door.

I liked Dan because he had always been nice to me, and he played piano. Though it was very rare (maybe once a month), he allowed me to accompany him in the chapel on the piano. He had played a lot piano bars, cabaret music and stuff like that. He once played a song called Dr. Longjohn that I liked. It was funny and had very sexual overtones. Other than that, he didn't care for my Elton John songs, but at least he let me play. Like I said, it was rare.

On this day, Dan and I were now alone in the laundry room. I immediately sensed why. He told me he knew I wanted a corner bed in the dormitory. A corner bed in an eighteen-bed dormitory is akin to having a mansion in a trailer park. You get space around your bed no other minor has, and you have the corner locker which is much larger than the others. The four corner bed areas were reserved for the boys who have been at Rancho the longest and were about to be released because they'd earned it through good behavior. I'd been at Rancho about four months, so I really haven't been there long enough for a corner bed, but if someone fucked up, I could get one, if a counselor said so.

Dan locked the door to the laundry room. His sweet, gentle demeanor quickly morphed into a sinister, controlling disposition. His personality was devolving before my eyes. He was enjoying the control he had over me. It's slightly disturbing, but not frightening. I didn't feel threatened. I was very familiar with being alone with the sexually insane.

"Do you still want a corner bed, Doug?"

"Of course, I do."

"Here's how you can get it. Suck my cock."

A thought flashed across my brain, "What do I get if I bite it off?" but I knew that was wrong. I had no right to be angry about his needs. I'm the bad boy, and I'm here to serve him. I need his approval to get what I want.

He unzipped his fly and pulled out a thick, massive erection. I was a bit ashamed, but I was horny too. I immediately knew what to do. I went down to my knees and tried to take his engorged penis into my mouth. It was difficult because of his dick's girth, but I got it in and started sucking. I looked up and saw his eyes roll back, totally immersed in his fantasy.

Dan began groaning and moaning, and my fourteen-year-old mouth was getting tired. He told me that he wanted to do something he hadn't done since he was in the Army.

"What's that?"
"I want you to bend over so I can fuck you in your ass."

"I've never done that before. Will I get a corner bed in the dorm?"

"You'll get one if you please me. We need to do this before anyone comes this way."

The voice in my head let me know that I was starting to bother Dan, so I rushed to unbutton my jeans, and pulled my pants down. Suddenly, before I could turn around, he grabbed my shoulders and threw me over, so that I was facing the wall. He pulled my jeans and underwear to the floor, and I heard him panting as he pressed both hands onto my back, forcing me to bend over. I had to hold onto the rusty sink in the small room, because there wasn't enough room for me to go down on my knees with both legs.

The next thing I felt was a searing painful stab into my anus. I screamed out in agony.

"Owwwww, fuck, fuck!"

I knew I was required to endure this, but it fucking hurt.

My screaming was my attempt to purge the torturous pain I felt as my asshole was ripped apart by Dan's thick penis. I could feel it tearing me open.

"Fuck, fucking, fuck, fuck, uhhhhh!"

Suddenly, I couldn't open my mouth anymore. Dan had grabbed my face and covered my mouth with the palm of a huge hairy hand. I was now unable to breathe normally. I hurt everywhere and was becoming a little fearful as to how long this is going to take. I certainly wasn't enjoying this. But Dan was. He ceaselessly pumped his penis into my undefended virgin boy anus, gaining speed, at the same time gripping my mouth to keep me quiet. I felt blood trickling out of my anal area and spilling down my leg. Dan whispered a warning in my ear to stay quiet, he's about to cum.

He was forcing his penis deep into my anal cavity. I couldn't scream because he cut off my breathing by strangling my mouth. I was worried about the blood I felt coming out of my butt. He finally grunted and yelled, and this thirty-five-year-old man shot his sperm deeply into my ass. I felt the warmth of his sperm mixing with the blood that was now flowing more rapidly.

And suddenly "OWWW! FUCK!" It was intense scorching pain as he pulled his penis slowly out of my anus, stretching and tearing my skin apart.

I quickly turned around. I panicked at the sight of the blood running down my legs.

Dan told me I had to hurry up and clean all of my blood off of the floor before someone came to the room. "I could get into big trouble, and you won't get your corner bed if you don't clean this up."

I felt guilty. I shouldn't have bled. I couldn't even get fucked to his satisfaction. I can't do anything right. I fuck everything up. The voice was pouncing, but I had no time for arguing with myself. I wanted that bed, so I grabbed a dirty rag and wiped out the inside of my anus. I washed out the rag and scrubbed my legs. I used the paper towels for the rest of the job. This is 1979, and sanitizer was fifteen years away from being available. I did the best I could. Dan hurriedly got dressed and told me to stay quiet as he opened the door to leave.

I couldn't tell the staff what happened, and I certainly couldn't see a doctor. I hoped it would heal. I wiped it out with the laundry soap and pretended I was ok.

But now my reward was due. Dan tells the rest of the guys that he's awarding me the corner bed. My dormmates were not happy. They didn't understand why I was receiving the corner bed when I was a troublemaker, and there were other boys who'd been there longer than me.

But I'd earned it. I proudly took all of my belongings and moved them over to the corner space, piling them into my corner locker, reveling in my well-earned privacy.

I'm gonna be fine. Of course, I am. I have to be. I'm gonna be a rock star someday, I thought to myself before falling asleep in my new bed.

PTSD

After telling Norman the psychiatrist about my sexual encounter with Catholic Counselor Dan, he gets a blank stare on his face and doesn't speak for at least thirty seconds. Although I didn't tell him every graphic detail — as a matter of fact, I think I minimized it and blamed myself for bleeding, after staring blankly at me, he finally speaks.

"Douglas, do you realize you were picking your skin while you were telling me about having sex with your abuser?"

"Abuser? You mean Dan? No, I didn't realize I was picking my skin."

At that moment I notice my fingers are picking at any skin cell they can find to make bleed on my right arm. It's as if my fingers have a mind of their own. I'm embarrassed. I immediately take my hand off of my arm and sink back into my chair still feeling embarrassed, but ready to defend myself. My motto has always been, "When embarrassed, fight back." I've heard it said that insecure people fight. Well, I guess I'm insecure, because a lot of people are dangerous, and I have to be ready to fight.

Norman the psychiatrist tells me that he is diagnosing me as having a disorder known as "Post Traumatic Stress Disorder," commonly known as PTSD. I've heard that guys who come back from the battlefield from wars are diagnosed with this "PTSD."

He tells me, "Yes, Doug, but you've been on that battlefield since you were a baby. You're still fighting that war and it's a severely painful battle."

He says that my childhood experience was severely traumatic, and prolonged. He explains that the "resulting trauma has set me up with a conditional emotional response of which I have little control over. I impulsively continue to go into a fight or flight response at the least provocation: traumatized people keep experiencing life as a continuation of the trauma and remain in a state of constant alert for its return."

I ask him how to cure this disorder and he says there's no cure. He wants to prescribe a drug called "MDMA." I've heard of it; my gay friends use it all the time to feel good. They call it "Ecstasy." But then he tells me the government is about to ban it and make it illegal because too many people are using it to enhance sex. That sounds like a good use for it to me — how dare the government step in and stop enhancing sex — I get two for the price of one! He tells me how complex this disorder is to treat. He says it's a long process and I must continue therapy and take prescribed medications.

This is a lot for me to process. I know this is true. I'm living with myself. No one has lived my life for me. But I need to make money to survive. No one's gonna help me, no one really cares. I'm more concerned about my bank account and fucking girls and boys than I am about this disorder I have. Serious as it may be, I write songs that seem to soothe me, and I'm gonna be a rock star anyway. I'll show the world how I beat this on my own. I'm the great I am.

5

My Sixteenth Birthday
(Happy Birthday to Me)

Now that I have my real estate license, it's just another day at the real estate office. I have appointments with a mortgage rep and an appraiser at a property I've listed, with the help of my broker, of course.

Usually, the voice would have a field day that I needed help to get a listing, but for some reason, its voice isn't chirping today. I walk into the office immersed in analyzing my colleagues. I've heard we were kicked off the Long Beach Board of Realtors for another shady transaction that Ed, our esteemed broker, approved. The deal was put together by my shady colleague, Mel Brooks.

Yes, his real name.

This guy can't seem to put a deal together that doesn't involve unscrupulous behavior. He thought it would be fun to take me along with him on his last deal, putting a notorious Long Beach drug dealer into a house for all cash. Actually, it was the simplest, fastest escrow I'd ever seen. Two weeks from beginning to end.

He took me to the drug dealer's home before the newest deal closed. Entering the house, I noticed bullet shell casings on the carpet. There was a fat man fast asleep on the couch, but in his hand, he clutched a large caliber weapon. I know nothing about guns, just whether they are big fuckers or small fuckers, and this was definitely a big fucker. Mel gets off on these kinds of deals. The seedier the better.

As we return to the office, behind his desk with his mouth wide open in a state of perpetual screaming hysterics, is Ken Friedlander. He's in another yelling match with a tenant over unpaid rent in one of the apartment buildings he owns. Ken's a nice guy, just too cheap to hire onsite managers, so he's constantly battling tenants over money. He's forty-three years old, drives a Porsche 911, and hasn't yet figured out it may actually be cheaper to hire someone to deal with the tenants.

Over in the middle, behind his desk, is Bryan Shannon, another old-timer who's made enough money over the years to have thoroughly lost interest in real estate. Why he even shows up to the office, I don't know. Maybe he needs somewhere to drive to every day.

My broker, Ed Soule', is lovingly referred to by his fellow agents as "irresponsible little puke." This seems an appropriate title for a spoiled rich brat, which Ed is every bit of. He's twenty-nine years old, younger than everyone in the office except me. He drives a Porsche 928, grew up in La Cañada, and sees life in terms of the haves and have-nots.

Ed, in his mind, belongs exclusively to the former group. He also, in typical spoiled rich kid fashion, displays a remarkable lack of insight into people and their motivations, including his own. Lately, he's been trying to convince me that he "relates" to me because I remind him of himself when he was my age. He wants to show me how much fun it is to rip people off. Sure, Ed. You relate to me.

The guy with the sleaziest personality has to be the fast-food chomping, chain-smoking, scrooge character, Al Williams. I hate passing by his desk for fear of bumping into it. The cloud of cigarette smoke obscures it. But the guy gets his listings. Twenty-three this month alone! He's a producer of money for the office, and nobody advises or despises the man who produces. For some reason today, Ken, Brian, and Ed are sitting on empty desks near mine, reminiscing about high school days.

"Brian?" Ken begins. "Isn't tomorrow your son's sixteenth birthday?"

"Yeah, can you believe it? It seems like only yesterday I was that age!" Brian answers solemnly.

And now, Ken is becoming reminiscent and nauseatingly sentimental about his teenage years. "Those were some great days — no responsibility, girls, high school, all that youthful energy, a fuckin' great time!"

I notice his belly, and I can't help but muse that his youthful energy has transformed into middle-aged stagnancy.

Brian chimes in. "One of the great things about being a teenager is looking forward to the next day, because of the freedom from worry. All you got is school and friends. It was great when Mom and Dad took care of it all for you. I'm sure that was your best memory about high school, Ed, right?"

Ed seems unperturbed.

"Hey, Doug! You're the closest out of all of us to still being a kid. Tell us about your sixteenth birthday, bud."

My birthday? Who the fuck cares? All I know is I'm feeling this horrendous deluge of paralyzing panic wash over my being. Everyone is anticipating similar teenage memories, and I have none to offer. On the spot and embarrassed, I fumble for an answer. But the voice gets here first.

Okay, you imbecile. You put yourself into this situation, now let's see you get yourself out of it. You know damn well they'll find your past disgusting. Ed will probably get rid of you. Best move he could make.

Fuck this! I answer inside. When in doubt, lie. But then again, I detest lying, so maybe I can just avoid answering directly.

"Well, I missed some high school activities, and most stuff is a blur." God, I hope that answer suffices.

"Really?" Ken seems to be the only one interested anyway.

The voice quickly pounces on this bit of information.
YOU aren't even interesting enough for them to care about anyway.
I hate it when the voice seems to be right. Brian's attention is wandering, and Ed's attention is caught by a pretty young thing walking by the office.

"Doug, I really would like to hear about your upbringing sometime," Ken voices reassuringly.

Just then his phone rings, and I'm saved by one of his obnoxious tenants. For once, the sound of Ken screaming is music to my ears. Brian has gone to the bathroom, and Ed is dealing with a rookie agent's problem.
And I'm alone again. Alone with the voice.
Your childhood? If they only knew where you were when you were sixteen, you fucking fraud..

My sixteenth birthday

I wake up in my cell at Los Padrinos Juvenile Hall this particular morning, not with thoughts of finally being old enough to obtain a driver's license, but cognizant of one agonizing fact: My abdomen is on fire!
I don't know what the fuck is going on here, I have no clue. All I know is that my stomach area is in intense pain. Fucking excruciating pain. I can't fucking breathe. Oh my God, it hurts so bad!
Who cares? I'm in Los Padrinos Juvenile Hall, Unit L-M, fifth cell on the right side of the hallway of the L corridor. Not exactly a suburban family setting. I've been locked up since I was twelve years old, and that's not counting my two previous stints in La Habra Community Mental Hospital at ages eight and ten.
I guess a better word would be "institutionalized." Boys Homes, mental hospitals, probation camps, juvenile halls — I've seen them all by the ripe old age of sixteen. But this morning, my past isn't on my mind. I feel only tremendous physical pain. I feel like a wimp. The pain is getting worse.
I don't want to yell for help, because the night shift always gets annoyed when a minor has any type of request. So, I hold my stomach very tightly, hoping (in futility) the pain will go away. But it doesn't.

I scream, "Help me down here! I've got a bad stomachache!"

I don't want to wake anybody. It's still dark outside. Since us inmates see no clocks in here, time is a concept that when focused on just adds more pain to an already too painful situation.
Light and darkness are our clocks.
I've learned to hope that it's later than it is. Right now, my clock says it's too early to be in physical pain. Physical pain is not acceptable here. To complain about anything means that you're a pussy. This is no place to be thought of as a pussy, especially a white one. I'm

not a white pussy. I'm known as the white boy who will knock your ass out if you try to take my shoes. Years of incarceration will do that to you. Locked inside this cage, my innocence turned to rage.

Fuck all that. This pain is different. It won't go away, and it's getting worse. I start screaming, the voice in my head tells me that I'm about to lose whatever tough reputation I have, but it's astonishing how tremendous physical pain will supersede mental hijackings.

Suddenly, I can't control my need to vomit. My stomach reflexively hurls its contents out of my mouth, splattering my guts all over the floor. I imagine this might dull the pain, but I realize almost immediately how wrong I am.

"Help me! My stomach is fucking killing me! I need help!"

I hear no footsteps. Nobody's coming.

"Shut the fuck up!" A fellow inmate has been awakened by my screams.

"My fucking stomach hurts BAD, man!"

I'm losing energy to even make a case for my pain. Finally, I hear footsteps. The night guard is coming. I hear one of the most marvelous sounds someone living in a cell ever hears: keys jangling, because that sound could mean they're coming to unlock my cell to go home, or to a boys home, or anywhere but inside these four walls and a cot. Most of the time it's a disappointment. But not today. The lock to my cell is opening!

"What's wrong with you, Probst?"

The inquiry produces scant interest in my suffering. She obviously doesn't give a fuck.

"I don't know. I woke up in a lot of pain. I can't even stand up straight. Fuuuckk!"

I'm doubled over with my arms crossed hands locked on my elbows. The night guy notices the vomit all over the floor. But my cohorts down the corridor are, unfortunately, up and aware of my plight.

"Shut that fuckin' white boy up!"

"Get Probst out of here so we can get some fucking sleep."

Ah, to be sixteen and among friends.

"Gee, Probst you vomited all over the place. Can't you keep it in the corner?"

The night guy is annoyed at my lack of vomitus manners.

"I'm sorry, man. But I hurt. I need some medicine or something."

"I guess so. I'll call the infirmary nurse, but it's 5:30, man. She ain't gonna be happy."

31

Please, God, take this pain away!

Why the fuck am I calling on God? It's not like he's ever been there for me. Besides, if he's got the power to take this away, then he had the power to prevent it. JOLTING PAIN! No time for theoretical mental masturbation. I fucking hurt. I hear the nurse down the hallway, and I visualize Florence Nightingale coming to my rescue.

"What's wrong with you, Probst? I know you be fakin' boy, cos' it's your birthday and you trying to get outside somewhere."

So much for Nurse Nightingale. Instead, I get nurse-bitch-a lot.

"I'M NOT FAKING!" I hope the vociferousness of my retort to her accusation makes an impression. It doesn't.

"Don't you talk like that to me, you little whiner. I'll have you taken to the box. You cryin' over a little stomachache. I'll get you some aspirin."

Ha. The box is no threat to me. I love that place. I can masturbate day and night with no interruption whatsoever. I proceed to barf right in front of her.
"That's so gross. I'll get you some aspirin, don't mess up the floor no more, ya hear me, Probst?"

I'm dying, and she's worried about the floor. She leaves, and I hear conversation between her and the night guard. They're concerned that this is more serious than a stomachache, sort of.

"Look, what if it really is more than a stomachache? If we don't get this kid in front of a doctor, we could lose our jobs."

"Yeah, yeah. If he'd just shut up. But he won't. Alright, I'll get the doctor."

"Probst, this better be real 'cos I'm calling the doctor for your ass."

I vomit again.

I can only muster a meek; "Is that real enough for you?"

My strength is declining. I feel awful all over. It hurts so bad. I still cry for help, and the guys down the hall still yell back at me to shut the fuck up. We battle back and forth until finally, after what seems like an eternity of pain, a doctor arrives with a much nicer and prettier nurse at his side.

"Where is the pain, son?"

The doctor's inquiry seems sincere. But by this time the pain has spread everywhere, and I can't locate a particular spot. I point all over my groin area. Actually, I point down there because I notice this pretty nurse eyeing me (at least in my mind), and I'm now trying to figure out a way to get my khakis off in front of her! I can't wait to show her my big white dick. For a moment, the pain subsides. Sexual thoughts always make pain go away. Oh my God, am I lucky! The doc is leaving me alone with this nurse. She asks me again where it hurts. I can't believe my luck. Happy birthday to me.

"Right here."

I exclaim as I pull my pants down, way down, farther down than necessary, revealing a semi-hard large penis. In my head, she's fascinated, but alas, she simply tells me to pull up my pants before the doctor gets back. Fuck that – don't you see my big white dick? Dammit. I know she was turned on. I'll bet she's wet. Oh well, she's right. The pain is too much anyway. She winks at me.

"You are cute," she whispers this in my ear. Fuck yes!

Of course, I could just be delirious. I can't tell because everything's becoming blurry. The doctor has given me something and I'm losing consciousness. I hear him mention to somebody my appendix may have ruptured, and that they'll have to transport me to LA County-USC Medical Center. Fuck yes. I'm getting out of here for a while.

In the meantime, I can't move at all. I feel like I'm turning different colors, and just then I hear the nurse mention my nice yellow color to the doctor. This is not good, so sayeth the doc. They lift me into a wheelchair, handcuffed to its arms (just in case I decide to make a break for it), and wheeled into a sheriff's van. Whatever the doc gave me is not taking the pain away. My mind is disconnected, and my insides are burning up. I feel floaty, as if I'm looking at my pain rather than experiencing it. Next thing I know, we've arrived.

What a fucking disgusting place this is. Bodies everywhere. Disgusting bodies. Disfigured bodies. Dead bodies. They wheel me past a bloody gurney with a bloody amputee still freshly bleeding all over the place. Brain matter and intestines everywhere.

It's hard to describe the smell. I've never smelled anything like this before. Because I'm in custody, I'm taken, while still handcuffed to my precious wheelchair, up to the Jail Ward. As I enter, I realize it's nothing but another fucking jail. Bars everywhere. Steel doors with huge locks. Men in handcuffs. In the room they wheel me into, the windows are all barred up. So much for a spa and a nice shower.

They run tests. I faintly hear one tech comment to another that my "Y" count is low. Or did he say high? I don't know.

The tech speaks to me. "Son, we think your appendix has burst, when that happens, it's a life-or-death situation because poison is now spreading throughout your body. So, we're gonna have to operate. The problem is, no surgeons are available now because they're all operating on a man who shot at LAPD officers and was shot by them in the head. They're in surgery trying to save his life. Although if it was up to me, we wouldn't be worrying about that scumbag."

Yeah, well, it isn't up to this doctor, and they are worrying about him. You're gonna die.

"You seem to be yellow which isn't good. We can't wait too long, 'cos you could be getting peritonitis, inflammation of the peritoneum."

"How serious is that?"

"Well, if we don't operate soon enough and take your appendix out, it is fatal."

Really? Thanks for the comforting news, guy. My life is literally in these fuckers' hands. This is where the injured nethermost of society end up. No one cares about us out there, so no one cares about us in here. I'm still underage, so I really have no rights whatsoever. I'm wheeled into an elevator for surgery. My next thought…

I awake.

My God, I thought the pain was bad before the surgery, this is fucking worse. I hurt really fucking bad.

"Nurse! Doctor, somebody! Help me! I'm in pain!" I cry and cry.

6

Three Boys In a Room

I look around. I'm connected by an endless array of tubes to some beeping apparatus. But this doesn't concern me as much as the pain. It's worse than before the surgery. I look down at my groin area, and oh my fucking God. I can see my insides. These fuckers forgot to finish the surgery. They forgot to sew me back up. This hole they've left in me is huge. I mean huge. It's gross. I could never be a surgeon. Wait a minute, I've got a tube coming out of the hole. Is it supposed to be like this?

"If you want a nurse, you've got to press that button on the wall behind you. But they never come anyway, homie."

Another voice that sounds like a cholo has spoken from somewhere in this room. Because it hurts so much to move, I don't even look in this voice's direction.

"Who said that?"

"I'm over here. Look to your right, white boy. I'm in the bed next to you."

Man, that voice sounds familiar. I look over, and it's Frank Ramos. I was in a Boys home with this guy. I'm delirious from the pain, but I remember he was a good person. In this world, it's comforting to know your future cellmate is someone trustworthy. But he no longer resembles the Frank I knew. He doesn't recognize me, and this isn't due to my appearance. As I look closely at his face, I notice fresh scarring. These are not small cuts. These are serious, deep, jagged lacerations, obviously the reason for his hospitalization. I wonder what happened to him.

"Man, what happened to you?"

"I'm not sure. They said I've been in a coma for three weeks. I just came out of it two

35

days ago. They haven't told me much except that I was attacked by some Samoans at a party. They cut my face up with a boxcutter."

No wonder the scars are so jagged.

"I remember you from Rancho San Antonio Boys Home."

I try to trigger his memory. It doesn't work.

"You know what," Frank begins solemnly, "I didn't even know who I was until yesterday. They showed me a picture of myself, an ID, with my name and birthdate on it. That's how I found out my own name. I don't know anyone or even how to walk. My brain got fucked up by the Samoans. They beat my head into a curb. It hurts."

"Where the fuck did this happen at, dude?"

"They told me it happened at a party in Compton. But they haven't told me why I'm in jail."

Suddenly, without warning, Frank starts convulsing. I'm in too much pain to do him any good. I can't even reach the button that supposedly brings the nurse. So, I watch, fascinated, terrified, helpless to stop his torture. His eyes roll back, his tongue disappears, and with his scarring, it all adds a monstrous dimension to his already hideous facial injuries. I guess I'm not so hardened because I feel for this guy's pain. For a moment, mine seems small. The huge, locked door is being opened and two nurses rush in. They prop Frank up, one pulls his tongue out of his throat, the other monitors some machine. My pain is great, but I wish these nurses were more accessible for his sake. They strap him down so he can't move. I don't see much else. I only notice the commotion has subsided.

"Nurse, I need something for my pain, please." My request is more of a beg.

"You'll be getting a shot of Morphine and Demerol, painkillers, as soon as we finish with Frank. Relax."

"Can you tell me why I have a huge hole in my abdomen? Are you gonna sew it up?"

"No, the doctor will explain it all to you, now shut up." Where the fuck do they get these county nurses from anyway? Then the voice creeps in.

Hey there, idiot? Now you're gonna have a huge scar on your stomach. You think you're so good looking. Not anymore. You're not gonna be pulling your pants down for anyone after you see the scar you'll be left with!

Appendix Scar (6 years later)

The voice always knows how to get to me. I'm in so much pain, fighting back is too much effort. I look up at the TV hoping for solace, only to see the dots of distortion. Even the damn TV doesn't work here. Well, at least they've subdued ol' Frank. He's snoring quite loudly. Here comes Nurse Hairychin with her huge needle, telling me to pull down my pants and turn on my side. Sure, so my guts can spill out of the huge hole left in my side by the wonderful jailhouse physicians. She assures me that my intestines will stay intact, and that with this shot, soon I will feel no pain. I just wish I was getting naked for someone sexually attractive.

With my naked, round white butt-cheeks exposed and ready, I feel that initial prick of the needle, and within seconds I'm feeling euphoric. The good sensations are so intense that orgasms pale in comparison. I've entered a world of "I don't give a fuck." I'm fascinated with the distortion on the TV screen in front of me. I know. I'll play "connect the dots" with the fuzz. I'm able to follow each dot's particular path slowly, like a mouse finding his way through a maze. Everything is moving in slow-motion, and…no pain. This is fucking heaven. No, better than heaven. God couldn't possibly have drugs like this. I feel so good, nothing matters. Time passes…

Next thing I know, I'm cognizant that my body's feeling pain again. I look at the clock and I see my three hours of pleasure are over. It's a fine line between pleasure and pain. I don't remember anything except the trail of dots. Now I'm turning over on my own, naked booty and all, ready for the next shot. I reach for my nurse-call button and press.

Nurse Hairychin is back with an even bigger needle. Fuck yes. Prick me baby. She admonishes me not to get used to this because they'll soon be lowering my dosage to fend off possible addiction, but I'm not listening. I'll take anything to ease this horrendous post-surgery pain. Poor Frank has become an annoying post-coma moron. He's lost most cognitive functions, including the ability to comprehend much for more than a few minutes at a time, making him a terrible conversationalist. So, for me, drifting into La-La land for a while is more preferable than a frustrating conversation with a derelict.

I drift off…

Abruptly, I'm awakened to a new a day by a new nurse. It's hard to tell what time of day it is through the bars and wire mesh on the windows, so I rely on the TV for that information. This post-surgical pain is constant and potent. I smell bad, and I notice I'm acquiring quite facial sores due to the stringy, dirty, long blonde hair resting on my face and neck. I'm a human open wound, infected inside and out. But this hospital/jail bed is certainly more desirable than the lonely cell existence offered by Juvenile Hall.

The doctor has come in to explain what's happened to me, and why I've got a huge hole in my abdomen.

"Good morning, Douglas, how are you feeling today?"

"Not good, doc. I hurt bad. I still don't know what happened to me."

"Well, Douglas. Let me explain."

Yeah, like I'm going to stop him.

"Douglas, your appendix ruptured. Because so much time elapsed between its erup-tion and when we surgically removed it, you developed peritonitis."

"What is that?"

"It's the poison in an appendix," he begins solemnly. "It spread throughout your body, so we had to clean it out. That's why we haven't sewn you up. This will drain the poison out for a period of time. But I assure you, the eventual scar will be small. You will heal, Douglas."

My intuition tells me I've just been patronized. He lectures me on being thankful that I'm not like Frank over there and exits hastily.

Almost immediately, my drugged blissfulness is disturbed by the commotion of a new cellie-patient being wheeled in. The guy is arguing with the nurses about something. It sounds like verbal vomit to me. The guy is parked by the empty bed, left to fend for himself. His mouth is rattling on nonstop. Black dude with a ponytail.

"Those fuckin' bitches," he swears as he begins to unwrap the dressing on his right leg. "They wouldn't give me my mail right now. I know I got a letter from my girl. Can't use the phone either. Mothafuckin' county jail hospital workers."

As he continues to unwrap his bandage, I'm transfixed by the endless swirling motion he makes as he's unbandaging his leg. Around and around his leg he goes, when he stops, not even he knows… What the fuck? He's got no fucking foot. A bloody stump that cuts off grotesquely at the anklebone is all I see. Talk about gross. It sort of looks like, well, like a slab of freshly cut roast beef, very rare. This dude's gonna have problems, 'cos he ain't growin' no new foot. I've got to find out how this shit happened.

"What the fuck happened to you, man?"

"What the fuck does it look like, white boy? My mothafuckin' foot's shot off! I was chasing this mothafuckin' blood through my hood with my 12-gauge, and I tripped and blew my mothafucking foot off."

Now I know he's a Crip. It seems like all black dudes are Crips.

He's not finished with his account yet.

"Mothafuckin' Bloods aint got no business bein' in 69 East Coast territory," he says an-imatedly, "but this mothafucka was lucky I tripped. I woulda blasted on that mothafucka!"

This dude hates "Bloods" so much, even after mistakenly "blasting" himself, he still wants that "Blood." It all seems rather pointless to me. Frank's moaning in the other bed temporarily interrupts us.

"What's up with that Ese'?" The black dude wants to know. "He sounds all fucked up."

"He is, man. He got fucked up by some Samoans big-time. He just came out of a coma. You know what? He doesn't even know who he is!"

Come to think of it, I don't know who this black guy is either. I decide it's safe enough to ask.

"What's your name, dude?"

"I'm mothafuckin' Big Dog from 69 East Coast Crip Cuzz. What you in here for, white boy?"

I hate having to explain anything, so I use the opportunity to make up outrageously cool sounding crimes. Having this hole in my stomach when I return to Juvenile Hall will give me all kinds of credibility if I decide to say I was knifed in a fight. Even right now, I lie.

"Assault with a deadly weapon. I stabbed this guy after he shot at me." My pretty face betrays my alleged criminal nature. Maybe he'll think that because of my cuteness, I had to be twice as tough. Uh, yeah right Doug. Guys named "Big Dog" don't analyze that deeply. I hear the voice making its usual leap into action.
You liar, Doug. You're a pussy so just admit it. The only knife you've wielded was when you've buttered your toast. You're the only one here whose injuries weren't caused through some violent action. You came in to this system as a little twelve-year-old wimp, and you're still afraid. All you do is lie.

"Yo, this shit hurts." Big Dog and I have one thing in common: PAIN! He now begins to furiously hit his nurse call button. My pain is killing me. I see Frank frantically hitting his button. I'm hitting my button too. Three guys in pain. All three frantically pushing our buttons hoping someone would come and make the pain go away.
But the voice has lied to me now. I'm not that frightened little wimp anymore. I've changed. It's true that I entered Leroys' Boys Home a twelve-year-old boy with hairless balls, cuter than a girl, and terrified as any pre-pubescent white boy would be in that situation. And yes, it's true, I got beat up numerous times. At times I screamed for my life without fighting back. I'm not sure how I even survived those times.
But I've turned the corner. I remember when I turned the corner. It was after I was kicked out of Rancho San Antonio Boys Home for being AWOL at night. I was sent back to Juvenile Hall and it all just clicked. My mom doesn't give a shit, my dad's never given a shit about me his whole life, and no one in my family cares about me either. This is my home forever. And I'm fucking pissed. I sat there and made my mind up that if I can't beat 'em, I'm joining 'em.
I recall immediately acted on this feeling. This black loud mouth kid, Williams who was always beating up white boys for no reason was sitting next to me talking trash. I el-

bowed him to shut up, which is a huge no no – you can get killed for doing that. He elbowed me back and got up to punch me. I went crazy. I grabbed his arm and twisted it behind his back, almost breaking it in two.

All the inmates yelled, "Fight!" And they ran over, lining up to watch. I could hear them saying that white boy's gonna get knocked out, but I changed that belief quickly. I rammed Williams' head into the brick wall, and started beating his face in really good, blood and teeth came out of his mouth, and he started whimpering. He was always a bully, telling me what to do like he was some bad ass, and there I was, beating the shit out of him while he begged me to stop.

I answered his cries with: "Fuck you you fucking bitch made punk, it's over for you. You're gonna die today, you bitch. I'm sick of you trying to control the white boys in here. This white boy is down for anything motherfucker." And I kept ramming his head into the wall, until he passed out. The officers came rushing in and grabbed me, and I slapped one of them.

"Fuck you too! I'm sick of this shit! Fuck all of you! Ain't no black ass punk, or Mexican motherfucker us EVER going to fuck with this white boy again. This is white power motherfuckers!"

There isn't a prejudiced bone in my body, but I was tired of getting disrespected by every one of every race. I never understood prejudice. I heard the term used so many times before I was ten years old that I had to look up the proper definition of it in my Webster's Dictionary. It read: Prejudice means to "pre-judge" something or someone before you understand it or them. I've felt the opposite. When I see something or meet someone who's not like me, I want to get to know them better. I want to appreciate our differences. Most of the time, I didn't think deeply about it, I simply didn't prejudge people. But, locked inside this system, I was tired of getting disrespected. And although throughout my life, the people I've loved the most dearly have been black and latino – my musical heroes, my best friends, my lovers – in this place it was different. The races stuck with their own kind.

It makes no sense to me. I don't want to be here. But this is my home. I have to survive.

They walked me to solitary and gave me thirty days in the box. I thought, so fucking what? No one's wondering about where I am anyway, and if they do, it's only because they want to fuck me or fight me. My anger at my parents, my whole family, the Priests, the counselors, the staff, and the animals I live with coalesced that day and transformed Doug Probst.

I've become angry enough and scared enough to hit them before I get hit. And I'm willing to go all the way; let them sort out the body parts later. I'm white and that means I have to fight or get the shit beat out of me. I prefer to keep my shit inside. I'm not gonna back down to anyone anymore. A few dudes have awakened from the ground wailing. "That white boy hit me!" And the two years between fourteenth and my sixteenth birthday were nothing but fighting. And I never saw one family member. It hurt, because I saw murderers with whole families on Sundays coming to visit them. A visit from someone who cares means so much. I have to be angry before I cry.

Now I'm sixteen and I have a hole in my abdomen. I'm vulnerable today and I'm in too much pain to put up much of a fight with the voice or Big Dog. Big Dog seemed uninterested in the details of my "crime" anyway.

The next morning, I'm awakened to the sound of voices surrounding Frank's bed. There's two uniformed police officers along with what looked like a professionally dressed woman. I assume he is being escorted to court, since he still could not walk on his own. As I listen closer to the conversation, I realize I am half-right. The woman is his court-appointed attorney and she's informing him about the charges against him. I can't make out much of the conversation (especially with Hop-along Jackson on my left), so I strain to listen. The cops and Frank's attorney leave our room.

"Frank! What's up, dude?" I ask,

"Well," he begins with a sigh, "they told me what I'm charged with, why I'm locked up."

"Really man? So, tell me." This has also seized Big Dog's interest. Frank opens up.

"Murder. They say I shot a Samoan at this party homie. I don't remember anything. They say they got witnesses, and that's why those Samoans beat me and cut me up. Now I might be locked up for life because of something I don't remember doing."

This is one nightmare I'm glad I'm not living.

"Mothafuckin' esa. You in here for murder, and you can't even walk." Big Dog seems to be enjoying Frank's plight. "Man, you got problems."

I can't help it. I've got to say something. "Like you don't have problems with no foot. We've all got problems, dude."

Big dog doesn't like a white boy giving him advice.

"Shut the fuck up, white boy!"

I seem to have triggered something in Big Dog other than anger. He looks rattled by my last comment, as if it is finally dawning on him that he's not going to be an effective tough guy ever again. To add to that, it's because of his own stupidity. In fact, I see tears well up in his eyes.

"Fuck you, white boy. I know I'm fucked up. It don't change that dude's situation."

Before I can answer, Nurse Hairychin comes in and informs me I have a visitor. ME? I have lived this existence in pure isolation for years, watching enviously as murderers and robbers get family visits faithfully, while I have seen no family member for months at a time. Sometimes years. Isolation. That is the sum of my existence. But today, a visitor? I'm all fucked up, and someone wants to see me. The nurse tells me it's my mom. I'm not able to move out of my bed yet, so she has to visit me here in the room.

The door swings open, and it's… MOM? The woman entering bears a slight resemblance to what I remember my mother looking like, but this one has bruises on her face, black eyes, and fresh bloody stitches in her scalp. Way to go, Mom. Always the drama queen. She looks worse than I do. Emotionally, I feel nothing for her. She's abandoned me, she's chosen a gangster over me, she's never visited me, she doesn't give a shit about me.

The many nights I spent in torment wishing she'd hold me and comfort me are gone. I'm not completely devoid of love for my mom, but right now I feel mostly contempt for her. I wasted too much time begging for her to love me. But still, there's something codified

41

into my DNA that tells me I must care about my mother. She makes it to my bedside and an awkward silence takes over as I'm not sure if I should exchange places with her. She's in her usual self-absorbed form. She cries.

Through the glass separating us, we pick up the phones and begin to talk.

"God, Doug. What happened? You look really bad, but the doctor says you'll be fine. Things haven't been too good for me lately."

Through her teary haze, I detect some slight, genuine concern. Yet even my hospital visit becomes about her.

"Mom, what happened to you?" I'm worried about her.

"Oh," she starts wearily, "Robert's been beating me lately. I'm not sure what I'm gonna do. Things haven't been too good at the house. He's been out of control. I'm worried about Steven."

Steven is my two-year-old nephew who lives with my mom because my sister is a full-time drug addict. He's my mother's obsession.

"I don't know what to say, Mom. I want out of this place. I don't think they did a good job with this surgery. Look at this hole in me."

On the inside, I think: Maybe since they almost killed me, we might have a lawsuit? Mom, if you sue them, you can have all the beer you want for the rest of your life.

She starts crying again. At no time does she offer to take me home. She can do that at any time. Right here, right now, she could call any authority figure over and say, "I'm taking my son home now!" She has that right. But she doesn't have the love. I don't even ask her, because I know Robert's more important to her. If she was gonna get me out of the LA County Probation System, she would have done it already. But she never has. Fuck you, bitch. I secretly hope Robert kills her. And one second later, I feel sorry for her and want to comfort her.

I'm screwed up in the head.

7

Navel Gazing

Long Beach California, 1986

Luckily no one's interested in my childhood, so I escape the line of fire for a while. The voice has tried but hasn't succeeded in making me believe I'm no good because of my upbringing. It'll keep trying though, I'm sure. My day isn't supposed to be about this shit anyway. I look at my watch, and it's five minutes past the time I was supposed to see the mortgage guy about these clients I have. Where the fuck is this guy? Everybody's late in this business. I hate it. I want people here on time, all the time.

A tall guy in a cheap suit waltzes in the front door. As he approaches my desk, I notice he's extremely handsome. My gay friends would label Chris as "Man Candy." Manly, good-looking, dark hair, blue eyes, chiseled facial features. His swagger tells me he knows he's gorgeous. I'm immediately intimidated and that rarely happens. I better get a grip right away, or the voice will have a field day with this one. I immediately have respect for him just based on his looks. I'm no different than anyone else.

"Are you Doug Probst?" I guess he missed the nameplate on my desk sticking right out in front. Oops! That's because the side with the name is facing me. I guess I love to see my name as much as I love looking in mirrors.

"Yes, I am." I stand up with an outstretched hand, offering my best realtor dude impersonation. "You must be Chris Menninger from American Mortgage?"

"Yeah, man it's good to meet you. I'd like to qualify your clients, but I'm hungry. "You ever eaten at Yesterdays?"

"Once. I remember there were a lot of college kids there."

I always forget I'm of "college kid" age. I don't feel like one. Yesterdays is the typical

1980's yuppie hangout. Short-haired preppie college guys drinking Coronas, looking to get laid. I immediately feel out of place as we arrive and as usual, the voice pounces.

'Here you are again Doug, in your fake job, your fake clothes, living your fake life. Why do you keep going to places where you don't belong? It's only a matter of time until...'

"Shut the fuck up!" I scream on the inside. Or so I thought.

Chris looks startled.

"Who are you talking to, man?"

My mind moves lightning fast for recovery. "Oh I'm just replaying a conversation I had with an asshole in a club the other night. I'm working on putting a melody to it."

"A melody to shut the fuck up?" Chris laughs.

Just then, a waitress greets us and shows us to our table. My eyes have descended upon a gorgeous Latin girl waitressing near us, and her eyes return the favor. She is beautiful. I can't believe she's eyeing me. She looks exotic, erotic, all the things that have already made her my wife in my mind. Today, I want to meet this girl, and I do.

"You're gorgeous. What's your name?"

"My name is Ramona. What's yours?"

I want to make a joke to show how absolutely witty I am, but my instincts tell me I'd make myself look like a fool. There's nothing worse for me than looking like a fool.

"My name is Doug. Chris and I have some properties we have to look at, and I see you're busy with customers, so I hope I'm not being too forward by asking for your phone number to call you later."

She smiles, as she writes the pertinent information down, and once again, I have another phone number to add to my burgeoning collection. For some reason, I feel so studly and cool after attaining The Phone Number. It's as if my whole life depends on her yes or no, I guess there should be a drum roll between the time I ask for the number and when the girl responds. I literally feel as though these are my moments of judgment. Am I worthy of her number, or am I a geek? If I receive a "no," I'm destroyed for quite a while. Usually, however, I've got it set up, so that I'm assured of no rejection. My encounters are risk-free, because I've had so much eye contact ahead of time. For a split second, it occurs to me how shallow and self-centered this whole charade is.

I really do want to do more with my life. I just can't seem to break this compelling need to meet and "conquer." I look at Chris with envy and sexual curiosity. I wonder if he's ever done it with a guy. I don't want to reach over and touch his crotch, that's not the way to get something going. Anyway, I've got other things to focus on. He's very good looking, but I lose interest in admiring him. I couldn't be in charge. I need to control the situation.

If I'm not gay, why am I thinking about him this way?

I can't wait to get back home and masturbate all night.

Momentarily, I wonder why I live a double life, but then the moment passes because I can't stop thinking about sex. I'm always either masturbating or plotting a sexual conquest. I'm on the phone talking dirty to a church secretary listening to her masturbate to a story I've made up, or I'm talking to one of many girls who masturbate while on the phone with me, or I'm actually fucking a girl (it takes more work to get the phone number and buy her at least one dinner), or I'm having my dick sucked by a paying customer, and so on and so on. It's cool to get paid and have my dick sucked at the same time. But here I am, going down (irony intended) the mental/sexual obsessive/compulsive path again. I want to be known for something else, but this "profession" and my own sexual obsessions dominate my life.

I think my head has psychological problems; it's definitely unsafe for me to think about me for too long, but how can I ask for help when it's my job to be perfect? I can't seem to live without acting impulsively. I act before I think. I admire and hate people with patience. Many times, I've cried out to God to grant me patience now! Maybe it's not hate I feel for patient, disciplined people, but jealousy. Fuck you God. If you were real — it's not even a debate, you can't be. If there is a God, he must be an atheist.

For a second, I recognize that I literally don't trust anything or anyone. But that second passes just as soon as it arrives. I worry about what people think of me. I argue with myself about what I think people are thinking about me. The "voice" enlarges my fears. I hear over and over, You're no good, Doug, you're no good; it's as simple as that.

Since I'm no good, reality sucks. So, I try to create my own reality; a world of sybaritic fantasies. I attempt to reframe reality. I invent and substitute illusions to soften the facts. I jack off all the time. But it's all a façade. There isn't any flexibility in reality. At least I'm trying. But this isn't trying. I'm a lazy fucker who takes the easy way out to get what I want. Deep down, I'm not shallow. Deep down I'm a fraud. I'm twenty-one now. I was supposed to be a rock star by this time. The world just doesn't seem to know it. Maybe I'm the one who doesn't know it. If I knew it, the world would know it. Someone, please discover me. I'm not getting accolades for being the iconoclast who breaks through the current shallow rock music with my shocking but truthful lyrics about real life. I'm writing them, but no one's hearing them. Instead, I'm naked, with my penis still fully erect, standing in front of a wealthy, obese, older man, thinking only about the money.

It makes sense to separate my lives. But can I separate them? I'm lying most of the time. I don't like lying. So, if I'm lying and I don't like lying, maybe I don't like myself. But how can that be? I love me. Is it possible to be confident and hopeless at the same time? If this is love, it's fucking malignant love. And I wonder if I'm taking all of my musical talent for granted? At the same time, I don't trust that I'll ever be successful at a "musical career," so I jump at any person who offers me money for sex. I tell myself that someone will discover me. I have time. Is that trust or taking my gifts for granted? How can I take my dreams for granted and yet act like I don't believe my dreams will ever come true? How can I crave success yet operate as a failure? I'm a mass of scar tissue that'll never heal.. And I don't know where to get the fucking medicine. Sometimes, I feel like there's no known cure. I don't understand myself or why I do this shit. Why do I do what I don't like to do?

8

Many Houses, No Home

I was born on April 1, 1965.

I was born into a dishonest world. Everything in our household was built on lies. My father, Kurt Probst, simply hated me. He was always angry, and he acted as if I only existed to annoy him. And I always annoyed him. I was being myself, a curious toddler, and suddenly he would hit me without warning or explanation.

On the other hand, when I was a toddler, the world was filled with wonderment. I had courage, and when I wanted something, I didn't wait for permission to get it. I was my father's nemesis from the moment I was born. I was investigative, impulsive, and I wasn't going to let anything stop me from doing what I wanted to do. Someone once told me I must have born with a penthouse in one hand and a cigar in the other. I don't remember who said it, but I remember feeling amused and annoyed at the same time when I heard it.

Now, I'm living in a world that was separate from the world most of you have grown up in. I'd been alive for seventeen years and thirty-five days on this earth, incarcerated at Sylmar Juvenile Hall, located in the San Fernando Valley. I had been incarcerated in Juvenile Hall or living in one of many Boys' Homes for nearly five straight years, since I was twelve years old.

At eleven years old, my parents placed me in La Habra Mental Hospital for three months. I was told I was "acting out" and I needed Psychiatric help. My father was raping my sister, but according to my parents, I was the one that needed psychiatric oversight. My parents divorced when I was eleven only after my mother walked in on my father raping my sister. My mom said she couldn't be with him after witnessing this. He wasn't trustworthy anymore. It had nothing to do with protecting my sister, Jamie.

My mother never reported my father to the police, and I stayed with her.

She then became involved with Robert, a Mexican Gangster from the Varrio Norwalk Gang in Norwalk, California.

When Mom and Dad deposited me in La Habra Mental Hospital, Mom was given an assessment from the psychiatrist as to his evaluation of what he thought the problem was.

Mom decided she was against psychiatry after the report held my parents accountable for their lack of interaction with me.

At the ripe old age of twelve, my mother placed me in Leroy Boys Home, in La Verne, California, because she claimed she could not handle me. I spent the next ten months of my life (September 1977 – July 1978) there. While I was there, counselors physically and sexually abused many boys. In fact, the second day I was there, a counselor known as "Uncle Ken" shoved the skull of a boy into a curb we sat on while lining up to run laps. After the screams and the blood were gone, the boy's head required thirty-three stitches. After seeing that, I was scared for my life every day that I lived at Leroy's Boys Home.

I was beat up a lot because I was pretty and noticeably young. Instead of being protected, Leroy's was just a continuation of traumatizing fear. I wondered why we were required to call all counselors "Uncle" when we weren't related to them. Although I wrote letters to my mother, I never received any responses.

She later said she ignored my letters because she thought I was lying. She never investigated. I tried so hard to please her, to be the best-behaved boy I could be while at Leroy's, but it didn't matter. I lived there for ten months, achieving straight A's and I was discharged with not one disciplinary problem ever.

The one bright moment of my life at Leroys' Boys Home was when I was taken to my first live concert at the Long Beach Arena in 1977. It was Aerosmith, but for me, the opening band stole the show. A counselor named Steve Depaolo took a liking to me and noticed my musical ability when he brought his guitar to Leroy's for me to play. I'll never forget the concert. I had no idea what I was about to experience from this unknown opening act. This little manic lead guitar player who never stopped moving was on the shoulders of this confident, dynamic lead singer through half the show. As they were playing a song called "Problem Child," the lead singer and guitar player rocked in front of each and every aisle of the Arena – and they stood rocking right in front of me for a minute as if I was a prince! I was blown away. We all were. They grabbed my soul and I found out the band's name was AC/DC. I was hooked for life. I went back to my lonely Boy's Home room, fantasizing about my future as a rock star. I knew that was me. It was also my ticket out of this hellhole of a world I was born into. Steve Depaolo was like a saint. He was the only counselor who treated me like a son.

It never got better than that night at the Long Beach Arena. I came back to Leroy's and the counselors and gangbangers continued abusing the weaker boys like me.

Years later, an investigation was done due to reports of abuse of the boys at Leroy's. My mother claimed she was never informed. Leroy Boys Home was later closed due to child abuse, but it was long after I was gone. I completed my stay at Leroy's and was released in July of 1978, when I was thirteen years old. My mother picked me up and I was overjoyed to see her. I was finally gonna have my mother. Then I noticed something. There was alcohol on her breath. She acted annoyed having to pick me up. We argued all the way home. This "incorrigible youth" had made it through a tough Boys' Home, earning straight A's at school, and never having one problem. I endured the beatings and never went AWOL. I endured all of this so I could go home to my mother who I believed loved me and wanted me home. I realized on the ride home that she had become an alcoholic and I was crushed. This was the commencement of my cynical nature toward life. I had been betrayed. But that was just the beginning. When I arrived "home," I met her boyfriend, Robert. Or, should I say, I met Robert's guns and fists. Robert was an extremely violent, terrifying gangster who was also addicted to heroin.

Robert gave me pot to sell at Bancroft Junior High School in Lakewood, California, where somebody snitched on me. They searched my locker and called me into the principal's office.

(This is the last official school picture ever taken of me. 1978 – Bancroft Junior High School – thirteen years old. You won't find any high school pictures of me.)

I was already high from smoking a joint of my mother's boyfriends' pot, so after hearing my name over the loudspeaker — "Doug Probst, please report to the principal's office" — I lazily strolled across campus. As I entered, red eyed and high, I saw a man with a military style haircut, sitting behind his desk, holding a large zip lock bag of marijuana in one hand, and a freshly rolled joint in the other. I recognized it immediately as the ounce of pot that Robert had given me to sell at school. He looked at me, still fondling the joint, appearing aroused by its phallic form.

"Douglas, do you know what this is?"

"No sir. I've never seen anything like that before. What is it?" I feigned complete ignorance.

"It's a marijuana cigarette," he said proudly, as if he'd solved a great scientific mystery.

"Wow. Where did you find that?" I tried to sound convincing, but I was high as hell.

"In your locker, Mr. Probst!"

"No way! I've never seen that thing."

He's not swayed by my protestations of innocence.

"We also found this large bag of marijuana in your locker."

"I don't know what you're talking about, sir."

Why would I worry? Everything's trivial when stoned.

He answered, "I'll make a deal with you, Mr. Probst. We have information that you've been selling marijuana on campus. We have evidence to prosecute you. But here's my offer: If you turn around and walk straight home, no detours, I'll only have you expelled. I won't file charges against you. I just want you off my campus, and you are never to come back. Is that a deal?"

"Sure. It's a deal."

48

Shit. The pot was wearing off I started walking home. Now I was going to get the shit beat out of me because I lost the dope Robert gave me to sell. And I couldn't get away from him since I've been expelled. I liked school. I liked learning. And there were so many girls to choose from. Oh well. I had no choice. I started my long, lonely walk home. My mother was going to have to find another school for me. Maybe she'd realize it was Robert's fault for giving me pot to sell, and she wouldn't blame me.

All of that was wishful thinking. As soon as I got home, and they found out what happened, Robert beat the shit out of me. Mom was too busy getting drunk and getting beat up by Robert to re-enroll me in school. I figured that mom probably wasn't making choices with my best interests at heart, so I decided it was safer to live on the streets.

I knew another boy named John Acosta who was smoking pot at his house just a few houses down from my mother's house. A lot of pot. He turned me on to Led Zeppelin. Just for that reason alone, I'll love him forever.

He was a good guy and we hung out together almost every day in the summer of '78. Then I hit the big time, got incarcerated, and disappeared on him and everyone for the next five years.

***

In November of 1978, I got caught burglarizing a house in Lakewood because I had stolen two kilos of marijuana from the local pot dealer. The police arrested me and took me to the Lakewood Sheriff's Station. The detective saw how young I was and begged my mother to come pick me up because he felt I did not belong in Juvenile Hall.

He pleaded with her, "Ma'am, your son is not a bad kid. He'll get killed in Juvenile Hall. He just needs some guidance."

She refused to take me home, telling the detective, "Fuck him. I really don't want him here," and I was transported to Los Padrinos Juvenile Hall. Her words reverberate in my ears to this day.

I had to appear in court and the pot dealer showed up in a hissy fit. He was pissed off at me and stared at me with a look that could kill. He spoke to the judge and wanted his "property" returned. The judge knew the "property" I had stolen, so he mocked the guy by saying: "Do you want to tell the court what you owned that Mr. Probst stole from you?"

And everyone in the courtroom looked at him to see what he'd say.

Realizing he had made a huge mistake almost admitting to a felony, he shut up.

I was found guilty and the detective tried to get me back home again but my mother wouldn't have me. So I entered the County bus in chains and I was ushered off with other juvenile criminals to Los Padrinos Juvenile Hall. It was a tough, dangerous place with a bad reputation.

Because I was now a ward of the court, I was assigned a probation officer, John Scott. He was a crusty, freckle faced, fifty-year-old man whose job has been to find places for me to live since I was thirteen years old. We had a relationship, but I didn't know how to characterize it. He was more of a Paper Report than a human being to me.

9

Incarceration

I called LP home for three months (November 1978 –February 1979). I was assigned a Probation Officer named John Scott who placed me in Rancho San Antonio Boys Home in February of 1979. For the next ten months, I resided at Rancho San Antonio Boys Home (February 1979 – January 1980). I was kicked out for leading a group of teenagers on a midnight AWOL for fun. I was sent back to Los Padrinos Juvenile Hall and moved to Central Juvenile Hall in Downtown Los Angeles for two months (January 1980 to February 1980). I was placed back in Rancho San Antonio Boys Home for three months (February 1980 – May 1980), was kicked out again for fighting, and this time I was moved up to a more hardcore place called Probation Camp David Miller, and then Camp Kilpatrick for four months (May 1980 – September 1980). I spent two weeks in the "box," solitary confinement at Kilpatrick, and then I was sent back to Miller.

Upon release from Camp Miller, my parents still refused to take me home, so John Scott had to find me another place to go. I ended up at Guadalupe Boys Home in Redlands, California for five months (September 1980 – January 1981), and then Sunrise Youth Community in Compton, California for six months (January 1981-June 1981) where I was sexually assaulted by the Director George Gybbs. Sunrise is also where I met a boy I loved named Ted. He was the kindest, sweetest young man I'd ever met, and he never refused to please me sexually when I was horny. I was then released from Sunrise into the care of a Perverted Wannabe Foster "Parent" in Long Beach/Lakewood for two months (June 1981-July 1981), a molester's home which I was able to get away from and live on the streets of East Lakewood for a month and a half. I was re-incarcerated when my mother turned me in for going AWOL from this perverted psycho's house. My next two months were spent languishing again in Los Padrinos Juvenile Hall and Central Juvenile Hall until October of 1981. I was then placed in Boys' Republic in October of 1981, where I lasted three months, until I was kicked out for fighting a kid who loved sticking a toothbrush up his ass. He crossed the line in the showers when he tried to stick one up mine. I was kicked out in January of 1982. Of course, I was sent straight back to Juvenile Hall in handcuffs. I spent many thirty-day stints living in solitary confinement in all three LA County Juvenile Halls. Most of them for fighting.

So, they arrested me at the Boys' Home and a Police Officer was assigned to drive me back to Juvy. Well, not exactly. This particular cop decided to park somewhere while I was in handcuffs in the back seat of his Patrol Car. He then told me he wanted to see my dick. This I will never forget because it was strange yet so familiar. He opened the glass.

"Hey, Douglas, I know I shouldn't be asking you to do this, but you are a very attractive young man. I'm imagining what your dick looks like hard. I really want to suck your dick. I want to see it."

Fuck, I'm horny too. "Well, if you take these handcuffs off, I'll pull it out for you."

I can't remember if I said sir or not. I hope I did though, it would have added a cool master/slave element to our interaction.

The cop is struggling with his horniness. He's caught between erection and sanity. He moves his head through the glass to get a better vantage point of my crotch area. He speaks again.

"Man, this is painful for me. I really want you to pull out your cock, but I can't let you out of those cuffs. I know it's hard, isn't it?"

"Yes, it is. I can show it to you, but not if I can't pull it out."

The cop speaks louder, "Fuck man, you look good, Douglas. I've got to take you to Juvenile Hall. I'm on a schedule. Man, I wish this was a different time and place. We'd be having a good time."

I guess the blood went back to his brain. Time for mine to travel back upward also.

"Ok, I understand." The voice ambushes me. You're going to fucking jail again. And you're still a fag. On the way to Juvy – what a fucking piece of shit you are. You're fucking pathetic.

I had to get my head on straight with handcuffs on, a horny cop struggling with his conscience, and the voice intimidating and berating me. And I would be locked up with the animals in Gladiator School in a few minutes. It really sucked to be sixteen years old and in Los Angeles County. He took me to Sylmar Juvenile Hall and a familiar cycle repeats itself again; the unpredictability of not knowing how long I'll be there, the mental and physical abuse, fighting every day, and total despair.

I was ordered to spend four months in the Psychiatric Program of Sylmar Juvenile Hall. After completion of four months, to my astonishment, I was taken to the Courtroom on May 6, 1982 and told that I was going to be "emancipated" while I was a minor and given my freedom. Apparently, the court and my Probation Officer John Scott agreed that they had run out of options for me and that since my parents' were uninterested and unequipped to take responsibility for me, the best thing for me was to emancipate me, make me an adult, and drop me off on the streets.

***

Now, I'm seventeen years old, and it's May 6, 1982. I've spent nearly every single day

51

of my life since I was twelve years old confined within the Los Angeles County Probation System.

I don't know much about your world. I've never been free to experience a teenage life for five long years. I have never played on a high school sports team. I haven't strummed a guitar except a few times in five years. I haven't heard a lot of music except whatever a probation officer decides to play on the intercom: It's usually "I fought the law and the law won," just to provoke us. I watched a lot of tv — mostly stupid shows meant for little kids. I never had a girlfriend. I've never seen a movie in a theater. I was in Guadalupe' Boys' Home in Redlands when I heard on the radio that my hero John Lennon was shot and killed in December 1980. I couldn't believe it, I was shocked. I could have cared less when that fat dude Elvis died, but this was my hero; a man who wrote his own songs, defied the world, created a rock band that spoke to me musically and lyrically. And somebody shot him? For a few minutes I sat by my radio, the tears welling up, ready to pour out from my eyes.

But I take another hit from my joint and I wonder if I'm just stoned. The tears don't fall. Life's better when stoned.

For months at a time, while in Juvenile Hall, I was not allowed to write or use a pencil. Pencils were considered weapons. I was locked in my cell for twenty hours a day, so I did a lot of thinking, but I couldn't write any thought down. At the time in my life when I needed the most brain stimulation, I got the least. I never ate a meal without worrying that I'd have to fight to keep it in my possession. I'm very skilled at taking a "birdbath," when you dump water from the steel sink in your cell onto your head and scrub it on your body. It's what you do when you can't take a shower with the general population, or you're locked in solitary. I spent a lot of my teenage life in solitary confinement because I fought for my right to eat. The "box" was my second home during my teenage years. Mental health professionals say that long term incarceration in solitary confinement does serious psychological damage to the person locked in solitary. But I loved it. Like I said before, I could jack off day and night, and I didn't have to interact with teenage animals who wanted to kill me for my shoes.

I never received any visitors during my teenage years, except once, when I was near death when my appendix ruptured. I guess no one came because no one cared enough to visit. I remember playing Pinball back in 1977 but I heard, through boys locked up with me, that there's these space age things called video games. I'd never played these video games. Vaguely I've heard their names, Pac Man or Space Invaders, whatever... Pinball was the latest hi-tech game I played. In 1977, I played music on 8 Track Tapes. Upon release, everyone was listening to music on Cassettes. I've never been to a prom; I've never graduated from anything. I entered the system in 1977 when Jimmy Carter was elected President, and I was released in 1982 when a Republican guy named Ronald Reagan was now President. I had never seen this thing called MTV, but it was apparently popular and controversial. The world had changed a lot without me since 1977.

I hadn't had much fun in the last five years. The only days I fraternized with the free world were a couple of months when I was fifteen and living in Guadalupe Boys Home in Redlands California. Though I was in the Boys Home, I was allowed to attend Redlands High School, and I lasted five months. I got high a lot at Guadalupe', and Redlands High School. I was eventually kicked out of Guadalupe', and sent back to Juvenile Hall. With the exception of those five months — and even then, I was living at a Boys Home — I'd been confined and caged with thieves, robbers, gangbangers, murderers, rapists, and child molesters.

And the molesters had the keys to my cell, the ownership to my freedom, and the rights to my body. The molesters were always in charge.

I just wanted a pencil and writing paper. I could have been happy fighting for my life, getting fucked in the ass, and never seeing the outside world if they'd just allowed me a pencil and paper. I wanted those items even more than a guitar and a piano. I'd ask, "Why don't you see that I'm different in here? I can be trusted with a pencil. I just want to write songs." They ignored me. It hurt so bad to be denied writing lyrics or putting my thoughts down on paper for so many years of my teenage life. I also couldn't create music on any instrument. I couldn't be me. It hurt deeply. I wanted to create something, anything. I didn't want to stab anyone in their eye. I prayed to god to get me out of here. But I realized there ain't no fucking God. I've been on my knees alone in my cell and his ass never answered one prayer. He gives the priests the boys, and us boys get nothing. Fuck him.

I grew my first pubic hairs while inside the LA County Probation world.

I imagined what it would have been like to kiss a girl or a boy. But I couldn't. Sex was either imaginary or with people who made it secret. I masturbated and shot my first ejaculate in a Boys' Home.

I learned how to juggle by smuggling tape into my cell. I'd wrap the tape around itself until I had good size balls (pardon the pun) and I taught myself how to juggle. I guess I practiced my own brand of self-discipline because it took a lot of practice and patience. I'd always been impressed with jugglers and never thought I could do it. But I learned! This is how bored I'd become after being locked in my cell for twenty hours a day for months at a time. I was imprisoned but I decorated my cell.

10

Entering Your World

On May 6th, 1982, after being incarcerated for five long years, John Scott came to my cell at Sylmar Juvenile Hall and told me: "Doug, the Court's decided you're capable of living your life on your own. The judge will emancipate you today. I am going to take you out of the Court to re-dress you in jeans, a t-shirt, and sneakers. Then I'll drive you to somewhere close to your mother's house in Lakewood. I will drop you off."

I was confused. Drop me off? Somewhere close to my mother's house? What does that mean? Actually, I realized, I didn't really care that much where he drops me off. I heard "Doug will be free" – that's it. He could have said he was dropping me off in Antartica. I didn't care if it was 30 degrees below zero; it was freedom.

I exited the gates of Sylmar Juvenile Hall without handcuffs. I would no longer look out a small window and see a brick wall. I got into John Scott's Toyota Celica one happy fucking teenager. A teenager who is going to start fucking people on my terms. I was already feeling like a stud. John Scott explained why he wants to drop me off near my mother's house, not AT my mother's house.

"Doug, we emancipated you because we think you're smart enough to take care of yourself. Your mother's an alcoholic, so I won't tell you to go there. I know you don't have anywhere else to go, but in my report, I have to say where I dropped you off. You're an adult now, so you can go anywhere on your own. I'm planning on dropping you off a block or two away from your mom's. I called your dad, but he refused to take you."

I'm an adult? I've never known a real adult. If there are adults in Los Angeles County, it's only because they act that way in public.

"So what do I do after you drop me off? I don't have any money."

"I know that, Doug. I'll give you $100. I'm advising you to stay away from your mom's house though. Her boyfriend is a gangbanger and drug dealer."

"Ok."

With a mixture of excitement, awe, and pure joy, I exited John Scott's Toyota Celica at the corner of Del Amo Blvd. and Woodruff Avenue in Lakewood California. I was happy to exit, and could care less that I only have $100 and the clothes on my back. Again, I was fucking free. I was free to walk wherever I chose.

I just wanted to fuck.

But I truly didn't have anywhere to live. I was told that my own mother's house was a bad place to be. I'm sure Dad's would have been worse. And I didn't like him anyway.

So there I was, walking down Woodruff Avenue toward Mom's house. I knew I shouldn't have gone there, but I went there anyway. Where else would I go? I tried to think of some alternatives. There were a three guys I hung out with for a time that might have a place for me: Johnnie Millan, Terry N. and John Acosta.

Of the three, Johnnie Millan was by far the most honorable. Johnnie was a great drummer who I had played with when I was 12 and he was 14. He also showed me a lot of respect as a musician. I was younger, but he was willing to see me as the leader of our garage band. He was trustworthy and kind. Johnnie made me feel cared about just by being himself. He didn't compete with me or try to control everything like Terry N. He made me feel cared about without wanting anything in return.

I'd known Terry N. since I was ten years old when we both lived in Bellflower, California. Bellflower is cushioned north of Lakewood; the southern borderline of Bellflower being just south of Artesia Blvd, running east and west. The Bellflower I grew up in was a city of bikers, tweakers, middle and lower middle class white folk who transplanted themselves from the Midwest. Its northside borders the city of Downey where The Carpenters' lived. Downey was the snobby older sister to Bellflower's intolerable little brother. The joke was that if you were caught in Downey and they knew you were from Bellflower, Downey would pay you to go back.

Terry was an older brother type who had a charming, engaging personality and we loved the same rock bands. Number one among those bands was Kiss. Terry was a musician like me, and also like me, he could actually play guitar with rhythm and emotion. But Terry had no regard for anyone's feelings. He made it clear when you were with him, you had to do what he said. I hated him, and I feared him. No one really liked him. He lied to himself by calling everyone who was afraid of him his friends.

One thing we both loved equally were girls. There wasn't a girl we weren't interested in fucking, and he was on equal par with me when it came to picking girls up. We both spent most of our time on the prowl in East Lakewood, Hawaiian Gardens, and Bellflower, fucking every girl we could. We used our charm and our looks to get 'em into whatever bed we (or they) had. There were many we met together, I don't remember all of their names; Mitzi, Traci, Sherri, Ranae' and Lisa; although Lisa M. became Terry's girlfriend, and she loved him. He didn't give a shit about her. She wanted to believe he did. But Terry thought of no one but himself. That's why they fought all the time. That's love to teenagers. I loved Lisa as a friend, but I was too busy trying to make money to have a real relationship with a girl.

To me, intimacy was seeing who could get naked first.

I had spent a month and a half living with Terry N. and Howard Dimmett in East Lakewood a year before in 1981. I met Howard and his mother, Phyllis Kelley, through Terry. Howard was a big, gregarious, loving, kind, and courageous white guy. I needed his love, and he gave it to me with no questions asked. Howard was a genuinely good person. He was the white gangster brother I always wished I had during those years I was locked up. Phyllis

55

was the sweet, wonderful mother I never had. She didn't judge us, she just cared about us. I'd never experienced such a nonjudgmental, kind, wonderful woman. She gave me the home my biological mother never did.

Back in 1981, the problem with living in Howard's garage on 209th and Roseton in East Lakewood was that I was in a fight every night. I got drunk with the boys in the hood and had to prove myself to guys who hadn't been to lockup like me. East Lakewood was an extension of being locked up. And I spent most of my time with Terry and that meant fighting all the time — win or lose. I hated it. I got sick of black eyes, letting loose all the pent-up anger I had inside of me for being locked up all my teenage life. Lisa Machado was a good friend and I loved her for her compassion and kindness.

But I was sick of fighting. I didn't get my freedom to fight all over every day again. But I still believed I needed that skill to survive in the outside world. The irony I faced fighting with everyone who angered me once I was released into your world, was that the skills I learned in danger required the presence of danger to be effective. It took me a long time to learn that I wasn't in danger every moment of every day of my life. And I'm still learning.

Although I feel a bit of happiness living in a neighborhood of people just as fucked up as me, I wanted to find somewhere to live without all the drama. Thank God for Howard, he was the only one I could trust who had my back. And his mother, Phyllis, was a saint. But I was sick of this shit. I'd been locked up or living on the streets too long. People that say living on the streets or being locked up makes you tough, have neither been locked up or lived on the streets. Being locked up and being on the streets didn't make me tougher, it made me suffer.

As much as I loved Howard, Lisa, and others in Lakewood, I had to get out. I'd still come back once in a while to visit, but I was intent on living the right way, especially since I hadn't been able to go to a high school, study, or accomplish anything academic.

I wanted to know teenagers who were going to college, not the penitentiary.

11

Your World is Not My World

I needed a home with a parent so I could go to high school and graduate, so… I chose Mom. I hoped she was different than how I remembered her. I was hopeful, but most likely delusional. Like my mother was gonna care. Fuck it, I thought, at least I might be able to pressure her into keeping me until I find a place to live. I'll be discovered soon enough by someone in the music or movie industry anyway.

I got to Mom's house a bit tired, but still hopeful.

I knocked. "Mom, it's me, Doug, your son. They let me out for good."

I heard an angry, bewildered yelp from inside the house.

"Whaat??"

The door swung open, and there she was. Fatter, angrier, and smellier. Only one black eye this time. It's fully closed but it's quite an improvement. Less bruising, and no visible stitching. With her one eye, she does not look happy to see me.

"Did you run away again? Why are you here?"

And hello, it's nice to see you too, Mom.

"I'm here because they released me for good. They told me they thought I was capable of going to high school and live without getting into trouble. Can I stay here and go to school?"

"Are you fucking crazy? Robert will kill me — and you — if he finds out I let you stay here. Robert's kids live here from time to time."

57

On the inside: So, you let Robert and his kids live in your house that you own by yourself?

Thanks for reminding me I'm NOT your prodigal son.

"Why did they let you out? You had to come here? Why didn't they take you to your father's house?"

"Mom, you know he won't let me live there. He doesn't want to live with anyone."

"Except hookers." She's right about that. He loves his hookers.

What's wrong with hookers? I could be a hooker too. Dad might be proud.

Thankfully, she backpedaled. "Where would I put you?"

Anywhere. I'd be happy to sleep between your budweiser cans, Mom.

Instead, I beg, "Please let me stay! I'm tired of fighting every day, I just want peace of mind. I want to feel safe. I just want to go to high school and graduate. Please just help me with that."

"Why the hell do you have to stay here? I don't know, Doug. We're not ready for this. But you really have nowhere else to go? I don't know what he'd say. I guess you could stay in the room that Steven sleeps in when he's here."

She relented and I had a place to stay.

Steven, my nephew, was now three years old. My mother took care of him because my sister Jamie shoots dope every day. She lived between the carcasses of automobile remains in the junkyards of Wilmington. Wilmington made Compton look like Newport Beach.

I didn't mind bunking with my three-year-old nephew. Living in a bedroom without fighting an Insane Crip Gangbanger for my shoes was the best fucking deal I'd been offered…ever. Of course, there was still Robert, my mother's Insane Cholo gangbanging husband. He's always angry, drunk and he carries a gun. But I couldn't escape to safety anywhere at Sylmar Juvenile Hall, especially if my head was being pounded into the ground by my cellie.

Maybe Robert's changed, I thought. If not, at least I can escape the house when Robert's drunk and insane.

So now, I was home. It didn't feel like home though. I was still nervous because Robert wasn't happy with me being there. Unhappy is an understatement. This guy was constantly belittling me, saying things like, "You're a fucking pussy gavacho motherfucker." This was not loving, but it seemed to be his only way of communicating with me. My real father never spoke to me and was never interested in me enough to even call me a name. He communicated by punching me in the face. It's odd, but Robert's attention was slightly better than no attention at all.

Luckily, Johnnie Millan had a job. He was living responsibly, and he was trustworthy. I called him, and he told me he could put me on his construction crew. He offered to pick me up because the job was in Redondo Beach which was ten miles away. Johnnie suggested joining the Laborers' Union because my job would be doing labor. I joined without a problem, even though I was seventeen, under the legal age.

I found out on the first day how tough construction labor work is. I could barely hold the heavy lumber I was told to bring to the carpenters' building area. I couldn't breathe while I struggled with the weight of the wood. I was getting cut up everywhere on my body, including a few places I didn't know existed.

I needed to escape. I'd been a captive most of my life. Locked up by your world. You wanted to be safe from me. I wanted to be safe from you. But I can never get away from me or you.

The construction job was simply too much for me. I'd already cut through a major power cable while racing a forklift and I almost killed someone trying to heave a sledge-hammer onto the roof to a carpenter. (The sledgehammer missed the roof and hurtled through the air, barely missing a human head that was still attached to their upright body.) After two weeks, I was given my check, $890, and was told to go on my way. As I left, I heard the construction crew's laughter, and I realized I'd been their comedy relief for two weeks.

And of course, the voice chimed in: You're too fucking stupid to work any job. You were handed this job and you blew it. You're a boy trying to do a man's job.

I had no response for this verbal diarrhea raging in my head today. In fact, I heard it confirmed by the Construction Crew Chief's own mouth when speaking to Johnnie as I got into his car to leave. "He's not a bad kid, Johnnie. You just expected a boy to do men's work. He couldn't hack it. Good luck to Doug." As Johnnie drove me to my mother's house, I wasn't listening to his "cheer up" speech.

But the difference between Johnnie Millan and Terry N. was like night and day. Johnnie was a good person who understood the shit known as my family, and he sincerely wanted to help me. Terry was a natural born criminal who only helped if he were in charge. They were like two fathers: One was light, and the other was darkness.

Johnnie, if you lived in my head, you'd know this: I'm probably not good enough to work in your world, no matter what job you give me.

I was going back to Mom's with money, but without a job.

As usual, Mom was drunk when I got home. She was in one of her rageaholic moods, cursing and screaming like the good christian woman she always claimed to be. I heard Robert smacking her with his open hand in the bedroom. I couldn't tell which body part he was striking, but it was probably her face. He loved to hit her in the face. I didn't like it, but if I were to intervene on her behalf, he would have stabbed or shot me.

She came out of the bedroom bleeding and screaming. She looked at me with an expression that could kill, as if I were to blame, while Robert was waving a knife and a bottle of tequila. Five years locked up, and this is the only home they could find for me? My mother was yelling about how he's the only man she's fucked, but I don't think the drunk vato bought her story. There were beer cans everywhere and these two stunk. You've heard of that show "Lifestyles of the Rich and famous?" This was more like "Lifestyles of the Poor and Ignorant." I didn't give a fuck if he beat the shit out of my mother. I felt slightly guilty about this, but I also wanted to get the fuck out of that place.

I decided to go to the Lakewood Mall. I had a few bucks, and somehow, I knew where a bus bench was. The bus dropped me off right where I wanted to be. Where the girls were. Where they would be looking cute and sexy, walking around; whatever their intentions were, was not important. They would see me. This was what mattered to me. I would be noticed. The mall was my nexus to paradise. Paradise, for me, was crafting the conquest, looking into the eyes of a girl looking back at me, stopping her, getting her phone number, holding hands, and finally making plans to meet and make love. It was all perfect in my head.

As I traveled through the mall, I was fighting the voice in my head everywhere.

Doug, you're stupid, you aren't cute, and no one you want will ever like you.

And then a girl stared back at me, and for a moment, the voice went silent. I felt excited. As I get stared at more often, I started to believe the press releases in my head. I must have been hot – and I would get laid. I was desirable because a girl looked at me with lust in her eyes. Then, I realized, I gotta pee. I found my way to the Lakewood Center Mall Men's Restroom. I pushed the door open and looked for a urinal.

And there they were — two men, standing upright at the urinals, looking like they're riding the elevator together, except that they're staring at each other's penises. I wasn't fazed at all, I just wanted to go pee. There was one available urinal, and I quickly walked in its direction. As I got there, both men, each well over thirty, stopped staring at each other, and looked at me with lust. Not the innocent "Hey, I noticed you're cute" lust. The men's lust was serious, passionate. Their lust was on a mission and I was the mission. I was the only person that existed in this bathroom at that moment. Nothing moved, except their eyes to my crotch. They both stared intently.

I wasn't bothered, offended, or outraged. It was normal to me. I didn't understand why this was a problem for people. These guys were just following their instincts – and it's not like they were grabbing me. I just turned and walked out. As I turned back to look, both men had their dicks out, and they were stroking them, staring back at me in a trance. They'd forgotten where they were. As one man stroked himself, I noticed he wore a wedding band.

I went back to my mission, and immediately a girl walked by who was gorgeous. In an instant, we glanced and then glanced again at each other, and I began planning our future together. But first, I had to get the phone number.

After glancing back a second time at this cutie (a blonde girl, which is totally different for me), I noticed she stopped to wait for me to walk over. I'll be the gentleman and honor her request, I thought. She was petite but shapely. Her body and face were attractive. She was dressed appropriately for her body and my mind.

I walked up to her and made this shit up on the spot, "You're really cute, and I'm heading home right now. I'd love to call you or get together. Sorry if I'm too forward, but if you give me your phone number, I'll call you."

The dreaded moment of waiting passes quickly.

She responded, "Sure, I'll give you my phone number. I live in Bellflower. I'd love to get together with you."

Yes!

1 2

The Forbidden Room

Mom: You could take everything she knows about the world, put it in a matchbox and listen to it rattle

May 30th, 1982

At my mom's house, there was a rule. I could never go into her and Robert's bedroom if they weren't home. If I was alone in the house, their bedroom door remained locked. No exceptions, even though the only shower in the house was in their bedroom. It didn't matter even when I came home from working construction, dirty, stinking, smelling and cut everywhere. If no one else was there, I was only allowed to take a bird bath in the kitchen sink. Robert hated me and he was adamant because he was jealous of me, but also he'd been in prison and knew I knew how to take a birdbath. This was a problem. I could never shower? What the fuck?

But there was no way in hell I was going to challenge Robert. I wanted him to be reasonable, but I knew that wasn't going to happen. Trying to reason with him would be like trying to get a dog to eat with a knife and fork. I couldn't negotiate with fear. So, I decided to try to reason with my mother.

I told my mother I was frustrated because I couldn't shower, and she actually listened. Mom actually decided to give me a key to the room on one condition.

"Doug, you know what Robert will do if he finds out I've given you a key to our bedroom. He'll kill you, and then he'll kill me."

That was true. But he wasn't going to know. For a moment, I wanted to savor this victory. I could shower when I wanted to! I just had to remember to lock the door behind me. Oh, and clean up after myself, so I wouldn't leave any trace of me behind.

I called the girl from the mall. It was then that I remembered how I really knew her, Suzy N., from years before in Bellflower. She arrived when I knew we'd have time alone.

I was excited beyond words, but I wasn't out of control. She looked hot. She told me she remembered me from when I lived in Bellflower on Hopland Street and she lived on Ives Street. We were little kids going to elementary school together at Ernie Pyle. I think we were the same age and in the same grade.

It was daytime, so we talked in the living room for a minute, and I moved in for a kiss. Suzy responded passionately. My heart and my brain told me to me to take it slow, but my hard-on told me to hurry up. So, I acknowledged our childhood friendship and went back to kissing her.

It got more passionate. My hand moved to her breast area and I began removing her blouse. She allowed this, and my erection became that much larger. It was time to go somewhere else. She understood, so we decided to move to the bedroom. I really didn't have one — Steven's three-year-old toys dominated the room I was staying in. It's hard to stay romantic while being stared at by Big Bird or GI Joe grimacing at me from inside his box of Adventures. Then again, that was just an excuse to use Mom's master bedroom to get freaky. I was so horny, I would have fucked Suzy in a toxic landfill. So, I decided to use the key to Mom's bedroom so we could enjoy fucking on a bigger bed.

I was transported into sexual bliss. I lost myself in ravaging her and I particularly took pleasure in exploring her body and vagina with my tongue. My face, my mouth and my tongue were between her legs for a long time. She remarked about the large size of my dick. She was enjoying what I was doing to her, and when we started fucking, she matched my passion. And she was vocal. I loved hearing her tell me how I felt inside of her. I rammed her over and over. She took it, and thrusted her hips upward, giving me everything she had. She'd have been my dream girl if she was a brunette. And not only was our sex everything I wanted it to be, she exclaimed, while I was in mid thrust, "You're wearing me out, Doug." This was coming from a girl who fucked me for at least an hour. I'm a stud. Suzy said so.

I had my orgasms, but I made sure not to shoot off inside her. Suzy left later that day, and I had the early evening to ruminate on what a Casanova I was.

I wandered off to the couch and drifted into unconscious serenity.

"You fucking punk motherfucker!"

I was awakened by the sound of Robert's rage. Before I could react, I was snatched by him and pulled off the couch. My face was hit hard, and I went down. I was stunned and I staggered to my feet. I tasted my own blood.

"You broke into our room, you fucking gavacho piece of shit. And you took a girl in there. I'm gonna fucking kill you."

I know he would. I ran towards the front door. My mother was standing there, looking disappointed. Suddenly, Robert turned around, disappearing down the hallway toward their bedroom.

My mom said to me, "We found a girl's wrist bracelet underneath our bed. What was a girl doing in our bed? What were you doing in there?"

Oh shit. I thought I made sure I locked the door behind us. Fuck! It wasn't enough. I didn't check underneath the bed. Didn't think I had to.

She continued, "I told you, the bedroom is only for using the shower. Now he knows you were in there. He thinks you broke in somehow. You better leave before he comes back out of the bedroom. I can't believe you had a girl in our bedroom. And you had sex?"

Well, Mom, I don't think it would have been romantic with Steven in the same room. I immediately felt angry at my mother, but I didn't vocalize my feelings. There was no time for that.

"Doug, walk fast. Out the front door. Go!"

What? Where was I supposed to go? I didn't know what to say to her because she wasn't willing to tell him that she gave me the key. She was too scared. I immediately realized that she was right. My mother was the only hope I had to stay, and she wasn't going to stand up to him. I knew I'd better get the hell out of there. Robert reappeared with a gun. He lifted his handgun and pointed it directly at my face.

"If you don't run right now, I'll blow your head off!"

Robert was practicing the Golden Rule while pointing a loaded gun. The man pointing the gun makes the rules. My mother yelled for him to stop, halfheartedly. She was afraid that if she told him she had let me in the bedroom, he'd shoot her too. She also yelled at me to walk out front. I was fucking scared. I knew his gun was loaded. Although I was convinced, I was bulletproof, now was not the time to test that theory. I walked out the front door, pleading with Robert to reconsider.

"I didn't break into your bedroom, Robert. I've got nowhere to go. What am I supposed to do? Mom, help me please."

"Robert, put the gun down."

This was the extent of her intervention on my behalf. I was now out on the front lawn. Robert was still pointing his gun at me, raging, telling me to get off the property, with nothing but the clothes on my back. I was angry at him, but he was the one with the gun. I had to walk to a pay phone now. Thankfully, I had a little money left from my construction job. Who the fuck would I call? All of my clothes were in the house. This motherfucker was accusing me of breaking in and it wasn't true.

But the voice in my head reminded me that I was to blame for everyone's misery, especially my own.

Doug, you fucked this up. You're an ungrateful punk. You wanted it all your way. You shouldn't have gone in the bedroom. Duhh! Stupid fucking idiot! Maybe you did break in after all. Robert knows something about you. He's right about you.

I fight back with the voice and shout at my mother who's just standing there staring at her only son with a gun pointed at his head.

"But Mom, you KNOW it's not true. Tell him."

Mom looked at me, imploring me to leave. Her eyes were distant, unfazed and cold. She had more important things to deal with. I worried whether she'd survive that night, but I didn't have time to worry about her anymore.

Goodbye, Mom and fuck you, Robert. I was walking away. There had to be something out there for me. I knew I belonged somewhere. In a different world. I'd had enough of your world. I didn't think you've ever wanted me in your world anyway.

Goodbye, Lakewood. Goodbye, Mom.

1 3

Looking For a Home

I was on the street with the clothes on my back. But I had a few hundred dollars in my pocket. The first thing I thought of was to call George Grand. He was a creepy fucker. George was the Director of Sunrise Youth Community. I met him when I was placed there to live in January of 1981. I had been kicked out of Rancho San Antonio Boys' Home for incorrigibility (whatever the fuck that is) and spent the latter months of 1980 in Juvenile hall waiting again for my Probation Officer, John Scott, to find another suitable place for my fifteen-year-old self to live.

The first thing I noticed after John Scott walked me into George's Director's office is that this Black man has one of the large "Permanent" Curl Fros' for a hairdo. He had the Barry White look. I always thought of those curls as looking more like they belonged on a woman's head rather than a man. George was a musician and a singer. He had toured with Billy Preston in the late 1960's. He had also appeared on Soul Train in the early 70's. He looked just like a 70's black musician with those curls. George was very cordial to me and instantly greets me with a handshake, a smile, and a "So, John Scott here tells me you're a musician and that you can play the keyboard?"

I noticed the Fender Rhodes electric keyboard sitting right in front of the wall to the left of where I was standing. I craved playing that keyboard. I was born a piano player and I hadn't touched one in at least three years. I could play Bach and Beethoven by ear when I was six years old, but I preferred to play Beatles' songs over classical. The Beatles were classical music to my ears. The first time I heard Paul McCartney start my "Meet the Beatles" record with "One, two, three, faaw!" – I was spellbound and hooked for life. Anyway, now George was tempting me with his keyboard. But first, he had other things on his mind. After John Scott left his office, George told me to take off my clothes to check me for contraband. I was a bit confused because it seemed like an odd request. I stripped down to my underwear, revealing my skinny white fifteen-year-old body to him.

"Now, take off your underwear, Douglas. I need to see everything to make sure you do not have contraband."

I submitted to his request and down went my underwear. He stared for a second, walked over to me, and felt my genital area with his hand. I was now wondering if he was being honest about what he was really doing down there. Even though he didn't act "gay" or effeminate, it was still unsettling. Though many men had already used me for their sexual needs, I still wanted to believe what an adult says is true. Maybe I was just stupid. I certainly felt that way. At least, these men made me feel that way. I felt desired and worthless at the same time.

During my six months stay at Sunrise Youth Community, George sucked my dick, and he forced me to suck his, on many occasions. He was a control freak with a devious mind. He used his position to do what he wanted with me, and I complied. He gave me privileges, and I caused a lot of trouble at Sunrise, especially since it was a co-ed facility. I fought with all the counselors who told George he should kick me out. George was afraid I'd tell on him for molesting me, so he let me stay. I milked this the whole time I was there.

So suddenly, when I'm on the streets with nothing and no one, George's name and image popped into my head as someone who just might take me into his home. At least, he might care enough to give me a roof over my head. I had his home phone number in my pocket, so I walked fast to a phone booth. It was getting dark and I was starting to feel cold.

I made the phone call to George. I told him what happened at my mother's house and he laughed. George had a cold, icy, emotionless demeanor that always made me uncomfortable. He liked to find humor in pain. Other people's pain. My pain. He laughed at me for being on the streets. But he did offer to let me sleep at his house, as long as I caught the bus there. He wouldn't even drive to pick me up. He lived in Fox Hills, which was near Inglewood, twenty miles away. I did what I had to do — find a bus and ask the bus driver where I could catch the next one going towards Fox hills. This required three buses and the last one was leaving at 10:03 p.m. The bus sucked, but it was better than being confined to my cell at Central Juvenile Hall or having a gun pointed at me by my mom's gangbanging lover.

As I arrived, I noticed George smiling. His smile was fake. It exuded great joy hiding intense pain. It was a façade. His smile also had a sinister quality to it. He was in charge and he let me know this right away. His house has a keyboard, but he had one requirement: If I wanted to stay and play, I had to have sex with him. His rule didn't work for me. It might have worked with a nicer man, but not with George. I was an adult, and I had a choice about who I was going to have sex with. It occurred to me that I would be better off on the streets.

I realized he didn't give a fuck about me or my homelessness, but I thought he cared at least a small amount. His gift to me was to allow me to give to him. He was a selfish prick. And I knew there was someone out there who would care about me. I might even fall in love with an older man who gives me a home, I thought. The sex would be wonderful if I was in love. I knew I was about to lose the only possibility of having a roof over my head, but if I didn't leave, they would be inserting pins into George's neck just to keep his head attached to his shoulders.

George and I fought. And I mean a good intense verbal battle. I could tell that this physically intimidating huge man was a coward. He couldn't manage his way out of a third-rate bar fight. With my fighting skills, I'd end up breaking his face in 30 seconds. But I knew if I hurt him, he'd call the police.

The voice jumped on this. Yeah, Doug Probst, you're fucking up, you're gonna lose this roof, you might as well beat the shit out of this self-absorbed coward.

Something new occurred for me. The voice wanted me to do what I wanted to do, and I refused to do it.

The night was cold. I walked and walked until I arrived in Inglewood, California, and the chilly air added bitterness to my new sweet journey. It was unusually cold for a mid-June Southern California night, but it didn't deter me from my goal. What the hell was my goal? Survival? Living my life had me feeling like a wounded animal. Wounded animals are angry, scared and think only about self-preservation.

So, I was a wounded animal, and I had to survive. Being selfish was ok. I had to keep walking, so I walked, walked, and walked. I didn't have a watch, but my guess was that it was one a.m. or so. No buses were running. Cars passed and drivers gazed at me with odd expressions, except the obvious gay guys. But out here, at Western Avenue and Marine in Gardena, these guys looked demonic. I was getting tired, but I knew I had to keep walking. But where was I going? My compass was pointing toward Lakewood, but that wasn't where I want to be. I hiked over to Rosecrans Avenue and kept walking east. The cold air sucked, but at least I had a coat on. By now, it was 2:30 a.m., I was yawning way too much, and I needed to rest. I was still on Rosecrans Avenue, somewhere under the Harbor Freeway.

I hated sleeping under a freeway, but I remembered something a counselor said to me once: "You're right where you're supposed to be, otherwise you'd be somewhere else."

It comforted me for five seconds.

My yawns were turning into closed eyes. I saw a bus bench, but it looked like a bed to me. The hard seat felt luxurious. I was glad I took a shower at George's apartment. I was fresh and clean. As I lay down wrapping myself in my coat, I contemplated where I was going. I wanted to go where there was life, activity and jobs. I wanted to go where there were people, tall buildings, businesses, and where the fun never ends. Where there were nice people who I didn't have to fight every day. Where I felt safe and in control. Where there was money. Where there were gay guys everywhere. Nice guys. A real city. My last coherent thought as I fell asleep on the bus bench is that I knew where I was going. I was going where I would be noticed. Where my face would be famous. The face that would launch a thousand hard-ons and open a million wet vaginas.

I was going to Long Beach.

14

Boulevard of Boys

I woke up. My guess is that it was 6 a.m. Growing up in cages will do that to you. I saw people gathered around the bus bench. I checked my ass to see if I still had my wallet and money, and remarkably, I did. This was it. I'd catch the next bus east on Rosecrans Avenue to Long Beach Blvd. I knew my Thomas Bros. Maps well.

When I was a kid, I was fascinated with those map books, connecting the pages, following streets and learning their names. I have the Los Angeles County cities, streets and freeways tattooed on my brain. I surmised from the many black squares that covered the paper mapped streets of Downtown Long Beach, that Long Beach was condensed, with a ton of buildings and activity going on. These were buildings that have businesses, and businesses have jobs.

I rode the bus to Long Beach Blvd. and ran across the street to connect with the RTD going south. Long Beach Blvd was the main boulevard into Downtown Long Beach. The ride was worth it. As I stepped off the bus, I felt like Dorothy in the Wizard of Oz when the movie changes from black and white to color. Instantly, I was amazed and in awe. And I loved it. Human beings were everywhere. Workers were working, street corner preachers were preaching, and homeless people were proudly displaying their contempt for shelter. There were also plenty of porno shops.

There was Mr. R's X Rated Movie Store, proudly displaying their latest porno movie technology – videotapes on VHS. My kinda place. There were more X rated movie theaters than regular movie theaters. But it was homeless people who engulfed the streets. There were more of them than anything else. I guess I was one, too. But I don't think I had that homeless smell, nor the beard. I bet that the number of bearded men per square inch here could have rivaled any mosque in Tehran. Every homeless person I passed had so many particles of food scattered among their long, scraggly whiskers; their beards could have substituted as snack bars. Some of the beards were so long they could have wiped their asses with them, and a couple of these guys smelled like they had.

I stepped over homeless man after homeless man. The streets of Downtown Long Beach were literally "littered" with these guys. Though not as ubiquitous as the men, there were quite a few homeless women there, too. They spent more time screaming into the sky, while alternatively disappearing and re-emerging from behind buildings in seconds. It was dirty and crazy, but I was already loving this place. I felt at home.

As I combed my long sandy blonde hair, I felt happy for the first time. It wasn't a momentary or fleeting feeling. This is the happiness I felt when I've played piano or guitar. It's also the feeling I get when I write songs. Things were looking up. As I walked down Broadway through Downtown, I saw an old run-down building at the corner of Broadway and Long Beach Blvd. It was called the Kennedy Hotel. It had to have been forty stories high. I was sure there were dramatic life stories being lived out on every floor. I loved these buildings and the old history, but the Kennedy Hotel was a bit creepy. I saw a lady sitting in a window talking to a rat. I also saw in the crowd — countless men and women who looked at me with lust in their eyes. I tried to make contact with each one, but it was impossible. I had to keep moving.

Across the street was Chili Don's Bar. This was not a "chain" food place. It was shabby and run down, with a sign that read "Navy" out front. The US Naval Shipyard was here in, Long Beach.

There were probably lots of drinkers fighting inside.

In fact, there were two guys battling it out in a fistfight in front of Chili Don's right there, as I stood watching. They were punching each other, and people were stopping to get a sidewalk seat. My mother and Robert would have loved it, but there was nothing in there for me. I looked away for a moment, and out of curiosity, I decided to see the fight again. Remarkably, the two brawlers were hugging each other and laughing while they were bleeding. Just another moment of insanity that emanated from everywhere around here.

I kept walking down Broadway. I waded through people as I passed Elm Avenue. And as I went by my third cafeteria and several crumbling archaic apartment houses, I noticed one modern condominium style building on the northwest corner of Broadway and Elm.

Its contemporary architecture stood out among the others. Although it sat in a world of madness, it radiated safety and sanity. This was a shining light to me. Only someone with money must live there. I wanted to live there. But I had to start making money. The voice instantly slithered into my thoughts.

You'll never make the kind of money you would need to live in that place you fucking worthless piece of shit, Douglas. You're a fucking boy. And you wouldn't be welcome there anyway.

The voice never allowed me to dream for very long. For the first time in my life, at this moment, my reality was better than my dream. I snapped out of the auditory grip of the voice and noticed a well-dressed man staring at my crotch. He was mesmerized. I looked at his face to draw his attention upward. He looked up at my face and then he said: "Hey, I don't know your name, but you're very sexy. Do you want to make $500?"

"How do I earn $500? And what's your name?"

"My name is Alan Berringer and I just want to suck your dick."

You're going to pay ME to suck MY dick? If I were you, I'd want it the other way around.

"So you'll give me $500 if I let you suck my dick?"

"Yes."

"Let me see the $500."

Mr. Belanger pulled out a wad of 100-dollar bills from his pocket. At first glance, it looked like more than $500. I've always been a capitalist.

"Ok, where are we supposed to do this?"

He pointed to his left.

"Follow me into the hallway in this building. No one ever comes in here."

I turned and saw that we were standing in front of the alcove to a very old apartment building on Broadway, near the corner of Lime Avenue. I told Alan to give me the money and I'd let him do his thing.

He opened a door to an empty room, and got on his knees in front of me. Obviously, he wanted to unzip me. I was not turned on, but he pulled out my seventeen-year-old penis and made an audible gasp, "Wow! Your dick is big." Ok, sir, get on with it. He put the head of my penis in his mouth and immediately I realized this guy was no amateur at sucking dick. I was barely seventeen years old (my birthday was in April), but my dick had already been sucked a lot. This guy was actually taking all of my dick down his throat. It was impressive and it felt good. He told me to imagine my favorite pretty girl doing it (as if I wasn't already).
. I started pumping my cock into his mouth. With his skills, it didn't take long for me to feel an orgasm taking over. I exclaimed that I was cumming. As I released a large amount of stored up cum into his mouth, I was amazed at his grip while swallowing every drop of it. Slowly and gently, Mr. Berringer removed his wet mouth from my softening penis. As I zipped up my jeans, happily counted my money again, and Mr. Berringer started talking to me.

"Have you ever thought about doing movies?"

"No. I'm a musician. What kind of movies are you talking about?'

"X-rated films. You could make a lot of money doing sex scenes on film. My friend, Larry Bronco, owns a company called YMAC, and he would pay you $1000 for a scene with a guy. You are sooo hot!"

"I don't know, dude. I want to have a career in music. I don't need to be doing something that makes me look gay to the public. They would find out after I'm famous."

"Here's my card. You just made $500 for ten minutes. Nobody knows. Call me if you're interested. I also pay more to guys who like to get fucked in the ass."

"No, I don't do that, Alan." Fuck that.

I asked him if he lived around the area, and he pointed in the direction of the building

I loved; the oasis in this sea of slime (I love the slime too). "I live on Broadway and Elm, in that new condominium complex. We shoot porn movies there, too." He gave me his card with his address and his phone number on it. Of course, I should have known. The rich guys make porn. And they live and shoot porn in the safe building.

Next thing I heard is how good his dick would feel in my ass. He told me lots of straight guys tell him that they never knew how good a big dick feels until they let him fuck them.

Nice try, Alan. It sounded like something I might say to a girl if I thought they were stupid enough to fall for it. Girls aren't that stupid. Neither am I. At that moment, I wouldn't have cared how much money he had, I wasn't going to be taking any man's dick in my ass. I have nothing against anyone who takes it up the ass, it's just not my thing. I remember how much it hurt and how much I bled when a counselor at Rancho San Antonio fucked me in my ass. I think I was fourteen.

After I waved goodbye to Alan, I started walking down Broadway again, with $500 more dollars in my wallet. The sky was slowly changing color, its amber turning black. I needed shelter. I noticed other young guys in the area. There was more than one hustler on this street. The men and the boys were already checking each other out. It was easy to separate the investors from the entrepreneurs. Most of the men were checking me out. I was new. I kept walking and I passed Broadway and Alamitos. The neighborhood was now residential, but it businesses dotted its sidewalks.

On Broadway and Orange, I saw a bar called "Lil' Lucy's." I wondered what it was like inside of a bar. I'd never been in one. I was curious about what went on in a place like Lil' Lucy's. Outside there were two transgender people arguing. I was fascinated and wanted to get to know them. During this time, transgender people were the first people to really love me and offer me their apartments to live in when I was homeless. I knew these were men, but they looked like they'd had the operation to make them women. I wondered what they'd look like down there. Did they have a vagina? How the hell would a doctor cut off a penis and make a vagina out of it? They must really be women deep down inside. This sex change operation had just been developed a few years earlier. I heard about it when I was twelve years old in 1977.

They were women but they fought like men. They were big and kinda scary. I would have loved to investigate my financial opportunities inside the bar, but I thought Lil' Lucy's wouldn't let me in. I was only seventeen and the age limit was twenty-one. I was a long way off. But rules and laws never applied to me. I knew I'd get inside. My way. And they let me in. It was a wonderful atmosphere inside Lil' Lucy's. I made many friends that night.

I also met a transgender person I liked right away. She and I became friends, and I was attracted to her. I didn't care that she had a dick, I fucked her many times. We stayed in touch for years. Later, I heard she became a transsexual adult film star.

Still, I watched the two trans turn and walk away. But one of the transgender people was very interested in me. She motioned to me and I walked over to meet him at the east side of the bar's wall. She offered me $100 to suck my dick. What the hell, why not? And, my God, could she suck a dick. I came in less than a minute. I shot loads of youthful cum down her throat. I felt breasts as I came. It helped. I love my life.

I realized I had over $600 in my wallet. This was enough for an apartment. I needed to keep moving. Two guys were walking fast toward me. One of them recognized me. How fucking strange. And then I recognized him. It was Ted from Sunrise Youth community.

I was surprised to meet someone I knew the first day I strutted through Long Beach. I guess I wasn't the only LA County Cast off to have arrived on the streets of Long Beach. The other kid was really good looking. He had shoulder length blonde hair with an all

American, blue-eyed white boy face. Not a common face, and it was a very attractive face. He looked like a surfer. His name was Rick Crawford. He had a big smile as he greeted me. His smile was infectious. Of the two of them, Rick was the Alpha Male. But ever since I arrived, that was over. No matter where I was or who was around me, I was always the Alpha Male. Rick can imagine he was, but one way or another, he'd find out that I was his superior.

Ted also received attention, but he was shy. I was his roommate at Sunrise Youth Community in 1981, just one year earlier. I was amazed and overjoyed when I ran into Ted on Broadway in 1982. We both knew we were here to make money and to meet dads & moms. In 1982, women also cruised Broadway paying for hot young male flesh. The sexual revolution was happening in our pants. We were convinced that selling our bodies would be the antidote for our poisoned self-images.

Ted and I bonded through the shared pain of tumultuous childhoods, drug addicted parents, and both having been sexually assaulted early in our lives and then again by our Sunrise Youth Community Director, George Gybbs.

We shared more than what people saw on film. In January of 1981 we were roommates at a facility for homeless and troubled youths, Sunrise Youth Community. This was a year before we met again on the streets of Long Beach California. Sunrise was located in Compton California.

Ted was quiet, but he would open up to me in our room at night. He was a fragile young man. He would tell me about how his birth "family" rejected him. It hurt him deeply.

Though I preferred girls, Ted was gay. I knew that the moment we met at Sunrise Youth Community. He was kind, slightly effeminate, and kept our room spotless. Being the horny sixteen-year-old I was, I didn't turn Ted down when he offered to please me sexually. He was sensual and he didn't hold back, especially when he wanted my approval.

The other hardened teens picked on him relentlessly, hitting him whenever they could. Ted was terribly out of place living with gangsters. We all know bullying is widespread in our present times, but if you think the past was kinder to LGBTQ youth, I can attest that history offers no such comfort.

I fought quite a few battles for him to let them know I wasn't allowing anyone to pick on my Ted. The gangsters were bewildered because I preferred to protect and aid rather than attack and harm.

Ted and I also shared a longing for approval that we sought to fulfill hustling on the corner of Broadway and Pacific in Long Beach California. But Ted was more than my friend. He was also the conduit, the vessel that helped me become a gay adult film star.

HOT HIGH AND HORNY: THE MOVIE LATE 1982

In the summer of 1982, Larry Bronco of YMAC Films offered me a role in his new upcoming gay adult film, "Hot, High, and Horny." He knew I was a "top," which is a term I learned that meant you fucked guys and girls, you didn't get fucked. My asshole was not open for discussion.

He said he wanted to film me having my cock sucked by Ted, and then climaxing by fucking him. It would be the first of a number of scenes in his new movie.

Larry set the scene. He wrote the movie scene's plot: I was Dirk, a jock from the local YMCA. Ted played Kyle, who spots me and is immediately attracted to me. I'm the unaware straight guy, but I sense his sexual interest in me, and he courageously invites me to his condo. I'm hesitant but curious so I decide to go with him.

I was initially uncomfortable getting naked and having sex in front of two men carrying heavy cameras on their shoulders and another pointing bright lights at me, but I was getting paid, so I started to love it. Complaining about something after I've agreed to do it is like closing the door after the flies are already inside. I learned that when I was locked up.

I didn't want to kiss a guy, so my reactions were sincere. But I knew Ted could suck a cock sensuously from the days we were roommates at Sunrise. So, we dived into the scripted scene on the carpet of Jim Slaton's beautiful condominium in a building called the Versailles on Ocean Blvd. in Long Beach.

I fucked Ted in many positions and I wasn't faking it on camera.

Suffice it to say, both Ted and I played our roles masterfully and the movie was made. I didn't think this movie would be as revered as it was among many gay men. I was just doing what I had to do to survive.

***

Back to our meeting on Broadway. It was all small talk. "Hey, Ted, what's up with you out here?" Rick said, "We're gonna make some money tonight." I admired Rick for being so open about why he was out here strolling down "gayway," Long Beach's main hustler drag. He was confident, straight, and admitted he was only gay for pay. He had two kids and a wife, and he was only eighteen. He wasn't judgmental. He didn't get into gay/straight debates, nor did he care what sexual act he was asked to perform for money. I'd describe him as "Trysexual." His wife didn't know he was out here supporting her this way.

I realized they wanted to entice one of these male cruisers to pick them up, and I needed to find a place to stay for the night. I wouldn't part with a dime of my money for a motel like they did. One night for $35? I'd have to be back on the street in the morning and I'd be $35 poorer? No way. I wasn't here to waste money like that. A motel room would also mean that I'd have to be around people who create drama. I'd been imprisoned with and shackled by drama all of my life. I wanted peace in my house. I needed an apartment. At least I'd have a month to live there before they kicked me out. Rick told me about a girl he knew who had an apartment. He gave me her phone number. I knew she'd like me.

I called her immediately, and she drove over to the phone booth that I called from. She was cute and it was obvious she was attracted to me. Her name was Jazmine. She had a studio apartment at 295 Bonito Avenue, three blocks from the beach. She knew how I was making money; in fact, she was doing the same thing for a different clientele. She also told me there was an empty apartment that the building's owner needed to rent. I had the money, and after my first night with Jazmine at her apartment, I talked to the owner in the morning. I made a good enough impression with him (it's called having the right amount of cash), and voila! Within five days of being thrown out of my mother's house, I had an apartment of my own in Long Beach.

I was three blocks from the beach in a studio apartment, and my monthly rent was $255. I had given this guy $450 in total and the utilities were paid for. I loved my new place, and I loved sleeping on the floor. I had a tiny kitchen, but I had a hot plate and a refrigerator. I had a drop-down ironing board. And I had my own bathroom. I felt like a king. I could piss and shit without interruption or complaint. I didn't have to fight to eat. I wouldn't be threatened with death or bodily harm when I coughed or farted. I could hang my clothes up or throw them on the floor. No one could interfere with how I lived.

This was the first time I would have a porcelain toilet in my own bathroom. I'd been sitting on steel since I was twelve years old. And I promised myself I'd never live like that again. I ran this show now. I was the fucking king. The owner thought I was eighteen — if he knew I was underage, I'd be homeless.

This was the beginning of learning to lie just to have shelter. I had to lie to survive. I had to lie to exist in your world. Your world has rules I must live by. I was underage though. Your world cannot know this. Your world locked me in a cage for five years, and then discarded me to fend for myself on the streets. I didn't want to exist in your world, but it was my reality. I quickly learned the art of lying. I was supposed to be in high school, but I was on my own. And my main goal was to survive.

I walked out of my apartment in the morning and I was immediately greeted by someone who would pay me for temporary use of one of my body parts, or even just to watch me adjust my penis in my pants. That usually occurred in the bushes in an alley. I got paid to stand there and look like me. The money was easy. I learned what I'm worth. And because what I'm worth depended on how much cash a person had at the time, I operated on a sliding scale, to a certain degree. I was earning money so fast that I realized I'd have to put it somewhere to keep it safe. The week I moved in, I bought a mattress. It sat on the floor and I realized it was gonna be my bed and my safe. Inside my mattress was where I start stashing my cash.

I had no ID, so I wasn't allowed to get a bank account. I didn't trust banks anyway. I was convinced they'd steal my precious earnings. And I saved every dime I could. Within a month, I squirreled away $3,500. I had it all hidden inside my mattress on the floor. I counted it every time I put cash in there. It was also the title I used for the first song I wrote, "My mattress on the floor."

I bought a guitar, and I played and wrote songs and poems every day and night. I had a way to temporarily shut off the voice in my head. It was music, my music. My poems and my music. I was insecure and unsure about how good they were. I didn't trust my own taste. Shit, I hadn't even heard much music in five years. Most of the music I'd heard was coming out of speakers in the yards at the three LA County Juvenile Halls. I heard it while we were marching in line, "squaring our corners" military style. I also heard music when other boys who shared dorm spaces with me played music on their radios. I listened at all times.

One new artist I heard on the radio in the dorm at Rancho San Antonio Boys' Home was a guy called "Prince." I was mesmerized while listening to this song called "I wanna be your lover" – it was so different than anything I'd ever heard before. I immediately sensed something special. I wanted to hear more. But, of course, I could only hear the radio when another roomie had theirs on. I never had a radio or a stereo. I've read very few poems. I wrote a lot of them in my head. I wrote poetry in my apartment. I also brought people home to fuck, some for pleasure, and some for money.

15

Gay Cancer

Downtown Long Beach/ Belmont Heights, LB. Summer, 1982

What a joy it was to live in Long Beach in the summer of 1982. On Broadway and Pacific, the young male hustlers congregated at night. There were some females there, too, but they plied their trade mostly up on Pacific Coast Highway around Long Beach Blvd. Though I hustled, I still distanced myself from the boys there. I thought I was different and was on my way to a better life.

As I walked down Broadway towards Pacific Avenue, I saw friends. Ted, my friend from Sunrise Youth Community, was strolling eastward across the street. He looked strung out and unhappy. I waved to him to cheer him up. The look in his eyes was despondent. As he kept walking fast, he managed a halfhearted wave in return. I saw Paul Andrews ahead. He was another young man I was friends with, while in Rancho San Antonio Boys Home. Paul was eighteen, blonde, and good looking, but what I remember most about him was his intelligence. When our eyes met, he walked up to me, and he was coughing. He looked tired and thin.

"Hey, Paul, man, it's good to see you. It's been a long time."

"Yeah, Doug, it's good to see you too. How the hell did you wind up out here?"

"I was gonna ask you the same thing."

"My dad kicked me out of the house. He's a minister and hates me because I'm bisexual. I told him I liked guys sometimes, and he told me God doesn't make faggots. Then he told me to get out of his house and never come back."

"I'm sorry to hear that shit. So you came to Long Beach?"

"Yeah, we live in Torrance. It's not too far." Paul coughed again and sniffled.

"You look like you have a cold, brother."
"You know, Doug, I have a feeling it's more than that."

Odd.

"What do you mean?"

"Since I've been out here, I've been sick, and I can't get rid of it."

"Have you seen a doctor?"

"They can't figure it out. I keep losing weight, and I'm tired a lot. I have white stuff on my tongue, and I got this purple spot on my neck. Check it out."

I looked at this purplish spot and I had no idea what it was.

"Does it hurt?"

"No. It's just sitting there."

"It looks like a bruise. But to be safe, if it gets bigger, go back to the doctor."

Paul yawned again. He looked skinnier than he did a year ago.

A man drove up in a Corvair. The passenger window came down and he yelled for Paul to come over.

"I've got to go. This is my trick tonight."

"Cool, man. Tell that dude to wait a second. I've got an apartment and a phone number. Call me, and if you need anything, come over anytime." I scrawled my new phone number down for him quickly.

Paul took my number and I watched him get into the Corvair. As I watched him get into the car, I grew more and more concerned. I was immediately aware of a new phenomenon. For the first time in my life, I cared about someone. I thought I cared about and loved people, but this was a new feeling.

I wanted to love my mother, but our relationship was broken very early in my life. She didn't care about my sister or me enough to get us away from my father. I thought I loved my sister. But she doesn't give a shit about me. I've always hated my father. Many people I've come into contact with have faked caring about me to get sex. Maybe some really cared, but I didn't know the difference. I played the game anyway.

Paul always asked me how I felt, and he wanted to warn the other guys to be careful. He sincerely didn't want them to get as sick as he was. He cared about us and he didn't want anything in return. I learned something that night. I learned you have to be cared for first before you can care about others.

I walked down Broadway watching the boys. They walked back and forth, looking for

76

tricks. The tricks were driving up and down, turning corners, staring at their prospective male escorts. As I walked back down Broadway towards my apartment, I became aware of how many cars were slowing down as they reached me. One car after another cruised alongside the curb. I realized I was in control here. I sensed neediness from these guys (and a few women), and I was surprised at how many cars and people cruise and stare at me. But I wasn't interested. I want to go home and relax. That night, I had enough money, and reading was the only thing I wanted to do. I wanted to get away from the tragedies I was experiencing.

I was starting to see more of my friends get sick on the boulevard and die. I didn't know what they were dying from. I remember Troy, who couldn't walk anymore and died in an alley between Atlantic avenue and Lime avenue. I remember Cesar, because he was a chicano kid who could speak Spanish. I think he was only fifteen years old. He died in the bushes at Broadway and Esperanza.

And then there was Paul. He came to my apartment one night weaker than ever. He was so skinny, I thought he hadn't eaten for weeks. But it wasn't a lack of food that was making him thin and frail. It was something else. He pleaded for me to let him stay. "Of course, you can stay here Paul. But I need to get you to a hospital. This is really serious."

"I'm not going to a hospital." Paul was adamant.

I wouldn't leave him that night. I stayed with him and gave him juice and comforted him with a bed and a pillow. He was falling asleep every two minutes. I left my apartment and walked to buy groceries and when I came back, Paul was unconscious.

I grabbed him and held him tightly, shaking him in a desperate attempt to wake up. He couldn't lift his head up to speak. I knew right then, I had to call the paramedics. I had heard there was a three-digit number "911" I could call to dispatch paramedics, firemen, or the police. I never heard of it when I was a kid. But I dialed it, and the paramedics arrived within two minutes. They had no idea what Paul was suffering from, but they assured me he needed immediate attention and rushed him to the hospital in Downtown Long Beach.

I didn't want to talk to anyone, but the EMT's and the police were insistent. I gave them Paul's full name. I was his only caretaker, so they searched my apartment. They were suspicious of me until they found no trace of drugs at all in my apartment. I answered every question with "I don't know" and they believed me. They wanted to know if he had family, and I told him I didn't know them, but I thought they lived in Torrance. I went to the hospital that night and Paul died the next morning, literally in my arms. I cried for the first time in years.

The hospital got ahold of his father and told me his father refused to claim Paul's body because he was a faggot. So, I called a wealthy trick I knew in San Pedro and together with a couple of other friends, we buried Paul in Torrance. Later, I heard his family moved him to their own chosen gravesite for him. I spent a long time feeling guilty that I didn't do enough for him. And I lost one of my only real friends. I was back on the streets the next night though. I really didn't need to hustle but I went out and told the boys that Paul had died.

It was dark as I passed the boys on Broadway and Orange Avenue. I stood there too, but I was just gazing at the hustlers and the johns. I'd made and saved so much money in the past six months, and for the first time, I didn't need to stand there and hustle. I noticed a well-dressed guy walking towards me. He was looking at me, so of course, I thought, he must be interested. He walked straight up to me and began a conversation, but it wasn't what I'm expecting to hear.

"Hey, do you have a minute?" he asked.

"Sure, what's up?"
On a mission, he related news to me that could save my life.

"I just wanted to warn you about something. There's about fifty or sixty guys who've gotten real sick and died. Mostly gay guys in New York and San Francisco."

I immediately thought of Paul.

"There's a few guys who are sick in Hollywood, here in Long Beach and Laguna Beach too. I think it's spread by having sex. No one's doing anything about it. They won't do anything if only gay men die. Please be careful out here."

I told him thanks for the warning. Like an angel borne of the nightly winds, he slowly disappeared into the night, without asking how much I charge. I realized he wasn't after my body. He was warning me, and he knew about something others didn't.

It was a strange encounter. I immediately started thinking about what he'd said. Paul was sick and looked sicker every time I saw him. He said the same thing. Ted and a couple of other guys were sick too. I got angry and imagined the government had planted something in the Gay Community to wipe them out. There was something weird and conspiratorial about this. This was a cause worth fighting for. I'd fight for my gay friends, but I never thought this would happen to me. I cared about other people, but I was bulletproof.

I've got dreams, and I'm going to have kids, so I'm not gonna die.

I walked home and fall asleep.

***

With the money I'd earned, I bought a TV, electric guitar, amplifiers, a couch, coffee table, and a bed. But I always made sure I bought the books I loved. I also acquired an old Kawai Piano, which I played constantly — enthralling some neighbors, infuriating others. I didn't care. I actually played to impress people, but I was insecure when they were in front of me. As long as they were in another apartment, I was cool.

I love to play in front of you, as long as I play what I want to play. Just another one of my oxymoronic pathologies. I know I'm the greatest piano player ever, but I'm afraid to hear other people's opinions.

That night, I wanted to read. I liked to read Almanacs. In fact, I had just bought the 1981 New York Times Almanac. I liked the World Almanac better, but this was the only one they had for sale at the bookstore. I absolutely fucking loved almanacs. I loved to read all the facts about our world. When I opened an Almanac, I was totally immersed in Everything Earth: Our world and every country's population statistics, along with every continent's geographical estimated land size. I learned the quantity and identifications of all the various ethnic groups in every country on Earth.

I also learned the aggregate totals of every country's religious denominations. I got to know the countries' capitals and major cities' population changes over the last century. I loved the sports statistical sections. I learned every baseball, football, basketball and hockey record holder's name. From Babe Ruth to Bobby Orr, from Wilt Chamberlain to Jim Brown, I learned it all.

I love me some almanacs. I didn't go to your high schools. I didn't learn whatever subjects you were taught. I missed your world's formal education. No high school for me. So, fuck your world. I read and learned my way. I still thirst for knowledge, so I read everything I can get my hands on. I became my own teacher. When I wanted to go to school, Mom and Dad didn't give a fuck, and neither did your LA County "teachers." I was seventeen and this was supposed to be my senior year of high school. I always wondered what high school was like. I was on my own, and I had to support myself. I had to keep paying for an apartment. I was underage, so who would hire me? I'm valuable because of my young cock. So, here's a message for all of you: Suck it good, 'cos I need your money.

As I walked home, hungering to read the latest population stats for Melbourne, Australia, I gazed at the black sky above me at the corner of Lime Avenue and Broadway. I liked this block because Mr. R's porno shop was located at the end of Lime Avenue. The black guy who ran it let me in even though I was underage. I let him suck my dick. But tonight, my mind was wandering a bit. I loved these old buildings that surrounded me. Everything in Long Beach was so old.

My grandparents lived here. Everything that's old and doesn't move anymore docked in Long Beach. That's why this was the perfect home for the Queen Mary Ship and The Spruce Goose. They were both ancient and can't move, but there's something wonderful filtering through all of this aged architecture. They're decomposing, but there is beauty in decay. These old buildings were protective and comforting, enchanting and mystifying. Even these lusts filled streets have a touch of sanctification. This was a sacred journey. We were collectively searching to fill our emptiness. So many people were out here are selling their souls for love in legal tender form. But you can trust us. There's no mystery to a prostitute's motives.

Maybe it's us, the outcasts of society, who are the true chosen ones. Didn't Jesus hang out with the harlots? Here we are; harlots everywhere for your pleasure. The lonely boulevard I walk on is hallowed ground. There are so many people, so fucking desperate and lonely, but there's a holy desperation to our quest. We have our own brand of worship. This trade is our religion. This boulevard is our church. Everyone wants someone else to save them, including me.

I read and read my newly bought almanac tonight. But while reading the facts, without even noticing, I picked my skin. I picked and picked at those imaginary bumps until they bled. If I didn't find one, I made one. On that night, I was particularly aggressive. I picked my butt cheeks until they were scarred and bloody. I started picking at 11 p.m. and then suddenly it was three in the morning. Fuck, I lost track of time while I was picking. Why the fuck did I do this shit? I swore, it would be the last night I picked my skin. But I've said that a thousand times.

I worried my scars would lower the value of my body, even though I knew I healed pretty quickly. Youth works that way.

16

My Succubus

September 1982, Long Beach, California

The fall of 1982 was spectacular. I made money every day and night. All cash and tax free. It was so easy.

Sometimes, all I had to do is wear my white pants, be shirtless, and adjust my penis so that the outline of the bulge was evident, and my congregation would begin worshipping. I could stop traffic on Ocean Boulevard faster than Superman on cocaine. And they offered me money just for walking down Ocean Blvd.

This was my job. To look hot.

I began to notice the more expensive cars. But I still loved the guys in the Ramblers and Pintos. Everyone had a chance with me. As long as you carried some cash, we could work it out.

And the women had opportunity just to get laid. Although the women who cruised here were not usually the highest paying customers, they craved seeing and sucking my cock as much as the men.

Everyone was horny in 1982!

There were reports on the news about police finding dead young men's bodies dumped on the sides of freeways and roads every day. In fact, I had begun tracking them, and from the 1970s until this summer of 1982, the numbers of bodies had reached over 50. There had to be more than one serial killer working the Southern California highways. I remembered seeing the face of one named William Bonin who was arrested in 1980. But I also saw the face of a real creepy guy with a stereotypical gay mustache trying to pick up one of my friends on Broadway and Pacific in the fall of 1982. I told my friend to get away from the car because this dude looked and acted like a weirdo. I remember the car was a Toyota Celica.

The next year, in 1983, I was watching the news when a crime reporter came on and said the CHP had arrested a suspected serial killer named Randy Kraft. When they displayed the picture of his car, I jumped off the couch. It was the same Toyota Celica and the same driver that I warned my friend away from the year before. Death came in many forms. It wasn't safe out there. But I felt a little safer knowing Mr. Kraft was behind bars.

And for me? My purpose is to teach the world to have more sex. The more I thought about it, the hornier I got. This was an important undertaking. I must acknowledge and accept this mission. To show you how having sex with me can bring deep fulfillment to our lives. I will show the world how all of us, male and female both, should participate in one global group orgy, and world peace will be achieved. The sexual revolution was happening in my pants. My life's mission was to teach sexual pleasure. I had a purpose. It must be true, why else would I wake up with a hard on every morning?

One September morning, I not only woke up with a pounding erection, but to pounding at my balcony window. Who the fuck was beating on my window at 7 a.m.?

Turns out to be Crazy White Power Joe and my mother! Crazy White Power Joe was a huge, scary, white dude I knew from somewhere, but I couldn't remember where. He was probably in one of the Probation Camps with me. He was a dedicated Nazi.

He had a swastika tattooed on his face. It adorned his left cheek. His body was a testament to cattle. He was a big thick fucking guy for a nineteen-year-old (my guess), which made him older than me. He was always older and bigger, he had biceps the size of cannonballs, but what really made him intimidating, was his personality and height. He was paranoid and nervous all the time, prowled to initiate fights, and he was crazy (hence the name Crazy White Power Joe). For some reason, he really liked me. I think it was because I fought hard as a white boy, and he saw that.

Most of the white kids in LA County facilities either gave up their food and shoes willingly or got beat up and had their food and shoes taken. I never gave up anything without a fight. Most of the time, I hit first. Of course, it took a couple of years of incarceration to make me like that. Inside, I wasn't like him. He was a racist asshole. I never understood judging people by the color of their skin. When I saw someone of another race, I wanted to get to know them. Why hate them? It never made sense to me. Your world never made sense to me, and it isn't getting better.

Anyway, what the fuck were Crazy White Power Joe and my mother doing here at my apartment? How the hell did they find out where I live? And why were they here at the same time? What the fuck? I opened my front door.

Mom looked like her usual shit self. She's got a black eye, her face was red and bruised and she looked haggard. She looked like what she is — an alcoholic. Crazy White Power Joe looked startled to be standing next to my mother, who was sitting on the steps.

"Wassuuup, Doooglas?!!"

"What's up with you, Joe?"

He awkwardly acknowledged there was an older female person sitting on the steps to my apartment door. "I'll come back, bro." If I had the courage to say it, I would have told him not to worry about it. But I told him to come back later. I was always agreeing to shit I didn't want to do. As Joe left, I turned to my mother, genuinely curious as to why she showed up at my doorstep.

"Why are you here, Mom?"

"Doug, I know you're doing ok now, and we're having trouble with money."

She must have forgotten that I was still seventeen years old and I was supposed to be in high school. Maybe I would have been in high school if you weren't an alcoholic. But nevertheless, my grandiose ego kicked in and I offered her an ear.

"What can I do?"

"Can you help me with $200?"

That's not much to ask for, but I hate to part with a dime because I'm cheap as hell. But my ego wouldn't allow it. "So, you need $200? That's what you tracked me down for?"

And then her ego kicked in. "Well, I've done all I can for you."

In my head, I'm thinking: "So you think keeping me in Boys Homes all of my teenage life, never once changing your lifestyle so I could have a home is doing all you can for me?"

I feel rage boiling up inside me. But she continues with her selfish rant. "I know you're probably a prostitute down here. You're making money. I need your help."

I'd seen many revolting things during the hellish years I lived in my parents' world, and then many more during my years confined to the Los Angeles County Probation System.

And now, three years later, Mom's on my doorstep, begging me for money, and simultaneously castigating me for how I earned it.

Had she forgotten?

Ok, Mom. The ringing of hypocrisy in my ears was so loud it had to have been to be palpable to the neighbors as well. But she knows about sex. She thought I was a pervert, and all I did was think about sex. Well, Mom, you oughta know…

Lakewood, California, July 1979

I'll never forget one of our special "mother-son moments" when I walked into her home for a weekend pass from the Boys' Home I was living in, only to be greeted with Mom's vagina and her legs spread wide open in front of me.

What a joyful sight.

My mind and my body were grasping for something genuine, desperately seeking love and guidance. Instead, I received cold rejection, bizarre sexualized encounters, daily beatings from my father, and the sum of everyone's fears and sexual desires – including Mom's.

I remember my mother's rancid pussy, when I dared to look at it, the moment I walked in the house.

I was fourteen years old, coming off a long, lonely bus ride from a Boys' Home that was 35 miles away from Mom's house. She refused to see me because she claimed it was too far to drive.

I left a Boys' Home infested with child molesters only to be greeted with Mom's wide open naked wrinkled hairy old vagina, her pasty white legs, spread open before me exposing the brown follicles that covered her thighs. I learned right then and there that a woman can be as hairy there as a man when they are too drunk to shave, or just don't care about hygiene. I like hairy pussies, just not Mom's.

When I was a young boy, I loved trying to get a peek up a teacher's skirt because I would get a hard on seeing that loose dark pubic hair sticking out of her panties. I don't understand the fascination with shaved pussies and assholes. It seems like everyone wants to imagine they're having sex with seven-year-old vaginas and ten-year-old boys. Maybe I'm just being judgmental.

But I digress… Mom is the subject matter here. I can never forget seeing her using her hips, thrusting up and down while she shrieked and howled drunkenly at me, faking her "sleep" as she pointed her rotten holy compass of torment toward my face. It stunk. I thought rotten fish had piled up somewhere. Ah, the aroma of a freshly fucked and unwashed dirty old vagina. It's an odor I'll never forget. I started calling it the "chimichanga sauce odor." It was filling my lungs like a dead catfish on the beach. She was still frantically begging and pleading for me to fuck her.

"Fuck me! Fuck me, Doug!" she screamed, eyes closed, pretending she was asleep.

I didn't come home for that. How about if we start off slowly, maybe a hug first? Fucking you was not on my agenda just yet.

I have to admit that even though the sight and smell were frightening me, at the same time, I was oddly fascinated. Seeing her in that position, on the couch with an empty bottle of vodka and fresh stitches in her head, was an exhibition of her own unique brand of trailer park panache. I mean no offense to anyone from a trailer park. When Mom exposed her vagina to me, begging and pleading for me to fuck her right then, she revealed openly and honestly her tremendous soul sickness.

She was my succubus.

She egotistically flaunted her inner demons and I resented her for it. I was not mature enough to understand why she did what she did, but I knew it wasn't traditional parental behavior and I needed to quickly clean this situation up. In a hurry, I became the parent. My life depended on it. Her current heroin addicted boyfriend could walk in at any moment, and I knew he would use this scene as an excuse to shoot me. He carried a gun with him at all times. He was jealous of my presence. I didn't understand why, and I was suspicious of my mother's motives.

Was she actually setting me up? That way, she could get rid of me for good. I will never forget how she'd scream at my sister, "You stole my husband!" She blamed a little girl for getting raped. I wondered how a nine-year-old could "steal" a grown man away from her mother. Instead of shielding her from the pain of being molested, she blamed her for her own pain. This was my mother, and she was one of the architects of the world I grew up in.

As I picked my mother up from the couch, she attempted a body twist and grabbed for my fourteen-year-old penis. She opened my zipper and put her head right there, making a mouth grab on to the head of my dick. I was desperately trying to swat her face away from my crotch while at the same time carrying her through the hallway so I could throw her into her bed. As we struggled in the hallway — her sucking my dick, and me fighting it while carrying Mom — I noticed her beloved portrait of Jesus above our heads, and Christ staring down at Mom while she sucked my teenage dick. But she sucked at sucking cock. The priests were better.

Back at my apartment:

I gave my mother the money she wanted so she would just fucking go away. I felt uncomfortable around her. I was supposed to love her, but I really hated her. She was an egotistical tramp — the oldest of three sisters, and she loved to imagine that she was smarter than them. She treated them with contempt, and they just accepted it, as if it were love. She thought she knows more than she really did. But she didn't know anything. You could take everything she knows about life, put it into a matchbox and listen to it rattle. But in her head, she was the smartest tramp in the trailer park. She thought she was an intellectual, and, strangely, she was. As Albert Camus said: "An intellectual is someone whose mind loves watching itself." She was an intellectual fool, always deriding anyone with formal education. She dropped out of high school at sixteen, but according to her, she didn't need school. She was so smart, she dropped out and got pregnant from a guy she never saw again. That's how my sister was spawned. My mom sure showed those high school graduates.

And she taught me a lot, mostly about sex. She sucked me, tried to fuck me, left me to rot in Boys' Homes, spent her life inside a bottle with no room for me, and yet all I hear everywhere is "love your mother." Your world enthrones mothers like they're all holy and divine. On the TV, on billboards; from people I know and people I don't know. It's all I hear. In this world everyone's supposed to love their mother. Your world even celebrates "Mother's Day." How about Abused Child Day? Your world tries to make me feel guilty for not sharing your love for my mother. I'm supposed to love and respect my mother? Yeah, right — the way she loved and respected me? Fuck you. And fuck your world. Fuck my mother too.

She stayed only until she had her $200. She departed from my Long Beach apartment while the sun was shining, and the sea breeze was still cooling the hot air. Someone once said, "Some people bring happiness when they enter, others when they leave." My mother always brought me happiness every time she went away.

My time was much too valuable to waste it on my mother. Out here in your world, there were many people I had to fuck, and a whole lot of money I needed to make. As I dressed for success on these streets of Long Beach, I knew I was changing the world. Your world was quickly becoming my world. The sunset came, and it was nighttime in Long Beach again.

September – December 1982, Belmont Heights, Long Beach

The fall and winter of 1982 were fun and glorious for me. I was seventeen, free, living life on my terms, turning the world on every moment of day and night, and making good money just being me. I got paid and I got off. Long Beach was a young surfer's dream. Not for surfing though. If you wanted to surf, go to Huntington or Newport Beach. Those beaches actually have waves. Long Beach was for young men who look like surfers and gay men who want to suck their cocks. Let's not forget the women who cruised Ocean Blvd. and Broadway on the prowl for young, male flesh.

It still felt like summer on this October morning. The sky was a gorgeous blue at 8 o'clock. I was awake, but still reasoning my way out of bed. In the morning, I sprung into inaction. In my line of work, getting out of bed was a career move. It was a tough decision, but even at this time of the morning, they were cruising and paying. I decided to get out of bed and hop into the shower, jacking off all the way to the bathroom. It didn't matter if I came, I'd get another hard-on five seconds later. It never went down. After I showered, I flipped my hair back and forth, so I had that surfer-meets-David Lee Roth-beach-dude look. I put on my "surfer" white pants, adjusting my crotch so that the outline of my semi-bulging penis was pressing against my thigh. Of course, I didn't wear a shirt. It's against regulations to cover up what brings in sales. It's 1982; tight pants, thongs, long blonde hair, and a young, muscled naked chest are hot. I know it, the world knows it, and I make my living being it.

This morning started out similarly to every other day. I walked confidently eastward down Ocean Blvd starting at Alamitos toward Redondo Ave. I had never made it that far, as I usually made my negotiations and get transported off to work well before Redondo Ave. Ocean Blvd. was a better street to hustle on during the day, because it ran parallel to the Ocean. I could wear less clothes and attract much more attention. Broadway was the boulevard at night. But actually, wherever I went, I attracted attention. This was just that kind of town. This part of Long Beach, known as Belmont Heights, is Gay Central. I guess that's why the locals affectionately referred to Belmont Heights as "Homo Heights." Another reason I love my gay friends. They have such phenomenal self-deprecating humor. This morning, I notice more cars with women cruising.

I was constantly playing my instruments and writing songs. This might sound like a wonderful life, but it doesn't change what I felt inside. I was making up for a lot of lost time. Music was my therapy. It doesn't completely erase my fears, but it is cathartic. For brief moments, I forgot about my inner demons and pour my emotions into my playing. I still had my paralyzing fears, self-doubts, and that inner voice in my head was always there, castigating and shaming me.

Some people are terrified of dying. For me, music is a brief respite from the terror of living.

I was getting more popular every day. As I walked up and down these streets of Long Beach, I was constantly stared at. I liked to look at me too, so I walked past businesses with large windows, cruising myself, making sure I looked perfect. Its ego feeding, but it's a hassle too, because every window reveals a flaw. I halted at my reflection and flipped my hair back over my head, letting it fall into place. I looked back to make sure I was still hot. This was business. One early evening, I ran into Alan Belanger again. He's the man I met the first day I was down here on Broadway. He paid me $500 just to suck my dick.

Alan noticed me and called out to me, "Hey, Doug!"

"How are you, Alan?"

"I'm good. Hey, I wanted to ask you something. Have you ever thought about doing movies?"

"Movies? I'm a musician, but I'd be interested in acting. I don't know if I'd be good though."

I was getting discovered. I'm thinking he might get me into a Warner Bros. movie opposite Jessica Lange – that chick that was in King Kong. That was the last time I saw a movie, but I remembered she was hot. I instantly created fantasies of stardom in my head.

"Well, I'm talking about porno movies. A lot of stars in Hollywood got their start doing porn."

"Really?" I believed him. It sounded logical to me.

"Yeah, quite a few did porn before they became famous. If you'd like to start, call this guy." He handed me a card with the name "Jim Slaton" on it.

"I live in that new building on Broadway and Elm Street. Jim is there all the time. We also shoot some scenes at his house on the beach."

Man, I thought, these guys are rich. I knew of that building he was talking about. Just the kind of place I would have liked to live in. I took the card and told him I'd call them both later that night. I had Alan's number already and wanted to know this Jim guy.

"Thanks, Alan."

"You'd be a star in porn. You could be bigger than Kip Noll."

I nodded my head as if I knew who Kip Noll was. I vaguely remembered hearing his name a few nights ago. I think one "trick" I met once, late at night, mentioned that I looked like him. I was at his house in San Pedro, and he was jacking off while staring at me saying that I was better looking than Kip Noll. I barely paid attention.

I sauntered back down Broadway, chuckling a bit at all the cars slowing down as I passed by. Yes, my ego was growing, but I was still grateful for my gay friends. I'd never been loved or treated with such kindness before in my life. These guys actually had become my friends. So, what if they wanted to have sex too? It was rare, but some of them don't care about sex. They were just nice guys. Respectful, kind, and compassionate people. I loved Homo Heights. Ain't no gangs here, I realized. I don't have to fight anyone. If I did, it was because of me and my head trips.

These guys, as far as I knew, weren't interested in fighting, robbing or stealing. They wanted to live in peace and harmony. They had no agenda, and the neighborhood was beautiful. It was simply a safe and peaceful neighborhood to live in. I never wanted to fight anyone in my life. I liked being kind to people just like my friends here in the Heights. I had compassion for others just like my friends here. I'd always felt different, isolated and persecuted. I'm creative and artistic, and my gay friends are very creative and artistic. They think about sex all the time, and so do I.

I was starting to wonder…does that mean I'm gay?

I was loving Long Beach more and more. As I walked, I glance into the alley and I saw my favorite homeless guy — the man from Glad. We called him "The man from Glad" because he wore nothing but Glad trash bags around his body. They were secured together around his waist. He was always bare chested. His shopping cart was also filled with them. His routine was familiar. He would lean over his shopping in the alley behind my apartment and look up at my window nearly every single day I lived there. He didn't just look at me, he stared into my eyes, with a burning intentional gaze. As if he was warning me about something too. He never accepted money, so I handed him food when I would pass him. His eyes were always locked on mine. I never felt in danger. It really felt like he was trying to tell me something. I wonder if I'll ever discover it…

He was so well known, when he died, the Long Beach Press-Telegram wrote a story about him called "The man from Glad dies." Apparently, he was a congressman from Minnesota at one time but became an alcoholic and ended up on the streets the last ten years in Long Beach. He loved the bottle more than his family or career. I don't understand how someone could think that alcohol can replace all that really matters. I don't spend much time asking why. I remember something I heard an older alcoholic person say in an AA meeting we were forced to attend, because they treated us like we were all drug addicts in Sunrise Youth Community: "It's not Alcoholics Analysis. It's Alcoholics Anonymous." Asking why is futile. Doesn't matter why you started. Just stop.

17

Dad

I went to the local Safeway grocery store, bought food for later that night and walked back home. It was Saturday and I was still trying to decide what to do when my telephone rang. I picked it up, and a voice I hadn't heard from in over a year said to me in that familiar ominous tone: "Doug, it's your dad."

I felt a rush of adrenaline surge through me.

My dad's actually calling me! He's thinking of me.

I was still anxious.

"Hey, Dad, how are you? What's going on?"

I wondered how he got my phone number, since I'd called him several times to give it to him, but he never answered the phone. He didn't even own an answering machine. He didn't want to converse with anyone. So how did he get my number? I was too afraid to ask.

He answered my question anyway. "I called your Mom, and she gave me your phone number. I wanted to ask you something."

"Sure, go ahead, Dad." I entertained fantasies of us together in my head. Was he proud of me for living and surviving on my own? I was not of "adult" age and I had an apartment, a phone, I paid my own rent, I wrote songs and hadn't gotten into any trouble. He would notice and want to tell me. I started fantasizing about the possibilities: He might want to take me to a baseball game. Maybe he wants to see me and have lunch. Maybe he wants me to play the guitar for him. Help him fix something; anything. I was just thrilled that he called me.

"I'm going to list you on my taxes as a dependent, which means I'm telling the IRS that you're living with me. I just wanted you to know."

"Ok, great!" I wasn't sure what that meant.

87

"So, now that I'm putting you on my W-4 form as a dependent, according to the IRS, you're living with me. You're saving me money."

"Of course, I understand. I'm glad I can help you, Dad." Of course, I didn't understand anything he said, except that he didn't call because he wanted to see me.

As we hung up, I wish I had said, "If I could actually live with you, I could go to high school and graduate."

***

My earliest memory of my father is being afraid of him. I don't mean fear in the form of respect, like he'd take away my toys. I'm speaking of terror; all-consuming terrorizing fear. From the moment I first remember interacting with him, I was afraid that he'd kill me.

The earliest interactive memory I have of him, is seared into my consciousness. I'll never forget it. I was two years old, almost three, and my nose was stuffed up. My mother and I were in the living room. I remember I kept sniffling and I felt bad, but I didn't understand why. I was having difficulty breathing, so my mother told me I should blow my nose. I couldn't understand what she meant. I didn't know how to blow my nose, so she took a tissue and told me to blow air out of my nose. She pretended to blow her nose to show me how, but I still couldn't understand. I sniffed instead.

My father was enraged. Terror engulfed me, and my little hands were trembling. The sound of his voice was like a monster. I was so scared; I couldn't perform this command. Why are you so mad at me, Daddy? I wanted to understand. He ordered me to blow my nose, and I sniffed again.

Smack!

I plummeted to the floor. I screamed, but I couldn't hear myself. Silence. All the sounds in the room were gone.

The living room grew darker. I was terrified and I didn't know what happened to me. I was stunned. My skull snapped upward after smashing against the floor. The force of his strike to my temple was powerful. I began bleeding.

I couldn't hear anything. My head hurt bad. I had no defense against this attack. I was suddenly aware of how helpless I was. My tender baby face and brain were vulnerable, unprotected, and exposed. He was God. I sniffed again. There was no warning.

This time, he punched my nose, my head snapped back, and I couldn't breathe. Something was happening to my face. It felt wet.

He hit me hard as a rock. Instantaneous terrible, terrible pain. Total darkness.

I cried and cried and cried. I couldn't defend myself. Crying, crying, crying out… please please help me, save me! I don't want to die!

Why, Daddy, why? Why are you mad? Why can't I make you happy? Why, Daddy, why? Why do I have to die? I love you, Daddy. I must be horrible to make my daddy hate me so much. My daddy's good, and I'm bad, so he must kill me. Please don't kill me. I understand how big you are. I'm small. You're a giant. You're stronger and bigger than me. I understand now. I promise to be a good boy. I promise I'll be good forever. I'm wrong; I'm stupid, but I don't want to die. Please don't hurt me anymore! It's my fault. Why is my face wet? The floor has red water on it. Scream! I can hear myself screaming now.

He knew what I was supposed to do and I couldn't do it. That was why he hit me in the face. I must be bad, I thought. My mother yelled at him to stop hitting me. She still thought I might be able to blow my nose, so she told me to try it again. I was pouring tears, and I was so terrified of what would happen if I got it wrong again that I didn't even try. I was too scared. Again, I didn't see it coming, but I sure did feel it.

I awoke on the floor, my sensitive toddler cranium now bruised. I was on my back. I felt tremendous pain. My brain was not working. It was throbbing. This is what it's like to die. I was trying to tell them I didn't understand, but I didn't know how to communicate it. I was so small, and I'd just been taught how helpless I really am. Everything had changed. One moment, I was almost three years old, confident, upright, communicating my thoughts and feelings and then…blackness, terror and fear. I awakened slowly. I was on my back, bleeding from my nose and ears.

It was physically painful, but the emotional pain was worse. With one punch, my father determined for me what I would always be — too stupid to think for myself, too weak to defend myself and too flawed to live. God decided I should be dead because I'm unworthy. I could feel wetness coming out of my nose. My father had punched me in the face. My mother said she yelled at my dad that if he hit me again, she would report him to the police. That's what she told me later.

She told me as she was attempting to stop the flow of blood from my nose, she noticed blood coming from my right ear. She said she was angry with him, but he didn't care at all. He said I was a wimp, and I should have listened to him and blew my nose. I guess he thought he could command me into learning. Or beat learning into me. And I became afraid. Not just afraid but filled with terrorizing primal fear. Fear is now my neural demon.

Being me frightens me because I'm not smart enough to do anything. In this moment, that thought of worthlessness became embedded in my brain and seems to have developed into an instinctive emotional lighthouse. I can't rewire this part of my brain. Those beliefs would override every talent I possessed, every crumb of confidence, any notion that I might have value, and any idea that I might be lovable. He commanded me with petrifying violence, and that ferocious beating provided my first permanent thoughts about myself: Worthless, disposable, unlovable, without value.

My father, Kurt Probst, grew up in Torrance, California. He had a younger brother named Lyle Konrad Probst. This is about as Germanic as it gets. His father, my paternal grandfather, was named Lloyd Probst, and he had a mother named Katharine. At any Probst gathering, they argued. In fact, every one of these Probst's were unable to get along with each other. My father disliked everyone. He was incapable of feeling compassion, kindness, or emotions.

To say he was cheap would be an understatement. He wouldn't give the waitresses tips at Spire's because "they were whiners, and they already received a paycheck" and so on. He was the most self-centered person I've ever known. From as far back as I remember, although I still wanted and needed his approval every day of my life, I also feared and hated him. He was always in a bad mood, never expressed anything except contempt for everyone and everybody, including me, and he rarely looked up from the newspaper, except to rape my sister or beat me. There was nothing more to him. He had no personality.

Being with my dad was as exciting as watching paint dry. He was unpredictable and volatile. I never knew what would make him upset. And when he became upset, he punched me in the face. That was how he "punished" me. It was always a punch to my face. I found out later from my mom, in an off handed way, that he had been slapping and hitting me much earlier than when I couldn't blow my nose. He was hitting me when I was in diapers.

Another early memory of my father is when he was charged with indecent exposure for standing at the window of our home waving his penis to the children walking to school. I think this was 1969. I was four, and the charges he received were minor. I remember my mother going to the police station, and they talked about it. He claimed he was innocently naked, but the kids reported he was swinging his woody so they would see it. Because we heard their discussion, my sister and I knew what he did. My father was twenty-seven years old at the time; he was born in 1942. Although he was arrested and charged, I don't think the police took his penis waving at schoolchildren action as seriously as they would today. If they had—

Oh well…they didn't. And the rest of my sister's life and mine became what it became.

My dad never cared about anything except to argue his point. He never spoke about much besides music and politics. I hardly ever saw his face because he never put down the newspaper, except when he was mad, or to complain about "Democrats." He loved Archie Bunker and All in the Family. He loved his soul singers, especially Jackie Wilson and Sam Cooke. I remember how he complimented them, "Those niggers can sing." I wondered why he referred to his favorite singers in that way. If you like them, why do you call them that? That was another moment where I realized I hated my father. He's a racist. I didn't like being the son of a racist.

I was a pest about information, so I asked a lot of questions as a kid. I got hit a lot for that, but it never stopped me. Gaining my father's approval was a powerful force. I guess getting punched in the face was better than total rejection. He believed kids should be seen and not heard. But he didn't even like seeing us. But I was gonna be seen. I learned he fought with his father, and my dad left home and joined the Air Force. His father was willing to pay for college, but my dad was stubborn and headstrong, to say the least. He thought he was smarter than everyone. His brother, my uncle Lyle, was very similar. He's convinced he knows everything, and he was never shy about telling us. He had his sexual issues also. He was expelled from North Torrance High School for getting caught masturbating on the roof of the girls' gym, staring through the window on the ceiling. It's clear that I come from a proud lineage, a long line of social deviants and self-appointed intellectuals.

My father was a dull person. I could scour thesauruses day and night to find a word that describes his personality, but they haven't come up with a fitting description. He only had two emotions: angry and horny. I made him mad, and my sister made him horny. He also loved his porn. Our house was self-storage for porn. My mother told me later how his idea of a marriage date was taking her to adult movies at the theater. This was the 70's and adult movie theaters were booming. That was an exciting outing for him, and he thought everyone else enjoyed it as much as he did. He thought for all of us.

We weren't people, we were objects he ignored, beat, or fucked. The times when I was beat the most was when I walked in a room and caught sight of him forcing his cock into Jamie's mouth, pushing her head down on it, or fingering her six-year-old vagina. He rushed to the door as I entered, and immediately punched me in my face because I interrupted him. He yelled at me to get out, and believe me, I ran for my life.

One time, I heard my sister crying and got the courage up to try to stop him, and he beat me so bad that the bruising lasted weeks. My teeth were knocked loose, and I urinated on myself, which I got in trouble for too. My sister and I finally realized this was wrong and we told our mother. It took a lot of courage on her part. Jamie thought it was her fault, and she didn't want to cause trouble. I was different; I liked trouble. And I believed mom would stop what was happening. We told our mother in the kitchen before Dad came home from work.

She asked, "What exactly is he doing?"

We told her that he was making Jamie put her mouth around his penis, and also ramming his fingers into her vagina because it was too small to get his penis into her. I was five and Jamie was seven. He had been doing this since I was three and she was five. So, by the time my sister was seven years old, she had been raped at least fifty times. I lost track of how many times he'd beaten me.

My mother was skeptical. I remember her saying she was going to question him, and if he said it wasn't true, we'd get punished for lying. Later that evening, I heard my father calling us liars from inside their master bedroom. My mother came out and scolded us for making up a terrible lie about my father. He yelled and smacked us both in the face. We cried together all night. I knew something was wrong. I had a hard time with being blamed for his actions. I knew this was wrong. But if they both said it, I guessed that I must be a liar, after all, they both said so.

It was worse for Jamie. I felt bad for her. She believed everything was her fault. At least I had an instinct that our family wasn't normal, but she lacked insight. My mother did a lot of damage to her. She berated and blamed Jamie as if she was jealous of my father's attention to her. So, she had not only had my dad's dick rammed into her mouth, and his fingers in her vagina, but she believed she was to blame.

He would continue raping her, and help would never come. We went to the only person we thought could save us from our father, but she blamed us. We turned the rapist into the police, and the police sent us back to the rapist.

My father was a volatile, unpredictable person to be around. He got into arguments with everyone, everywhere. We couldn't get through the drive thru at Jack in the Box without him arguing with the clown. I cringed in the backseat when the clown asked him something, because I knew he'd say something he thought was funny, and when the clown didn't respond the way he expected it too, the fight was on. He loved arguing his point, even with a voice inside an inanimate cement clown. And wouldn't you know it – the clown always won. I probably ingested a lot of boogers and spit whenever we ate fast food. My dad never thought it through. You don't mess with the people handling your food.

His insecurity extended into our time spent playing music. He loved music, and he knew I was a prodigy on all stringed instruments. The problem was that he thought he had talent. He could barely play notes, let alone keep up with me. I dreaded those times when he pulled his guitar out and tried to play along with me. He had no rhythm, and he couldn't keep up with me. I was scared of his temper, so I was always making excuses for him. Invariably he got mad when we played together, because he couldn't play as well as a six-year-old.

We'd start "I saw her standing there" by the Beatles, I'd be jamming fine, and he'd screw up within the first 30 seconds. I had to stop and let him curse whatever excuse he created that placed the blame somewhere else. The guitar was not operating incorrectly, or I was playing too fast, usually I received the blame for his ineptitude. Of course, it wasn't his fault. Somehow it became mine. This was weird. I halfway believed him because he was my all powerful, all knowing father. But I had moments of clarity: He's just a fucking insecure dumbshit who's also a shitty musician.

91

18

I'm a California Tourist Attraction

November 1982, Long Beach, California

I decided to call Jim Slaton, the name of the pornographer on the card that Alan Belanger gave me. He answered and said he'd heard about me and wanted to meet me. He invited me to his Oceanfront Condominium. He actually lived a block away from me, but upon entering his 25th floor high rise condominium with ocean front views, I realized I had stepped into opulence. This impressed me. I was a seventeen-year-old kid with no education, no family, no skills, and was struggling to survive on his own.

I'd never seen such a grand display of wealth. He had the glass coffee table situated ostentatiously in front of his flamboyantly grandiose white sofa. The kitchen had a bar area that resembled a nightclub. I turned to look out the huge sliding glass balcony doors, and I saw both a telescope, and film projector sitting on tripods, directly facing the beach. He was watching and filming the boys on the sand. And he wasn't shy about bragging.

He wore the wealthy man's coat of tan. He immediately asked me what I like to drink, and before I could say "Dr. Pepper," he handed me a scotch on the rocks, saying, "It's the best." Glen Livet. Sounds like dog food. What the hell, I'll try this Glen Livet. I wanted to live this kind of life. I had to know how soon I could live like this, how he obtained this stuff, and how I could get rich. I wanted money — this kind of money. He asked me if I liked his home, and of course, I said yes. He boasts and complains about how many people are jealous of his lifestyle. I loved Glen Livet. It became my drink of choice.

Though he's a braggart, my first impression of Jim was good. I liked him. He seemed interested in me. He sat down near me on the white couch, but he didn't get uncomfortably close. He sipped his Glen Livet and asked me about me. I told him I write songs. He said he'd like to hear me play guitar sometime, and then asked me how I felt about performing in a movie. I was very interested in money, but I wanted to know what he expected me to do.

"Well, Doug, the guys who make the most money are the ones who get fucked. If you're willing to do that on camera, I'd pay you $1,000."

I told him emphatically that I would never do that. I was a slave to money, but there ain't no way I'm doing that, especially on camera. That would ruin my musical career. I might get this new disease that's already killed nine of my friends from getting fucked in the ass. It hurts anyway. It would show me doing something on film that the world hates and never forgives you for.

And I don't want to die.

"I'll jack off, and that's it."

"Okay, we're shooting scenes this weekend. I'll give you $500 for that."

"Ok, it's a deal."

And the best part was I was already experienced at what he was paying me to do:
Masturbate in the bathtub.
And here I am. I'm a star.

That cover made me well known all over Long Beach and the world. When I began traveling, I realized I was popular worldwide. I remember walking into a bookstore in Hollywood and people were gawking and fawning all over me. It was the same thing in New York City. People wanted my autograph, especially in the porno shops, mostly because I liked to walk around the X rated sections. I guess "7 up & cumning" sold well throughout the 1980s. I went to pay a parking ticket at the Long Beach courthouse in 1984 and as I got to the front of the line, a young, effeminate, guy behind the counter became star struck and started shaking.

"Oh my God! You're my favorite porn star! I can't believe you're right here!"

I was with my girlfriend, Laura, and I made a motion with my finger across my lips signaling him to zip it shut. She was looking the other way, so he made the same motion across his lips, assuring me he understood. He did it with more panache than I ever could.

"I get it. She's your...I promise, no problem...my lips are sealed," he whispered.

I was flattered.
Another time my face on this cover embarrassed me was when I took Laura into the porno section of the bookstore. This must have been about 1984 — I was so happy to have a VHS video tape machine at home, so I could rent porno movies and get my girlfriend horny. See what a romantic guy I am? Anyway, I proudly strut her into the X-rated section

of the store to see what kind of porno movie she might like to see. I turn to my right, and… there I am! My smiling face is staring back at me.

My acting debut in "7 up & Cumming" is facing me on the rack at eye level. I quickly push her from behind, into the opposite direction. I've got to get her out of here before she sees me on a gay sex tape. I get lucky this time, but I realize something — I'm doing things I'm ashamed of, but I like doing them. But I don't want the girls to know about this. Whatever. Of course, later, I discover many girls get excited watching two men have sex. Laura was one of those girls.

I realized I had to let go of the shame I felt about what I was doing. At that moment, I needed the money, and I liked the attention. Plus, America loves to watch porn. It's more real than those fucking music videos I watched on MTV. Music was, and is, my life, and I'm not sure what to make of lip-synching songs. I did realize a change though. In the music business, you can't just write a song, and expect only a listener's imagination to make it a hit. Those days, any song needed a video to accompany it. It was now a video world. Music videos and pornography – maybe there was some way I could make them magical together? Only one of these mediums lures you in by faking it, and that's the music videos. You can't lip sync a blowjob.

I wanted to buy a car. Shouldn't a porn star have a car? I was tired of being a passenger in life. I was still underage, and I didn't know anything about cars. I received very little outside information, especially about cars. I knew nothing, except that I liked Camaros and trucks.

My friend Rick Crawford's mother owned a car lot. I didn't have a clue what to ask about, but I was willing to spend $3,000 cash. I had more than $10,000 in my mattress. I still wasn't willing to put it into a bank. I didn't trust them, and besides, I wasn't eighteen yet.

Rick's mom had a 1978 Datsun pickup truck for $3,000. It looked good – Black, orange and sporty. He came to Long Beach and we rode the buses out to East Jesus (Azusa), and I bought the truck. Now, I'm driving. No lessons, no experience, just able to get where I wanted to go much, much faster. There's not a lot to know about driving — just don't fuck up.

After our transaction was completed, Rick's mom invited Rick and me into a corner office up front where we followed her, and she shut the door. She then pulled out a bag of cocaine and a mechanism known as a freebase pipe with an acetylene torch and ether. I'd never seen one before and didn't know what to do. She lit it up, inhaled the smoke that was swirling in the glass and passed the pipe to Rick.

I watched Rick and his mom freebase coke together, but when they passed the pipe to me, I refused to smoke from it. I remember thinking it was a bit odd that Rick and his mom were sharing cocaine, but I stayed away from judging them. My life experiences affected my judgment paradoxically. I didn't judge, but I didn't practice good discernment either. I was still a bit frightened of drugs. Later in my life, that fear left me, and I regretted for a long time that I tried coke. I've learned that regret is wishing for a better past. Wishing is for children.

Some families go on picnics together, others smoke crack together.

Behind the wheel of my 1974 Datsun pickup, I no longer walked down Broadway like a star. I drove like a star. I wanted to visit Alan Belanger in that nice Condominium complex on Broadway and Elm Street. I called him, and of course he was free to see me. I wasn't free, but at least I was affordable. I knew that just by showing up, I'd leave with at least $300. I knocked on the door, and Alan immediately welcomed me with open arms.

Alan had a friend visiting him today. He introduced us. He introduced himself as John Movido but everyone there called him Robby. He told me Robby wasn't his real name, but his "Escort" name. He named himself Robby Leonetti after Robby Benson. I remembered Robby Benson from a 70's TV show – he was a good-looking dark-haired guy who had piercing blue eyes. I immediately liked Robby, mostly because he was not trying to get into my pants the very second he met me. He was very intelligent, and we conversed as if we'd known each other forever. Robby started talking about the porn business, and how I don't have to get into that, because there's not that much money in it anyway. Alan didn't look pleased with this turn of conversation, but he was graciously quiet. Alan turned to Robby and reminded him to tell me something they wanted me to know about. Robby suggested to me that if I really wanted to make money on a larger scale, then I should put an ad in the Advocate Magazine.

"What's the Advocate?"

Robby explained to me that the Advocate was a nationally distributed Gay Centered magazine that focused on news, the arts, and entertainment. It had apparently been around since the 1960's. He told me it was published before Stonewall. I had no idea what Stonewall was, but my ears perked up when he suggested that I should advertise as an escort in the Advocate classified section. He said he made thousands of dollars a week this way and had met many wealthy men who he now counted as friends, through his advertisement as an escort. Robby wanted to drive me to one of his upscale client's houses. I kinda wanted to show off my new truck, but Robby had a BMW. That doesn't impress me, but I knew it was impressive to other people. Off we went in Robby's new 1982 BMW. As we drove, I was still wondering why I didn't relate to what's popular. The voice in my head told me: It's because you're fucking stupid.

Robby talked a lot while he drove. He was also coughing a lot. He showed me a magazine with pictures of him in it. It was called In Touch. It was a Gay porn mag, and he said he wanted to introduce me to the photographer who took these pictures. I could get paid the same amount of money for still photographs. and they wouldn't damage my future career plans. He said this photographer named Kurt Deitrick was a good guy and was serious about producing quality work. I could see by Robby's photos that this Kurt guy's photography skills were superb. In fact, he asked me if I wanted to meet Kurt today. I said, of course I'd like to meet Kurt. All I had was time, especially when there was money to be made. I noticed Robby coughing again, and he was having a hard time breathing. This was more serious than just a cough.

"Are you ok, Robby?"

"Yeah, but I can't seem to get rid of this cold."

I instantly knew he had this disease that had already killed six of my friends.

Robby had a degree in Mechanical Engineering, and was very smart, but I don't think he was smart about downplaying the seriousness of what was wrong with him.

I'd already seen my friends from the Broadway area of Long Beach get sick and die. Their health deteriorated quickly as I watched, helpless to do anything. Every time I'd see them it was worse. Their bodies were shriveling up and they couldn't breathe. Something was filling up their lungs. I was there in an alley behind the Kennedy Hotel, when a young sweet kid named Johnny, so thin and pale, painfully gasped his last breath as the ambulance took him away. Johnny, Ray and Tristan died the previous week. Johnny was nineteen, Ray was twenty and Tristan was only sixteen. And now, they're dead, along with Paul, Cesar and

Troy.

I'd only been out of the system for six months, and the closest group of friends I'd made were dying one by one. I already knew ten guys who'd died. If I knew ten guys who died just in this small area of Long Beach, there's got to be many more dead around the country. How come I didn't see news coverage on this epidemic? I read the Long Beach Press Telegram and the Los Angeles Times every day. I hadn't seen one report in either newspaper on any day. And I read them cover to cover. I also watched the nightly news. Nothing there either. It was fucking obvious something terrible was going on. All I heard about was the Tylenol thing. As tragic as it was, only seven people died from taking Tylenol. I personally knew ten guys who were dead. That's three more, just in my life. What the fuck? Where was the media?

I thought Robby might have the sickness. He opened up to me.

"I'll be honest with you, Doug, I think I might have the Gay pneumonia that's going around. I've got a purple spot on my leg too. I just can't believe I'm that sick – I'm too young. I'm going to my doctor again this week. He can't figure it out, but I'm sure some specialist is working on this, and I'll be fine."

He pulled up to a big house in some other city's hilly estate section. We knocked on the door, and an immaculately dressed man in a suit answered. He greeted Robby warmly, and locked his eyes on mine. He was undressing me with his eyes. I didn't think Robby was expecting to cease existing the moment this man saw me. Fortunately, Robby was a gentleman. He was gracious and briefly interrupted the man's fixation by whisking him into another room for their intended conversation. Whatever their conversation was about, I didn't care, I was focused on learning from Robby. My instincts told me he knew how to make money. As the two of them returned, the man asked for my phone number, telling me that he'd love to call me. I gave it to him. He also gave me a card, telling me to call him anytime.

Everything was ok as Robby and I exited. Robby informed me that this guy was one of his "upscale" clients who he had met at a restaurant in West Hollywood called Numbers. He suggested I go there with him sometime, because (in his words): "You could make a fortune just standing still in that place."

I'd love to make a fortune standing still. But I needed a little help formulating this advertisement in the Advocate first.

Robby suggested that I use a name that evokes fantasy. Robby's real name was John Movido. I told him they called me Dirk in the video, and I couldn't stand that name. He also suggested that I cut my hair. It's the 80's now. Long hair is so 1970's, it's ancient, archaic, and not in style. I had noticed that everyone's haircuts were now short.

The music world was changing, and the fashions were changing. Hair was short and going up on heads instead of falling down to the shoulders. I agreed that it was time to cut my long locks. As much as I loved my long hair, I wanted to be "in." I immediately went to a stylist who cut my hair and dyed it blonder. Robby loved it and declared that I was ready for the world of the elite. I needed a name for my advertisement. I decided that no name would be better for now, so I decide to call myself "Long Beach Fox." I placed the ad in the Advocate "escorts" classifieds section in November of '82. I was ready.

I got more calls from the advertisement in the first day than I could ever imagine. And of course, just the first day yielded more calls than I've received from every member of my family in six months.

I realized that I'd have to get an answering machine. I'd entered the modern world now. I had a business. I needed to return calls I might miss. I got calls from men in New York City, Alabama, Colorado, and of course many here in California, mostly from Beverly Hills and Orange County. The majority of calls I received were from Orange County. Oh, that bastion of Republican Conservatism. I love my conservative gay men here, even though they're hypocrites. I immediately discovered they pay the most. Besides, society hates gay people so much, they have to hide themselves.

One man who made an impression on me was Karl from Huntington Beach. He was a real estate developer who owned apartment buildings everywhere.

We struck a deal over the phone for an $800 meeting, which would mean that I would get paid even if all we did was talk. I didn't know how much to charge for services, but I always started at $500 on the phone. $750 and up if I had to drive to your place.

He drove to my Long Beach apartment, arriving right on time. I was immediately struck by the immaculate convertible 450 SL Mercedes Benz. He appeared, displaying that radiant tan we see on the wealthy elite. Of course, he was dressed like a rich man, walking confidently, dressed in a tailored suit, expensive tie, and sporting a perfectly sculptured, grey haired CEO haircut. I'd say he was about sixty. I'd never seen or paid attention to what a rich person looked like until I started living and hustling on the streets. Now I can spot wealth faster than a clergyman can spot a boy scout.

Karl and I saw each other quite a few times after that. He encouraged me to get my Real Estate License when I told him I was considering it. He genuinely cared about me. I liked him too. One night Karl took me to a restaurant in Laguna Beach named Ron's. It was the owner's first name. Ron's was the most spectacular dining spot ever. The food was exquisite, and it was beautifully served. I'll never forget the salmon-colored flags that hung in the restaurant.

Ron's had a piano bar, and I wanted to play. I remember the regular piano bar being annoyed, but Karl called Ron over and they told the guy to move and let me play. I entertained everyone, playing Elton John songs which, I thought they'd love. This crowd wasn't interested in hearing Elton; they wanted Gershwin and Broadway show tunes. But I made a good impression with both Karl and Ron. We eventually drifted apart as his real estate empire grew to mammoth proportions and he settled on the east coast. He made New York City his home.

Karl told me I could make money at a bar called the Boom Boom Room in Laguna Beach. Laguna Beach was about 40 miles south in Orange County, but I drove there anyway because Robby had also mentioned how popular it was.

I was still only seventeen years old, but they let me in anyway. I did make money at the Boom Boom standing next to the restroom with my back against the wall. Guys would offer me $100-200 to suck me off and I obliged. I think I came in three mens' mouths and walked out with $500 the first night I was there. I met and made friends there too. I was learning that relationships were more important than quick money.

Sadly, one by one, every friend I made at the Boom Boom Room died. They were now calling this thing "The gay plague," "Gay Cancer" or "Gay pneumonia." By my eighteenth birthday in 1983, thirty good friends of mine were dead from this disease. And no one, I mean no one cared. I wasn't seeing any reports of it in the news or anywhere. How can thirty of my friends be dead from the same disease and society not care? Because as long as it was homosexuals dying, it was fine with society.

19

Music, Sex and Drugs

The ad began earning me more money than I ever dreamed of. It also connected me with people who were interesting and diverse. I got calls day and night, from one extreme to the other. I got calls from horny guys who just wanted to talk dirty, to extremely wealthy men who flew me all over the country to meet me. Many wealthy men flew out to California to spend time with me. Sometimes I was paid and tipped well over $3,000. And it didn't always depend on what act I sexually performed.

I learned that a lot of guys are just lonely. Some are married with stone cold wives (according to them) and at times I was simply paid to listen. They felt judged by their wives, and I wasn't a judge. I became a psychologist.

There was Joe in Kansas, who was the primary investor in a network of private hospitals. He was so sweet, he took me out on his boat, to the ballet, an expensive dinner, and wanted me to show him how I pee. He jacked off while I urinated in the toilet. He got off a few times and provided me with plenty of water to keep me hydrated and ready. He also paid me handsomely for a cup of my pee that he could keep and cherish forever. Or drink it, or whatever he wanted it for. I didn't care. That's what he liked. Ahh, memories.

Nowadays, I wouldn't give anyone my pee, unless it's through a court order. Back then, I gave no thought that people might have sinister motives, but I certainly learned differently later. Maybe the reason I never encountered any people who wanted to hurt me was because I was fearless. That fearlessness served me well in those days.

In early 1983, I heard my phone ringing. I saw that it was George. He only called when he wanted me to come over and jam with him. He knew he wasn't getting any dick, but he was a good musician, and he knew I could play any instrument. Now, since I had every instrument — keyboards, guitars, basses — he called me. Last time I was there, he had a young guy playing drums, while he played the keys, and I played guitar. I think he wanted to stare at us while we played, and meanwhile, I was finding out that I could play the bass and guitar better than most guys I'd jammed with.

I'd called other musicians looking to form bands from the recycler musician classifieds and jammed with other guys in Long Beach. Hardly anyone could play well except black musicians. When I jammed with them, they never disappointed. Maybe I hadn't looked hard enough, since I spend half of my time scouting girls to fuck or being gay for pay. George was a pro. He toured with Billy Preston, he's a singer and songwriter who has appeared on Soul Train, and he's cut records. I did like jamming with him, even though I hated him.

He said he wanted me to go to a Music Industry Christmas party with him. Of course, I go.

George wanted to drive, so I showed up at his place early enough to get to the party with time to spare. We were having a lemonade in his apartment in Fox Hills before we went. He still stared at me with saliva drooling down his chin, but I wasn't not concerned. I was to go. He told me the party was over by La Cienega and Pico Blvd. at some guy's house he used to tour with. Cool – lots of professional musicians would be there.

As soon as we entered the house, I realized how right I was. A lot of famous black and white Recording Artists were there. Right away, I spotted Chaka Khan of Rufus. She was over in a corner laughing with some big black dude. I saw Howard Hewett of Shalamar, who sees George and walks toward us. I like Shalamar's songs, especially "A Night to remember." Howard walked up to George and asked him how his record was coming along. Doug replied that it was slow, because "You know how long the studio time is."

Howard answered in the affirmative and put his hand out to shake mine, asking me my name.

"Doug – just like his." I answered. Howard chuckled and said it's nice to meet me – and moves on. He's a nice guy, I thought to myself.

Ralph Johnson of Earth, Wind and Fire and some other people who are George's friends came up and greeted us. I was George's prop. It was obvious that was how they viewed me. I observed people snorting cocaine throughout the house. There was Billy Preston, snorting coke, staring at me. Billy was larger than life to me, because he's a phenomenal keyboard and organ player. He also played with the Beatles, my heroes. I love Billy's music; "Nothing from nothing" and "Will it go 'round in circles" are two of my favorite Billy songs. I know that Billy co-wrote "You are so beautiful" because I read everything about music. I love that song. It's beautiful. He kept looking at me, and in that moment, he wasn't so beautiful.

His stare was so intense, it could cut through steel. Ok, so you think I'm attractive. I'd rather be admired for my musical abilities. I'm among fellow musicians, I thought. I knew I was young, but I wanted to find a way to prove my musical skills to someone who would listen.

I see there were a few musicians who were walking down steps into a basement. I surmised that it led into a studio, which I deduced this when I heard live musicians jamming. The sounds emanated from wherever the steps lead. I decided to leave George's side and travel to where the music was.

I went downstairs and there were three guys jamming. My ears, heart, mind and soul were loving this. I'm enraptured when I hear great music. I saw three black dudes, one on drums, one on keys, and one on bass guitar. They looked at me and smiled. No sexual overtones. And the ones that had expressed sexual interest in me have now valued my musicianship over sex (except George). Every black musician I've ever met has been kind and encouraging to me (except George). Anyway, these guys jammed for a little while, and I nervously picked up the guitar. They looked at me with surprise in their faces. I asked if it would be ok to play, and they skeptically nodded their heads.

I hooked up the Gibson Les Paul and easily slid right into the music. I felt every note. I instinctively knew the chords, and I could sense the changes. I simply jammed along with them. They looked stunned, but they become even more charged. The music was now taking on a funked up, groove-oriented energy. And with a white boy. We attracted Billy Preston, and he jumped on the keys. Now it really felt like magic. I could feel what everyone was doing individually. My guitar was musical fluid, and I was laminating all the parts. My fingers were unstoppable. I was in command. I fit. This was nirvana; this is what I was supposed to do with my life. We sounded so good.

I knew then, for sure, music is who I am.

Billy stopped when Ralph walked in. Everyone stopped and looked at me. They were all wearing huge smiles.

Billy exclaimed, "That white boy can play!"

They all chimed in with the same.

I heard it over and over. That white boy is bad ass! These are the highest compliments any white musician can hear. Praise from professional black musicians.

When Billy got up, I jumped on the piano bench and started playing. Though I'm not quite at Billy's level, I played well enough to earn more praise. I was fucking good. I must have been good; this praise was real. George was watching, with jealousy. His sneer makes this event all the more enjoyable. I was more than a prop. I'd gained attention because of my talent. I was more than a face and a cock. I was basking in the spotlight. It was a musical spotlight, and it felt good. Wasn't he supposed to be happy for me? Maybe that was too much to expect. Maybe I shouldn't have expected anything. Expectations have always been a problem for me. But I digress.

Of course, there was still a sexual component to whatever I did. Billy Preston was grinning at me in a sexual way. In fact, there were quite a few gay black men staring at me. And beautiful black women too. There were a lot of gay black male musicians here. I had ultra-gaydar just by standing here. Chaka Khan wasn't staring at me, but damn she was sexy. And then I did catch her staring at me. I found out her real name was Yvette. I introduced myself to her and told her I was a fan. Although I could see she thought I was cute, she seemed more interested in something else. I lost confidence quickly.

The voice pounced: They only want you because they're faggots; and so are you! They don't give a fuck about how you well you play any instrument

Fuck you, Fuck you, Fuck you, Fuck you, Fuck you...I repeated to myself over and over again.

Billy noticed me and called me over. I knew he was attracted to me, but I wanted to separate myself from that with him. I wanted to play music. He asked me how long I'd been playing.

"My whole life." This was true. But what I really wanted to say was, "Oh, I began playing by ear when I was a kid, my parents noticed I was a prodigy, and got me a piano teacher. I must have been good, because these were two fucked parents. I learned how to read music, but I hated playing by sheet music. I wanted to play music the way I felt it; especially classical. I liked playing Beethoven, I just didn't like reading Beethoven. I argued with the teacher, he said I was hardheaded, and that was that. I played on my own since. I'm a hustler now. But I'd sure love to play with you."

"You are damn good. What's your name?"

"Doug."

Billy told me he was having a party at his house in Malibu and would love for me to come. I jumped at his offer. He gave me his address and phone number. George saw us talking and the green-eyed monster was evident. He told me to watch out for Billy 'cos: "He's a predator."

I guess it takes one to know one.

I knew Billy did a lot of cocaine. And he was gay. So what? I knew he savored my musical abilities more than my cock. I wasn't worried about drugs. I didn't have a problem with drugs. I smoked some pot, and I used acid more than few times. I'd done cocaine twice. Once, Jim Slaton had offered me a "line" to snort. I did it, and I felt very amplified. I liked it. I walked away and didn't think about it again, until a guy whom I met through my advertisement called me to come to his house. His name was Bob Abernethy. He was a cheap son of a bitch. He offered me $300, and I went because he said he'd give me more if things worked out. He lied. When I arrived at his Manhattan Beach home, he was in his pajamas, drinking scotch and basically seemed sleepy. He gave me $300, and I was hesitant to do more than have conversation. He asked me to go upstairs where he had porn movies. Being the young horny sex addict I was, I didn't have to think twice. I stopped hesitating and went up there with him to see what he had. He had a straight sex tape going. It did its job.

In any case, Bob walked in the room, and asked me to go with him to the bathroom. I followed him. I saw what looked like a fat, round, glass vase sitting on the bathroom sink. Right next to it were long tweezers next to a bottle of rubbing alcohol. I also saw acetone. On the other side of the glass vase was a pile of thick white powder in a dinner plate. A torch was visible. This was a coke smoking facility, and I was intrigued. This was no ordinary glass vase, I thought, as I noticed the glass stem sticking out of the side. I'd smoked pot out of enough bongs to know this was a large glass pipe used for smoking cocaine.

He lit the torch and put a large rock of hardened cocaine on the bowl. He lit the bowl slowly and told me to get ready to put my mouth on the stem. I didn't understand, but I was curious to know. I watched as the smoke slowly filled the pipe. He was patient and obviously a professional smoker. He waited until the whole pipe was filled with the smoke of freebase cocaine. Bob told me to blow out all the air in my lungs and get ready to suck on the stem slowly. This was important. Slow. I put my mouth on the stem and I began slowly sucking in the smoke. For a few seconds, I felt nothing but smoke going into my lungs. I was surprised at the amount I was continuing to take in. At about ten seconds into this massive hit, it began.

This is unreal, I thought to myself. I'd entered a sexual cosmos that was light years ahead of the pain I was usually feeling. I wanted to feel cocks, pussies, and assholes immediately. It was incredible. I felt this way for at least fifteen minutes, and then, slowly, the high started to wear off. My state of arousal was replaced with reality. I started to lose my hard on. The drug's effect was fading. I couldn't continue to feel this way unless I took another hit. Somehow, when he offered one, I say no. My erection had been defeated. I wasn't frightened of cocaine, I just stopped myself.

I'm bigger than cocaine. I have a destiny. I know I can't stop my horniness, but that's biological. I've been sexualized since birth. Sex is integral to who I am. I've heard people say they lose all rationality and logic when they're aroused. For me, to be aroused is rational and logical. I can't choose whether or not I get a hard on. Erections happen all day and night. But I don't have to pick up a drug. I have control over cocaine. I have a musical career ahead. I know it. Nothing can stop me, not even cocaine.

Billy Preston and I became friends and we jammed together many times. He introduced me to Richard Penniman, more famously known as Little Richard, the architect of rock n roll. Little Richard was world renowned in a way that only few people in history are. And he didn't miss a chance to remind me. I loved being around him and watching him play the piano. He wasn't classically trained like Billy was, but he played with even more passion. I'll never forget those times with Billy and Little Richie. Both of them treated me with respect and as an equal.

MTV dominated a lot of my free time in late 1982 and 1983. I was hooked on the videos, and the songs. It seemed like they were playing a lot of the same ones over and over. All day and night, I saw and heard, "Who can it be now?" by Men at Work; "Electric Avenue" by Eddy Grant; "I ran" by A flock of seagulls, and "Jeopardy" by the Greg Khin band. Every day, I sat on the couch and watched this stuff. I still practiced my instruments every day, and I wrote my songs, but I felt like I was behind the times.

I realized that music was changing. One thing I noticed was that MTV wasn't playing many R & B Artists' videos. Black people weren't represented. In fact, Eddy Grant was the only one in rotation. MTV was run by bigots. Like the rest of the world.

I read four different newspapers on a daily basis, and never see any reports on Gay cancer or Gay pneumonia. I wrote a letter to the editor asking why no one had reported on the sickness that was killing gay men, but they didn't publish it.

I learned from my gay friends in the Heights that many guys were starting to stay away from bathhouses. My friend, Mike Dewitt, and his partner, Eddie, were not going to the 1350 club anymore. It was starting to sink in that something serious was going on. These guys were hard core sex fiends. And they were starting to wonder if the fun and games might be over. Mike was a construction worker, and Eddie was in the Navy. They met at the Mine Shaft.

The Mineshaft was a gay bar on Broadway, where wannabe cowboys, leather daddies and pretty boy studs competed for restroom fuckfests. It was "role play," but a lot of Navy guys went there to drink. Long Beach has a naval shipyard, and there's a lot of horny, young midshipmen available for the cruisers. Mike was a sweet man, and he was loyal to Eddie, that is, except when he went to the 1350 club. And Eddie approved of Mike's bathhouse escapades. I think they accept that they like to fuck other people. They had their three-ways once in a while, but Mike was concerned.

I was over there for dinner, and he told me that his friend Randy had two purple spots on his leg. I knew Randy. His boyfriend Chris was a domineering, possessive and jealous guy, but always ready to help if I needed anything fixed mechanically. Chris joked around a lot, and he was a pathological liar, but he worked at the Porno store, so I used him to get sex tapes. Randy was a model; he flew around the world (the perfect boyfriend for a jealous guy eh?) – and he was honest and forthright. He was originally from Texas and had that "Southern Belle" charm.

I went to Randy and Chris's house, and Randy was coughing a lot. Randy spoke up.

"I think I might have this thing they call Gay Cancer. They're calling it GRID now — Gay related Immune deficiency. It's a syndrome of problems. They should call it a syndrome."

Chris answered: "You're being melodramatic Randy. The only syndrome you have is buttocks spreadeth syndrome. You've got a cold. Just relax. I'll make it all better."

"This cold isn't going away, Chris."

"Are you still going to your alcoholic anonymous meetings?" Chris asked Randy.

"Yeah, but I don't feel good. Look at my tongue, you guys." Randy stuck out his tongue.
I saw white fungus. It reminded of me of the white fungus on Paul's tongue and other friends who had died. It seemed to be the first symptom to show up.

Chris continued to joke. "Yeah, you've probably got dried up cum stuck on your tongue. You should start talking at the meetings. Your ass and mouth have had so much anonymous cock they could start their own twelve step meeting."

Randy answered, "I wish you'd shut up and stop joking, Chris. Honey, I love you, and I'm scared. We've had friends die from this already."

I piped in, "Yeah, I've already seen twelve friends die. It's weird. Young guys are wasting away."

Chris was having none of it. "Alright, you two, I want no more negativity in this house. Think good thoughts. Beautiful thoughts, and beautiful things happen."

I wondered why Chris wasn't taking this seriously. Many gay friends of mine weren't taking this seriously. I also thought that Randy probably had the sickness.
Chris was an older, big guy, over 250 pounds. He'd been in a relationship with Randy for over two years. Randy was gorgeous, and could have gotten a better-looking guy, but I was learning that this is how a lot of Gay relationships work. The older less attractive man wants the younger hot guy, so he pays for it. It's not direct, like a prostitute, but the older guy will let the younger guy have free rent, he'll buy all the food, he'll help the young guy with school, etc… And the young guy gives him sex. And love, if the young guy has that capacity.
In the end, it doesn't matter if the older guy is ninety-three and the younger guy is eighteen. All that matters is do they love each other. Are they satisfying each other's needs? I'm no one to judge any relationship. I'm just an observer. And an older man/younger man relationship is what I've needed most of my life.
Oh well, tomorrow was my eighteenth birthday. Tomorrow, I'll be an adult.

20

Numbers

Long Beach, April 1, 1983

My phone rings. I imagine it's either a hot latina I've been fucking, or one of my gay benefactors. I pick it up, and a familiar cold, stale voice is on the other end.

"Hello?" At least three seconds pass before I hear the voice.

"Doug? This is your dad."

Fear and excitement rush through me. My father's actually calling me on my birthday. And I'm still excited to hear from him.

He says he has something for my birthday. Now that I'm eighteen, he's going to give me a birthday gift.

My dad has money, maybe it's something expensive.

"Thank you so much, Dad. Can I ask what it is?"

"Yes – I'll tell you right now. Come over to my house. I have a porno movie just released on VHS with Ginger Lynn in it. She's my favorite porn actress. She can take it and doesn't fake it. It's a great movie. You can have it. But I'd like it back after you watch it – because it's Ginger Lynn."

"Thanks so much, Dad."

I'm always horny, so for a moment, my libido overrides rational thinking.

Ginger Lynn is a firecracker, but I'd be looking at the hairy brunette women. I love me some hairy brunette women.

My dad's gift to me for my eighteenth birthday is a porno movie.

And he wants it back. Oh well, I'll take it. At least he thought of me.

June 1983

It's almost summertime in 1983. I get a call from Robby, who says that Kurt Deitrick wants to do a photo shoot of me. He's heard about me and saw me in "7 up and cumming" and" Hot High and Horny," my two porn masterpieces.

YMAC called me Dirk. Larry gave me that name because he thought I resembled Dirk Benedict, the actor. Kurt is the best male nude photographer around. His work is highly regarded. He took over the title of the most popular male nude photographer from Bruce Bellas. Bruce was apparently "the man" in the 1970's. I'm learning so much about gay culture I could teach a class. Bruce died in a car accident in 1974. He created a huge following, and this Kurt Deitrick guy has capitalized on that following. Kurt is very good at photography; Robby showed me his pictures.

They are appealing to the eye, and they capture the male physique in a sexual but not slimy way. He uses lighting well, and he makes Robby's dick look big. The bigger the dick, the bigger the sale. I never thought about selling "male sexuality" before this. Now I'm learning. I had mostly sexualized women – beautiful curves, breasts, shapely bodies, small feet; there is so much that is sexual about a woman. Gay men understand male sexuality better than women. Gay guys worship male sexuality. I guess I've got that sexuality they crave.

I listen to Robby tell me how Kurt's pictures translated into worldwide recognition for him, and it piques my curiosity. For now, meeting Kurt Deitrick can wait. Lately, I've been making a lot of money from my regular clients, and Hollywood has become a favorite place for me. I had a client who called on my ad, picked me up in a limousine at my apartment in Long Beach and took me to his estate in the Hollywood Hills. He was a popular actor. I thought a lot about what he told me: "You should be here in Hollywood, Doug, this is where you'll meet the people who will help you along your journey to stardom."

Why should I settle for Long Beach? Although, I haven't really defined "making it," I go to Hollywood. And I'm just as popular there as I was in Long Beach. I get a lot of attention everywhere I go: Sunset Blvd., Santa Monica Blvd., Hollywood Blvd. I love the restaurants and the nightlife. The Rose Tattoo on Robertson Bl. is one restaurant/club I really like. John Thompson took me there for dinner; it's another upscale restaurant that offers an expensive and exquisite dining experience. There's also gogo boys who dance. I got coaxed on stage to dance one time; I danced sheepishly, tore off my shirt, and made $300, but I want to be known for my music, not go-go dancing. I danced there a couple more times for the money and the food. One night I made $800. The Rose Tattoo also served incredible food.

I've now eaten at many expensive restaurants with John and other wealthy clients; the Velvet Turtle, Chasen's, Morton's on Melrose and Robertson, La Boheme' on Santa Monica Blvd, Orso's on 3rd Street, The Ivy, Bob Burns and Las Brisas in Newport Beach, and Ron's in Laguna. I'm becoming accustomed to fine dining.

On Santa Monica Blvd., there's a club called Rage. I walk in, order a drink and stand by the bar. I buy my own drink, even though I'm eighteen, and it's strong. A guy next to me buys my second drink; a long island iced tea. They don't skimp on the alcohol here. I'm getting buzzed. Within minutes, I'm mobbed. I'm surrounded, and it's a little freaky but fun. I'm enjoying myself, and I like the attention I'm getting from every man (and a few women) near me. I drink three drinks and decline the offers to have bathroom sex.

I decide to stroll out to the dance floor. I sway a bit due to the alcohol, and I move my body to the thumping of the dance beat. The atmosphere is electric and ultra-sexual. It's a huge dance floor, and boys wearing clothes are in the minority. Most men are naked, and they bump and grind against one another, swallowing MDMA pills like M & M's. The fresh aroma of poppers fills the air. The music's too loud to have a conversation, but no one wants to talk anyway. I feel like an outsider among these meaty, sweaty bodies, but I'm stared at everywhere I walk. Finally, someone goes too far. I feel a tight squeeze from manly hands onto my butt. Someone has grabbed a hold of my unprotected ass. They squeeze hard, and I angrily pull away. I like being admired but grabbing my ass without permission is not ok. As I walk, they part in waves to let me through as if I'm royalty.

I love you guys, but even I don't fondle girls or guys without their permission. C'mon, get control of yourselves. I'm starting to get angry, but it's not enough to explode at the Rage.

I'm not logical when I'm angry. I lose the ability to explain why; I'm just mad. I love you guys; don't you realize you're lucky I'm here? So many of my childhood friends would come here with an Uzi and slaughter you just for being gay — who you are. I love you for who you are – but don't fucking grope me! They sense my uneasiness, because they know they're out of control. Guys start to back off of me and let me be me. I realize I'm among friends. I don't have to fight. They're sensitive. The cage that turned my innocence to rage no longer holds me captive. A sense of calm permeates my soul. I listen to the music and start to dance. Now I'm grinding with everyone; I'm going a little mad, but mad with happiness. I'm swinging my hips, undulating, dancing with numerous guys, and drawing attention. Music is in my blood, and I can dance. I really love you guys.

Gay men have decency, respect, and compassion. Fuck the straight world. All I get are guys who want to fight, judgments, coldness and competition. There are some scary gay men here. I've read about them in Drummer magazine. They have Green Beret queers too. As I depart the crowd of admiring queens come to sit by me, and I love the that they're spending time with me. It's not always about my dick. Maybe I just think it is.

As I sniffed, I became incredibly horny.

It was orgasmic. The guy near me could see the change in my face, dropped to his knees and began sucking my dick. Unfortunately, it didn't last long. I felt a huge psychological meltdown, and pulled away, almost paralyzed from the fear. He suggested I sniff the bottle again. I did it, and the process started all over again – but not as intense as the first time. These "poppers" were powerful, but their duration period was short. It wasn't worth it all the time. Still, I encountered poppers everywhere. They seemed to be an indispensable component of a Gay man's sexual equipment. Every Gay man I knew who frequented the bathhouses, carried poppers

There's another spot in Hollywood that I hung out at more than any other. It was called Numbers. It was a restaurant and bar where investors scouted young entrepreneurs. Robby suggested I go there, advising me with words I'll never forget: "You could make a fortune just standing still in that place."

I want to make a fortune standing still. And so, I shall.

Numbers is a restaurant and bar that attracts the famous and powerful Hollywood Directors, Talent Agents, Actors, Make-up Artists, etc. — all the successful gay talent and power brokers in the Entertainment Industry. It has dinner tables that are situated against a circular wall, making them seem like a Disneyland ride. I think they're situated that way just in case the boys want to dance in front of the diners. The first time I made my entrance at Numbers, I knew it would be profitable. I'm not impressed by "powerful" people, they should be impressed by me. Some people say, "It's not who you know, it's who you blow." But I like to remember what my hero Prince said, "It's not who you know, but do they know you?"

I went to Numbers many times over the years, usually when I wanted to earn some extra money and meet famous, powerful people. I had some great dinners and met some really nice and some not so nice people. I remember being grabbed by this repugnant guy who asked me "how much?" – to which I replied,

"Probably too much for you, but I'm open for negotiations".

Of course, his ego wouldn't tolerate that, and he answered back with an obnoxious retort:

"Do you know who I am?"

"Yeah, you're some drunk asshole with a fake tan and a bad facelift."

I didn't give a shit. I'm always nice, unless you're an obnoxious ass. He sucked in his breath, as if to feign shock. A friend of mine laughed and said that the guy's name was Sandy Gallin. I'd never heard of Sandy Gallin, and I didn't care. My friend said Sandy was the biggest talent agent in the world. So what? What is an agent without the talent? I'm the talent; he's a bookend. It was rumored that Sandy was a cheap prick too.

I made many friends at Numbers. One of the first men I met was Allan Carr, who produced the movie "Grease." He had won awards on Broadway for Producing "La Cage au Folles." He also produced the cheesiest movie I'd ever seen called "Can't stop the music." I didn't see it when it was released in 1980 because I was in Rancho Boys Home. But I saw it later at a friend's house on videotape. I couldn't believe how bad it was.

Allan was a braggart, but he was nice to me every time I saw him. He ate like a horse. I told him more than once he needed to go on a diet. He never did.

He was a vulnerable man with a fragile ego which he compensated for by living in a house the size of a mountain. Inside it was a large dance floor with a disco ball. He complained about the movie industry a lot. He didn't demand much in bed, he loved sucking me off and swallowing every drop of my cum. He was loud and he was generous. But he belittled a lot of his employees, blaming them for his failures. I wanted to get close to men I met at Numbers, but Allan was a man no one could get close to. There was a difference between friends, lovers and clients. Allan was a client. He called me one time crying after he was mocked for producing the 1989 Academy Awards. He wanted my company, and I gave it to him. I felt sorry for him. His productions were flamboyant and creative, but this time he went over the top. He thought having Snow White sing Proud Mary in a girly voice would be a hit. It bombed, and Hollywood is cruel when you bomb. I think he passed away after we hung out one last time at his house.

There was someone I met at Numbers whom I truly loved. I was walking by a table and I heard this man ask me my name. I told him and he said I was gorgeous and wanted to know if I was available to have dinner with him. I said yes, and in the middle of my filet mignon, he gave me an off handed compliment by saying "You're smart and gorgeous. I don't know if I can afford you. How much to come home with me?" I laughed and quoted a price. He hurriedly agreed, and I followed him to his home on Heather Road in Coldwater Canyon. His name was Michael Filerman and I'd never heard of him.

He told me he produced 300 and something episodes of the TV Show Knots Landing. He also produced the hit show Falcon Crest. I never saw one episode of either one, but I could add. 300 or more episodes meant he had a boatload of money.

Knots Landing was the most successful television show of the 1980's. But he wasn't like anyone I had met before that was as successful as him. Michael didn't act like a big shot. He was a genuinely good man who was thrilled to be with me. In bed, we always 69ed, and he never complained if he didn't cum. He was more worried about how I felt. I remember going to Laguna Beach with Michael and he attended to me with those small courtesies that made me feel special. When we were at the beach, he worried if I was too hot, how I was feeling, and if I wanted new sandals for comfort. He opened doors for me, and he was genuinely concerned about my well-being day and night. He asked me questions about my plans for the future, he listened to me, and we stopped at a music store.

I could see his glowing admiration at my musical ability when I played the keyboards and the guitars in the store. Right then and there he offered me a chance to write a musical score for one of the TV episodes he was producing. He treated me with respect. Michael was a man of his word. He had integrity and wanted nothing more than to share his time with me. He helped me whenever I needed it. He loaned me money when I wasn't managing my finances well. We had some fun times at the beach and at his house. I loved his house in Coldwater Canyon. I loved him. Michael was one of the good guys. He hired me to write music for an episode, but it never came off. I was scared his people wouldn't like my music and we never let it out of his house. He eventually bought the Coronet Theater on La Cienega and spent his later years producing plays.

He was responsible for many hit television shows. Michael won a lawsuit against a chief entertainment from Fox for stealing Michael's characters for a show he called Melrose Place.

Many of his TV pilots got cancelled, but the huge hit shows were still brining in money and attention, He bought the Coronet Theater on La Cienega Blvd. and hired an unknown actor named Noah Wyle to star in a play he was producing. He introduced me to Noah and Peter Berg. Once, years later, when Michael and I were having dinner at Numbers, I noticed the younger guys getting a lot of attention. I worried aloud to Michael about whether I was getting too old to be appreciated and loved for my looks, he advised me: "Don't define yourself by this profession. You have so much more to offer." I loved him for saying that to me. I never forgot it, but the voice would pounce.

I met many civilian people at another restaurant Michael, and I frequented called "Orso." I loved the outside patio at Orso. "Civilians" is a derogatory term used by arrogant Film and Television Industry folk for the people who watch their banality. Civilians spend money on their vices too.

One man I can never forget was a Gay Christian Pastor who was the head of a large church and congregation in Orange County. This man came up to me while I was standing at the bar and asked me to have dinner with him. Of course. I'm always flattered to be asked to have dinner no matter how narcissistic I might be.

I notice this man is dressed differently than many others here. His clothes are casual, he's wearing shorts and sandals as if he just came from the beach. We sit down at his table, and he asks me what I'd like to have for dinner. I like the veal piccata, and he's happy to oblige. I must say, before I go any further, that this was the ugliest human being I'd ever seen in my life. He looked like the elephant man in shorts. Mirrors had to be a cruel punishment for him. I know I use my looks as bait, but tonight I've reeled in Frankenstein. I hate judging others on their looks. I'm here so any nice person can get laid, no matter what you look like. Not so attractive people are usually loving and kind, only the movies twist the reality. It's the shallow beautiful people I'd like to see wiped out. I'm not cruel. I feel compassion for people who aren't physically attractive. I'm grateful for what I've got. But his face is so repulsive, I don't know if I can perform any sexual act with him.

He begins the conversation with a compliment, "You are so gorgeous. What's your name?"

"I'm Doug. Thank you for saying that. What's yours?"

"My name is Stephen. I'm new to Numbers. Do you come here often?"

"Not really. But I like this place, they have great food."

Stephen is a poor conversationalist. I surmise he's shy because of his looks. He's uncomfortable in this atmosphere, but he knows why he's here. He immediately asks me how much I charge.

I ask, "What are you looking for?"

"I don't know, because I don't usually do this. I'm a Pastor from Orange County."

"You're a Pastor? That's interesting. What's the name of your church?"

Stephen looks frightened. "I can't tell you that, it's a very large church, and I'm the Senior Pastor. I'm the leader of a large congregation. Our services sometimes have thousands of people."

"Wow. Can you tell me what city in Orange County?"

Stephen confesses it's in Santa Ana. He admits this, because he wants me to follow him all the way to Orange County and spend the night.

"I don't usually travel that far for less than $1,000. How does that work for you?"

"Well, you must be a real pro to charge so much, but yes, I can pay you $1,000."

I say to myself: Oh no – please, God, Satan, whoever, I don't know that I can get sexual with this guy even for $1,000. But I'll give it my best shot. Please, please don't try to kiss me, Stephen. And please, please don't ask me to fuck you.

Stephen doesn't want small talk. He wants to get back to his home in Orange County. It's a long drive, and I ask him if he wants me to drive, or is he planning to drive and then pay for my cab back to Los Angeles. Stephen wants me to spend the night. Shit.

I decide to drive my car. I don't want to get stuck being dependent on him if things don't turn out to his liking.

He gives me directions; he lives in Tustin. I know the way. I sleep with my Thomas Bros. Maps. I know the page to look for - 101 to the 5 South to the Newport Avenue exit, blah, blah – I'll be there. This fucker has handed me $200 up front and has promised to pay me $800 after we do the deed. I still don't know what the "deed" is.

It's a long fucking drive. I've had a couple of drinks, but I'm not drunk. We make it into Orange County, and I follow him into his driveway. He has a modest house. Tustin is middle

109

America suburbia. It's quiet.

We enter his home, and I notice bibles, crosses, and mountains of books. This is the home of a reader. I pick up a book on St. Francis of Assisi and see more books that form a religious library. There is methamphetamine on the glass coffee table. He sits down and offers me a line of meth. I say yes, and I sniff it – but not very well. I was never very good at sniffing or blowing my nose, so I only take half of the line he offers me. He snorts a huge one.

The next thing he does is grab me to kiss him.

"Whoa there!" I tell him I'd like to talk a bit first. I really do like conversation. I'm an intellectual whore.

I ask him, "So when did you realize you were gay? Was it before you became a pastor or after?"

Stephen is truly uncomfortable with this conversation. I don't care. I sense he's hiding a lot. "I don't know that I'm gay. I believe in our Lord Jesus Christ. I teach salvation through the blood of Christ. Homosexuality is a sin."

"So why are you paying me for gay sex?"

"I think I have a problem. But I don't want to talk about that. I just want to get what I'm paying for."

"You've only paid me $200 so far, and I've spent $20 in gas just driving here. What do you want to do?"

Stephen begins to undress. The meth is affecting his brain. I can see the horny closet case is feeling frisky.

His face is getting uglier by the second. This man is hideous. And his hypocrisy makes him even uglier. But I've got a job to do – for a thousand dollars. You'll see a different side of me if you try to rip me off. I sense he's a game player.

"You're getting undressed. That's cool, Stephen. Where's the rest of the money?"

"Here's $500 more. I know I'm not the best-looking guy, but I'll give you the rest after we finish."

Ok, $700 is good enough to get started.

The meth has a sexual effect on me, but it's not enough to keep me aroused with this guy. I can get rock hard with good looking solidly built men with confidence, who also know who they are – I'm attracted to confidence. I'm very kind with guys who are shy; I understand the bigotry that they have to face, and how difficult it is to be who they are. Many are married, and many are kind, loving men who live in a society that hates them. But I think Stephen hates himself and he hadn't been courteous to me. Maybe my apprehension with Stephen stems from my experience with the hypocrisy of Christians. From the Catholic priests to my mother, they're all phonies. I ask a couple questions.

"So, do you want to suck my dick?"

Stephen says, "I want you to fuck me. Fuck me hard."

Shit! This guy is fat and ugly. Do you have a strap on? My worst nightmare has now come true.

"Ok, bend over."

"No, I want to lay on my back and kiss you while you fuck me with my legs in the air."

I feel ill. This has gone from bad to worse. No one can save me now. I'm supposedly a pro. But this is asking a lot of me. Ok, Doug. You can do this. Now I'm the one who's full of shit. I don't know that I can.

Stephen lays on his bed, fully naked, displaying his grotesque body, and spreading his legs wide for me to enter the cavern of hell.

I get on top of him with force.

"You want me to fuck you, Stephen?!" I feebly try to summon up excitement.

My limp dick isn't fooling him.

"Yes, yes, please fuck me. You're not hard though. Aren't you a professional? Can't you just turn it on and off at whim?"

He knows how grotesque he is. He's paying for sex he can never have without money. I really do feel sorry for the guy, but he thinks I'm a robot. He expects me to satisfy him. He's never going to be a friend, which half of what I look for, so now that I have this knowledge, I don't need to fully perform. I'll get paid no matter what because I'll never see him again. But my ego tells me I've got to give him some satisfaction. How the fuck am I gonna do this?

"Do you have a magazine of naked girls I could look at while I fuck you?"

"Why do you need that?" Boy he's stupid AND naïve.
"It helps, Stephen."

"But I'm paying you. Isn't that enough?" Now he's pissing me off, but I still must try to fulfill his needs.

He grabs me, pulls me close, and locks his lips onto mine. I feel bile rise in my throat.

He knows I'm struggling. "Doug, fuck me, please fuck me. NOW!" This guy is demanding.

Even worse, he wants me to fuck him missionary style, so I'm forced to look at his face while I fuck him.

I stick my cock in his asshole, and it's wet and slimy. I know he cleaned himself out (that's a pre-requisite) but I'm still having trouble staying hard. I pump my semi-hard cock in and out of his ass, and he's not happy.

"Come on, Doug. I'm paying you to fuck me and kiss me. Make me happy."
"I am, Stephen. Don't you feel it? C'mon, take all eight inches. I'm fucking you!"

He looks up at me, begging me to kiss him while he tweaks both of his nipples.

Do you know what you look like, dude? Qausimoto comes to mind.

He's reached a feverish frenzied state of arousal. His nipples have grown enormously.

He's super excited. I see him take one hand of his left nipple and stroke his tiny weiner, and to my amazement, in ten seconds he whispers it feels good! His other finger slowly leaves his nipple. I shout out that I'm going to cum – although that's a huge lie.

As he continues to tweak his nipple, I hear this from his lips: "Do you really believe in homosexuality? I don't think I'm a homosexual, Douglas."

I don't have time to analyze.

"Don't you know there's no such thing as homosexuality? I'm not a homo."

I look up and right there on the wall is Jesus — hanging from a huge metallic cross. He looks defeated, he's crying and dying; and there are metallic tears engraved in Jesus' eyes. For Christ's sake, why do you want to witness this man's death on your wall? I don't understand this celebration of your Lord's death. If Jesus does come back, wouldn't a cross be the last thing he'd want to see? That would be like someone coming back after he's been electrocuted, being greeted by electric chairs everywhere he goes.

Your religion never made sense to me anyway.

Life after death is a fantastic product — no one comes back to complain.

There are books of medieval literature, bibles, and books that analyze the "writings of God" everywhere. But on the walls, there are crosses, and more crosses. I've got to take my mind off the celebration of death and get back to work.

I pump my semi- hard cock deeper… at least I'm trying.

"Oh God," he exclaims. "Forgive me, I'm not a homosexual."

"Another three inches and you will be!" I'm pumping madly trying to go deep.

Finally, he's cumming. Like doggie cum. He spews his jism all over his big fat belly. Yes! It's over. I've done my job. I can roll over and get off of this fat weirdo. I'm exhausted. He's clinging to his God now. All of a sudden, he feels guilty. He says all of this while he continues tweaking his right nipple. I let him talk.

"Don't you know that God ordained man and woman to be together?"

"So why do you have sex with men?"

"I think I have a problem. I need to pray to God to forgive me. Homosexuality is an abomination. We'll go to hell for this. You need to repent too."

"What do you expect me to do? Unfuck you? I don't need to repent. I need my money. Just give me the rest of the money. I'm glad you're happy, or guilty, or whatever state of mind you paid me to put you in."

I should charge an extra $500 for guilt.

I tell him that if he feels this way, one way to clear his conscience would be to be honest with his congregation. Since he said they follow his words, and they love him, surely, they'd love him through this. They'd understand and forgive him. Be honest with the very people you teach.

He emphatically says he can't do that. There are a lot of little old ladies who would have heart attacks if they knew he had homosexual sex. They would vote him out. They would turn their backs on him.

"Well," I reply, "then they don't care about you, and they certainly don't practice forgiveness."

He's not listening, While I'm counting my money, he's on his knees, eyes closed, praying and begging his God for forgiveness. He admonishes me to do the same.

"I don't need your God's forgiveness. I gotta to get home." Actually, I just want to get far away from another Christian hypocrite.

At least he paid me our agreed amount: $1,000. It took every bit of dissociative disorder I could morph myself into to fuck this man. And now he's not gay. Whatever, dude. I've heard this before. I don't want to engage this nonsense, but he keeps it up.

"I'm so sorry, Lord. Please forgive me. I know this is not what you made me to be."

"You should see a psychologist. You hate yourself. God made you gay. Accept it. You became a Christian later. Being gay came first."

"Oh my God," he exclaims. "We need to repent. We have defiled the name of the Lord."

How do I explain to him that he's gay? Explaining being gay to a born-again Christian is like trying to explain what water tastes like.

I don't have time for this bullshit. I've had sex with Priests, Pastors, Born again Christians (every denomination and hypocrite including my mother): I've had sex with Arabs, Hindus, Buddhists, Indians, Atheists, I've had sex with nuns, catholic schoolgirls, white girls, church girls, deacons, brothers of the Holy Cross, Jewish Rabbis, Mormons and Jehovah Witnesses, black men and black women, Latin men and women, every fucking race and a majority of countries around the world – every fucking religion, every political party, you name it – I've had sex with it.

I've been in bed with all of you, you've all craved my cock, you've all licked my asshole, you're all horny, and the only difference between you is that some of you are honest and some of you like to pretend and lie about it. You think you're smarter than a whore like me. I was born into a family of sex addicts, liars, and hypocrites, and you think you can fool me? On top of that, your world dishonestly pretended to "protect" me from my family, only to house me with more liars, sex addicts, and phonies.

I've never known honesty. But I certainly smell the pungent odor of dishonesty in this house. This guy is leading his congregation straight to hell. I've heard it said that "self cannot reveal itself to self," which is why man created God, psychology, and drugs to "uncover" itself to itself. Because we all know we're full of shit. Well, you made me what I am. I can see through you. I admit, I might also need to see myself better. But right now, I need to survive. And I have my youth. It's working for me. I play YOUR game. I didn't make the rules. I'm just riding the waves.

21

Catholic Girls Love Bisexual Boys

1983 – 1984, Long Beach, CA

I started a new hobby during this time making dirty phone calls. I'm not proud of it, and I never called anyone that wasn't a willing participant. But I did waste a lot of precious time sex talking, listening to the person talking dirty, and masturbating furiously. At least I know the reasons I did this, and there are two of them.

The first is that I'm simply a sex addict. I'm horny all the time. I jack off day and night. It takes up a lot of my time. I don't know if it's because I was locked up for so many years, or what the reason is, but it's not enough for me to just jack off alone by myself. I had enough of that while I was in solitary confinement. It was ok, but I would have liked to touch and feel another person.

Reason number two is that I like to get people to do what they won't admit they really like to do. This is the more foundational reason. I like to hear the hypocrite become horny and know that I gotcha! I developed my own elaborate scheme to accomplish this, and amazingly, I was highly successful at it. I surmised that the church staff would be the easiest women to manipulate. I have men call me every day, so it's women on my list now. I usually call the Catholic churches first. It's 1983, so there's no caller ID, and I'm not concerned about being found out. In addition, the majority of the girls and the nuns would participate, so no one had anything to report. They'd be telling on themselves. I don't feel any shame, I'm not going to lie, and I don't have a reputation to worry about. What others think of me is none of my business.

I'd look in the yellow pages for the Long Beach "St. this or St. that" because I didn't want to pay for long distance yet, and Long Beach has hundreds of Catholic churches.

I masturbate as I pick up the phone. I call and, invariably, I'd get the church secretary. I can tell right away she's probably eighteen, maybe younger, and right away I know I'm halfway to a sexual release for both of us.

Me: Hi, my name is Jesse, and I'm calling the church today because something happened to me, and there's no one else I can talk to about it. I can't tell my family. I'm a catholic, and I know I should open up to someone at the church.

Her: I can put you through to our pastor, or you can talk to me. Our pastor is more experienced.

Me: I don't know how comfortable I'd feel with the Pastor knowing about this, it's something that happened to me at a party, and I don't want anyone to know. I know you probably deal with a lot of things, and you have to be a psychologist at the church, so could I open up to you?

Her: Sure you can. Everything you say to me is confidential.

Me: Thank you SO much. I can't tell my parents, and I know you're experienced. I don't have to be ashamed as I tell you? That's what you do right? I can just get it all out?

Her: Yes, that's what I'm here for. Go ahead.

Me: Well, like I said, my name is Jessie, and I'm eighteen. I want to be honest with you, but I'm embarrassed. None of my friends know this, but I'm a virgin. You're the only one who knows. But everything's confidential right?

Her: Yes, go on.

Me: I went to a party the other night and my parents don't know about it. They're real strict, and that's why I appreciate being able to tell you, and I know it's confidential. At the party, everyone was drinking, and it got late. I stayed back with my friend, Mark. He's older than me, probably about your age – I think he's twenty-four. That's why I feel comfortable telling you this; you're older and you've heard everything at the church.

Her: Yep, I have. I'm here for you Jessie.

Now I know I've hooked her, and even though I know she's seventeen at the most, she believes me when I say I think she's older. I cater to her ego and her sense of wanting to help. Yeah, it's manipulative, but she could hang up anytime. A few actually did. Most proceeded like this:

Her: Jessie, your secret is safe with me. Just tell me what happened.

Me: My friend Mark and I were alone on the couch, and before I knew it, he put his hand on my leg. You promise this is confidential? I know I need to get everything out, and not hold back, but you are experienced in hearing everything right?

Her: Of course, Jessie, no one will know. Just let it out.

Me: Well, before I said anything, he put my hand on his… and I'm not sure how to say this, but he put my hand on his…on his…penis.

Her: Ok. What happened next?

Me: Well, I started feeling aroused, and my dick…oh I'm sorry, I meant to say penis…

Her: No, say it like you normally talk, Jesse. You must tell it like it happened. We've heard it all, and we need you to get it out. Use words that you normally use. If you have to curse and be descriptive, do it. Let it out.

I can hear her breathing change, and I sense her excitement. Now I know she's titillated, aroused, and as much of a phony as I am.

I start describing, in very graphic detail, a sexual encounter with "Mark," which included 69ing with him, a detailed description of how "big" his cock was, and anal sex.

One of the first successes was at St. Hedwig Church in Long Beach. I don't remember her name, but the girl started masturbating and literally told me to tell her more because she was so hot. We had many conversations until she no longer answered the phone.

As my endeavor became wildly successful, I expanded on the stories. I called Baptist Churches in South Los Angeles. I loved hearing the black women get aroused, and some were very honest. "Fuck it. Tell me, baby, how big your dick is…" I'll never forget one Black Lady who really got into it. She was listening to me, I could hear her masturbating, and she knew things that I didn't even know. "You makin my pussy sing, Jesse."

I'll never forget describing how two of us guys shot our cum onto a girl's face. The woman stated: "That's called shooting stars." What the fuck? I'm the pervert here, and I've never heard that term. I suspect I'm not gonna find out about this in no science book. A church lady (a prominent woman) has now schooled me in descriptions of sex acts. Wow! I'm enthralled, and excited. She was like many who I had phone sex with; there was never going to be a second phone sex call. They exposed their freakiness once, and it wasn't going to happen again. They needed to get back to being prim and proper. They simply felt guilty. But I didn't. Then again, I'm not masturbating in a church while listening to a man describe two men having hard core sex. Many of these women, including two nuns, went wild with this, only to declare that homosexuality is still a sin, and I needed to repent. If I came, I just hung up when they started this shit.

Another result of these phone calls was that I met a few girls in person. A couple of them became obsessed with me. Even after they knew what I told them, they wanted to meet me. We would exchange pictures in the mail, and to my astonishment, a couple of them were really hot. I'll never forget Lucy, a latin chick from some Catholic church in El Sereno.

She really liked white boys and seemed to forget my whole "Jesse" persona. When I received her pictures in the mail, I knew I had to get to that church soon. I drove up there, and we kissed passionately in the rectory when no one was there. She was cute, but I lived far away. She became obsessed and wrote me love letters, showing my pictures to her friends telling them I was her "boyfriend." This was a little worrisome. I drove to the church, met her and fucked her in the back of the rectory. Soon I had enough of her obsession with me and I spent a month letting her down.

Most of these women legitimately wanted to help a young man in distress, but dived in enthusiastically when the story became sexual, and I expressed words that released them from feeling guilty.

No one is evil here. To me it's just another example of how people like to hide their turn-ons, and how bigotry and hostility toward gay people is so deeply ingrained in our culture. What other reason could there be that women and men would masturbate and be excited at the description of two men sucking and fucking, and at the same time advise me that it's a "sin." An abomination. That I was going to hell. All this while they are masturbating to the imagery of men fucking each other. The psychology of that extreme cognitive dissonance is above my paygrade, but I think Albert Camus sums it up: "The evil that is in the world almost always comes of ignorance, and good intentions may do as much harm as malevolence if they lack understanding."

When people don't understand it, they fear it. Simple as that.

***

At this same time in 1983, I met a girl named Laura who became my first girlfriend. I had moved to the Bixby Knolls section of Long Beach. It's a wealthy enclave, with large estates mixed with upper middle-class homes. I had accumulated a large amount of cash by this time (well over $50,000) and my friend Mike Dewitt finally convinced me to deposit it into a bank. I still harbored deep distrust of banking institutions, so I only deposited a good portion of my cash. I only felt comfortable because I was over eighteen and I had a Driver's License and was starting to feel a little more attached to your world. I was still frugal however and did not trust that my income stream would last. I decided to rent a large bedroom in a home located a wealthy section of Long Beach known as Bixby Knolls.

It was rented by Chris, a man I met at a Gay nightclub in Orange County called DOK. Chris was one of the men who cornered me at DOK at the Gay Adult Movie release party for my friend Troy, better known as Jeremy Scott the porn star. One of the men there was a guy named Bill Higgins who took notice of me real fast. I overheard him telling anyone who would listen that I was going to be his next big porn star. He didn't even know my name.

I noticed he was making movies where the boys took cocks up their asses without protection. The gay plague now had a name: AIDS. It was an acronym for Acquired Immune Deficiency Syndrome. Scientists at the CDC had figured out that this was a sexually transmitted disease that attacked a person's immune system. Once it colonized your immune system and destroyed it, you died. There was no surviving AIDS. This was very early days of AIDS, but he knew he was killing kids. The doctors were stunned because every drug they gave their AIDS patients failed. That's because every drug developed by mankind had been developed to join forces with the immune system to fight off attackers. No immune system, no help. And everyone died.

I took Chris's number and later found out he was an engineer for the Los Angeles radio station KLOS. I went with him a few times to the station and met the famous DJ's. I loved Shawna – we became friends, she mentioned me on the air a few times, calling me "cute." I smoked pot with Frazier Smith, and we hung out with Bob Coburn a couple of times. I attended the huge "US" Festival, which was a three-day event, as a guest of Craig and KLOS. I worked as a gopher and sat in on interviews with David Lee Roth, Danny Elfman, and many more musicians who were playing the festival. I brought my guitar & keyboards and played songs at the Festival and at KLOS. Stevie Nicks was there once, when I was playing guitar and she complimented me on my playing. My playing at KLOS led to musical opportunities I later took advantage of.

I was standing in the driveway of my new home in Bixby Knolls washing down my new Datsun 260Z, a fancy sports car to me. Of course, I'm washing the car without a shirt on. I bought a set of barbells, and a bench press, and I had been lifting weights every day to improve my physique.

I need to show off my chest because I know when the high school day ends, the girls will be walking home on my street. One day, Laura and her friends walk home down the street and I'm shirtless washing the car. I look over, and they're all staring, but I notice Laura's the cutest. She's also bold, as she calls out, "Hey, you're cute!" And I say thanks, and she replies, "Why don't you come up here? What's your name?" I get to play older teenage boy to the younger girl. I ask her for her phone number, but since I know she walks down the street every afternoon, I invite her to come inside anytime she wants. And she does.

This girl's got courage. She's cute too. I can tell she wants to act older, and I love that. We're teenagers, after all. Isn't that what we do? I love impressing young girls. Laura's the lucky one at this time. Of course, it's all a facade. Inside, I'm a defective mess that quivers with fear. But I never reveal fear to anyone at any time. Especially to Laura — I want to impress her. To her, I'm the Prince, the Knight in shining armor, the man of her dreams. She's younger and easily impressed. We talk about teenage shit. I'm genuinely interested in her plans for the future. She wants to be a cosmetologist. She's not dumb, but she's gullible. I love looking down into the eyes of a girl looking up to me.

My concept of love is really just that famous four-letter word. Laura suits my needs.

I imagine I'm the lover every girl dreams about, but I really just want to fuck Laura all the time. I take her to concerts; a memorable one was David Bowie. She and I both loved his music. I also took her out to fancy fine dining, although it was now becoming routine for me. Every day I had lunch alone at The Velvet Turtle. I was accustomed to expensive restaurants, and I ate at them every day. But my favorite nights with Laura were when we watched porn together. It was exciting to see her excitement as she saw sex on the VCR. It was thrilling to feel her get wetter and wetter as she let herself go and stared at the cocks on the TV screen.

When we fucked, she was a screamer. In fact, out of all the girls I fucked, she was the loudest ever. One time, at an apartment I had later when I moved back down by the beach, I stuffed a pillow in her mouth to muffle her screams. When I walked into the hallway, I was greeted by an ovation — my neighbors were clapping in unison, congratulating me on a job well done.

Sometimes I sat with her friends and watched MTV. It was funny listening to them wail about how cute George Michael was. This was later in 1984 when "Wake me up before you go go" was played every five minutes. I couldn't believe how naive they were thinking he was straight. No straight guy moves like George Michael or writes a song as gay as "Wake me up before you go go," but still, Laura and her girlfriends were convinced he was straight. Whatever. Let them imagine what they want. I still think George Michael does more harm by lying about his sexuality. Tell the fucking truth, and maybe you'll lessen the prejudice and ignorance. But of course, he didn't until years later. His career, just like many gay men's careers were more important to them than being honest. But maybe if they showed some courage, people would respect them more. There's so many gay men who can't seem to figure that out. You get respect when you demand it. I won't be a hypocrite. I do the same thing.

22

Becoming Shawn Mayotte

May 1983, Long Beach, California…

It's another beautiful day in Long Beach when my phone rings. A male voice on the other end asks if this is Doug. I answer yes, and the voice tells me his name is Kurt Deitrick. I'd given Robby permission to tell Kurt it was ok to call me. Kurt asks me if I'm interested in being paid to be photographed nude. All my brain heard was "being paid." It was the single most important phrase in life to me. I get paid. I have the same mindset when my true musical aspirations conflict with my love for easy money. I'm getting calls to play on sessions, and they pay up front. So instead of focusing on what I want to say, and being an artist, I focus on the quick buck. I learned that long term thinking isn't compatible with a short term brain.

I don't ask questions, and Kurt sounds excited that I'm interested in posing for photographs. I assume it's because he knows what I look like and is horny for me like everyone else. I have a momentary thought that he might be excited because he lives to make money too. But it can't be that. He's excited like everyone else. I'm the great I am, the alpha and omega of every gay man's fantasy.

Kurt lives in Rossmoor, an upper middle class unincorporated section of homes near Los Alamitos. We set a time on a Saturday morning to meet at his house. Kurt encourages me to work out and be tan for the photo shoot. We agree that he'll pay me $750, which is bullshit money for this. He originally offered me $500 and I refused. But, of course, I only had $250 more worth of courage, so we agreed on that. Over the phone, it's now become easy to deduce that Kurt's a businessman. He's thinking with the big head, the one down below is not controlling him. He's fucking cheap. He knows I'll make him a lot of money. I don't think about this enough to hold out for more cash up front. I'm still convinced that I'll make millions with my musical talent, and that this is all just a prelude to my future cornucopia of capital.

As I arrive at his home, I wonder if this is where he's going to take pictures of me. I wonder if he's the one who takes the pictures. I wonder why this isn't a Hollywood movie set and why I don't have my own trailer with catered food. I'm already lost in my fantasy. While I'm wondering all of that nonsense, Kurt comes to his front door and greets me before I knock. He's fast to talk and perspiring heavily. This is a nice house; it has four bedrooms, a large kitchen, and a backyard with plenty of room for parties.

As I enter, I see old furniture, old pictures on the walls, old wallpaper, old, old, old. I get the feeling this was his grandmother's house. He's old too, and not interested in small talk. I've been here a few minutes, and he asks no questions about me or my family or how I became interested in doing porn. Oh well. He and I are here for business, and Kurt wastes no time. He shows me the rooms where he photographs the models and tells me he has a partner who helps him with the photo sessions. Kurt lets me know his real name is Kent Schlesselman. I appreciate that. By telling me his real name, Kurt (Kent) has trusted me. In the world of gay porn, hustling, escorting, role play, and all things related, there are many people I get to know, but who never reveal to me their real names.

The gay world is a world of secrets. They hide. And they use their creativity to hide behind outlandish costumes and masks. In my youthful opinion, gay men create masks because, number one, they instinctively know they're hated for just being different. Number two, they're afraid of straight people, and with some justification. Most straight people don't like to see gay people and use any reason they can to justify hating them. Straights don't realize that most of their favorite costumed and made-up superheroes, villains, damsels and leading men in the movies are created by gay artists. This is why Halloween is a gay holiday.

Kent says he's heard about me, and that I'm very attractive to a lot of people. Suddenly, an older woman walks into the living room, and introduces herself as "Kit." Maybe this is Grandma. Kent informs me that this is his photo shoot partner. I'm surprised that she's his partner. She's gotta be in her 70's if not her 80's — wrinkled and spotted, her tits resting comfortably on her knees. Kit doesn't mess around with small talk either. She's all business. She asks me if I'm ready to do some test shots today. Of course, I am — pay me first. Kit says she wants me to tan out back first. I'm not tan enough for them. That's fine with me. I ask how much they're going to pay me today for test shots. We settle on $250, and this does not include the $750 Kent's paying me for my photo shoot. Kit and Kent were the first people who recommended to me that I should use these new things called "Tanning booths." They helped create a tanning salon addict out of me. One I saw myself with a glowing tan, I couldn't stop my quest for it. They became another weapon in my armor of beauty.

After I lay out in the backyard, tanning in the speedo they gave me, I showered, and then the test photography session began. Although Kent took most of the test shots, it was fascinating keeping a hard on while being photographed by a seventy-five-year-old woman. She asked me if I needed straight porn magazines to look at, and I answered yes. She threw a couple of Penthouses at me, and a few with mmf threesomes and they did help my erection stand tall. We got through the test shoot day – I'm sure they got what they liked, but I didn't let them get too much for just $250. Of course, all the way home, the voice was telling me how stupid I was to trust them. I argued with myself to no avail. We set up a date in June for the full Kurt Deitrick nude photography session. I showed up on the agreed upon date. And so, we began.

He and Kit escort me to the "family room" where I take off my clothes and sit on a couch. It's not hard to get hard, so that happens quickly. Kent has a huge camera around his neck, so he looks like a very professional photographer to me. He's focused. He tells me how to position myself to get the best possible photo.

I haven't seen anyone work so hard for a picture. He strains. He perspires. He's too old to be doing this. He tells me to sit with my erection resting on my abdominal muscles to make it look larger. He captures fifty photos in less than an hour inside the house. I strike many poses. I loosen my underwear, so my dick hangs low, I grab my dick through my underwear, I thrust forward on cue, Kit commands me to stroke my cock to keep it hard. It's fascinating and funny to have an older lady instructing me on how to use my penis to make her money. Alas, my penis has dominion over all.

Of course, there is a paradox here. Although everyone's focused on my penis, neither Kit nor Kent reveal any sexual interest in me. I'm not bothered by that at all. I'm focused as much as they are. I'm doing my job. They photograph me all over the house, as well as outside. I'm on the couch, in the bed, standing (inside and outside in the sun), and I'm laying down outside in many poses. They work their asses off to get these photos of me. I admired them for having a tireless work ethic at their ages. Kent perspires heavily, but I understand why. I don't balk at or judge anything they ask for, except shots of my ass. I don't want to look effeminate or advertise my ass for sale. Even the piss shots didn't faze me. Kit wanted me to pee for the camera, and she needed to know exactly when, because as soon as I started to urinate, she had to capture it quickly in sequence. Snap! Snap! Snap! Snap! Apparently, they've got buyers who like shots of streaming pee. I'll piss all day and night for money.

As we wrap up my first nude photo shoot, Kent mentions "the cum shot." I already know. That's the climax; the apex; the zenith of my show. It's the most important event of the day. I've had my dick sucked a thousand times in the last year. Gay guys crave cum. Many women do too, they love to have me shoot it down their throats, but nearly every single gay man requires a cock-sucking to end this way. Kit and Kent position their cameras as I stroke my cock. They tell me to let them know the instant I feel it. As I get closer, I mentally distance myself from them. I imagine my latin dream girl spreading her legs in front of me while I eat her pussy. I get there quickly.

"I'm coming!"

Snap! Snap! Snap! Snap! Snap! Snap! The sequence of loud camera clicks by both of them seems to last longer than my orgasm.

My first nude photo shoot takes all day. I think Kent and Kit combined for over 300 shots. The last item on Kent's list for today is my name. I need a new name that people will like. It has to be a name that represents me and agrees with how I look. He agrees that "Dirk" is awful, and he wants to use a sexier one.

He and I both hit upon Shawn, because everyone said I resembled Shawn Cassidy.

This was one of the only pictures taken of me in my teenage years. It was on a home pass I'd been allowed to take for my sister's wedding. I was not happy because my mother tried to have sex with me the night before. After this one, I didn't have another photo taken of me until I was seventeen, No teenage pics for me.

Kent proposed the last name "Mayotte" after a professional tennis player named Tim Mayotte. I liked the sound of the name. The name "Shawn Mayotte" flowed well. And now I've officially become Shawn Mayotte.

As I leave Kent's house on that day, driving home, my mind wanders. I know there's something wrong with me. I don't like myself most of the time, the voice in my head is always telling me I'm no good, and I believe it. But a baby can't be born hating himself? How did poison get into my self-image? I start to think back to when I was a baby. It begins to dawn on me — I remember vividly when my father first hit me in the face. I remember my thoughts were: "I'm worthless, and I deserve to die because I'm so bad." Maybe I was so little, that my brain recorded this, and it replays this recording all the time. I think that's where my self-image became poisoned. I keep thinking, but now I'm receiving praise from people. How can I continue to hate myself if so many people like me? I've read somewhere that the antidote for a poisoned self-image is affirmation of your self-worth from people who love you. I get constant admiration from people for how I look. Maybe these pictures will be the antidote for my poisoned self-image. But I wonder, are photos of my naked hard cock the antidote for a poisoned self-image, or are they the product of one?

The very next night, I hang out and drink with a few of my straight male friends. Rudy and Jim are two guys I know here in Long Beach. They've done prison time, and somehow, I struck up a friendship with them while I was playing the guitar in my apartment. I think they overheard me loudly blasting out the chords to Judas Priest's "You've got another thing comin" on my Marshall amplifier while they were walking through the alley. I remember they ran up the stairs to my apartment and praised my guitar playing, telling me: "Dude, that was fucking awesome! Was that you playing the guitar? We could hear you down here. We got to meet you."

I can tell by the number of tattoos that Rudy and Jim are no choirboys, but I love 'em for complimenting me for my musical ability. I let them in, never thinking they just might be there to rob me. They weren't. They genuinely wanted to hear me play more songs. I obliged them. They wanted to hear AC/DC's "Dirty Deeds," Van Halen's "Somebody get me a doctor," and the Scorpions' "Can't live without you." I know them all, and we become fast friends. They drink beer while I play them songs I've been writing. I hang out with them for a few nights over the next couple of weeks, and now, the night after I return from my nude photo shoot, here we are, three angry men looking for trouble.

We go to downtown Long Beach and drink all night. Of course, my friends and I choose to drink at Chili Don's – we're guaranteed a fight. I started mouthing off to six drunk sailors.

All I remember is that I swung and hit one in the mouth and, then… perfect darkness. I woke up in my truck, with Rudy and Jim telling me, "Wow, you fought hard, and we tried to help, but first there were only six, and then there were three more who jumped on us. You're lucky to be alive, Doug. We dragged you out of the alley where they were beating the shit out of you."

"Did you guys at least try to fight?"

"Yeah, but there were too many of them. They knocked you out and your tooth is fucked up. Look in the mirror, bro."

I look up to see my reflection in the rear-view mirror, and I was HORRIFIED! No

123

fucking way! Not only did I have a blackened, purple grapefruit size closed eye, but one of my front teeth had been knocked out! FUCK! Oh my God. I guess this shit can happen to me. I'm fucked forever as a gigolo or a rock star if I don't fix this immediately. I get mad at Rudy and Jim. I don't want to blame them – I know I'm an asshole, but couldn't they have saved me from losing my tooth? They argue that they saved my life. Maybe they did, or maybe they're just cowards. So what, we're all cowards. I've got to fix my tooth. I'm not letting anyone see it until I see a dentist. I don't have medical insurance. Luckily, I have plenty of cash. Cash is king anyway.

Unfortunately, Laura shows up at my house in the morning before I can see a dentist. She disturbs my hangover. I was out all night, and she got worried. I try not to open my mouth, but she sees the gap where my left front. Surprisingly, she finds it attractive.

"You're so cute without that tooth."

What the fuck? She's just dumb. But it dawns on me. I've recognized that she likes bad boys before. When I've asked her what guy she thinks is cute (from pictures in a magazine or in a mall), she always points out the rough, greasy, bikers with beards, stupid looking dudes. So then why is she with me? I know... because I'm attractive to them all. Of course. But I can't be seen with a missing tooth.

Laura is just a speed bump on my way to conquering the world. I've got to have all my teeth intact (especially in the front) if I'm ever going to look myself in the mirror again. So, I immediately get on the phone with the first dentist I can find in the yellow pages. I make an appointment to get my tooth capped that very day. You know why the dentist worked so fast? Because I paid cash. When they asked if I had insurance, I said no, I'll be paying cash. They warned me it was $600. Warn me? That's a mere bag of shells.

The very next day after I lose my front tooth due to my anger and big mouth, the dentist caps my tooth, and all is well again in the world of Shawn Mayotte.

23

My Sister Jamie

Long Beach, Summer 1983

As I drive, I smile, and I turn the frowns upside down. I not only get calls from gay clients, but also from no name recording artists, as well as recognized artists, who request my services to play on their sessions. Kent (Kurt Deitrick) calls me and says he's selling more of my pictures faster than any model he's ever photographed. I feel I deserve some of the money he's making off of me, but I don't dwell on that very much. I have an array of friends from disparate lifestyles. Whenever I walk into downtown Long Beach, I always pass my homeless friends. I love to listen to their life stories they're so eager to tell me.

I feel good helping them with food and cash. I go to the store for them, and I'll give them five bucks if I have it on me. My favorite guy is the "Possum" – he used to tell me that he was like a "Possum" – because he worked at night and slept all day on the street. He knew I didn't judge him. He opened up to me, when I'd sit down with him on the corner of Broadway & Lime. It was his corner; his house; his spot. He told me about growing up in Wisconsin, and how his dad was a great guy, but he drank a lot. He loved his parents, and said "we got whippings with a belt, just like every kid did back then."

"That's what's wrong with kids today, parents don't whup 'em like mine did."

I asked him how he got from Wisconsin to here, and though he attempted to answer; his memory was damaged by years of alcohol abuse – I tried to follow his story, but he would take me on colorful journeys into madness.

Most people ignored him or taunted him. In my opinion, he was an outcast, just like me. I identified with him. I wanted to ease his pain. On the other side of Los Angeles, it was different. When I'm in Hollywood, hanging out with the big shots, I quickly recognized the superficial was their truth. Though I was fascinated with wealth and power, I was nauseated by the insincerity of most of these "power people." In Hollywood, you're just someone they're with until they see somebody more important walk through the door. It was confusing to be tantalized and desirous of what they possessed, and yet be repulsed by their lack of humanity. They did things for people out of pure self-interest. I guess it was a way of absolving themselves of guilt. I was a prop to them. I want to live like them, but I don't want to be like them.

My life at this point is still a mixture of excitement, joy, and paralytic fear. I feel happy at times, and I'm realizing that my need to impress people is more important than liking myself. Although I portray self-assurance, in actuality, it's a camouflage for feeling like a fraud. I guess it's because I act like one. I inhabit separate worlds, and the chasms I create between the two are becoming larger every day. I thought life would get better now that I'm free from custody, and no longer have to interact with my family. Maybe it really was my parents who were the problem, not me. But why am I living two separate lives? Half of my life I live in the straight world, and the other half I live in the gay one. In the middle is Laura. She is my "girlfriend," although I'm fucking other girls, and having sex with men and women for money. I feel guilty, but that's a normal state of mind for me, so I don't bother with changing behavior. But I know she's committed to me. I'm the handsome sexy older guy that she's obsessed with, and there's no other guy like me. She's faithful.

I continue getting calls from Kent, telling me that his customers want to meet me. He mentions a wealthy guy from Alabama who wants me to send him an envelope containing my fingernail clippings. Kent implores me to do this and meet the guy. Apparently, he's very wealthy, and I could get rich quick just by flying to Alabama and living with him for a year. He's some oil magnate. No fucking way. I'm not living in Alabama for a year. He can have my fingernail clippings — I'm honored (a little frightened by this, but still honored) — but I'm not living in Alabama, no matter what. My life is here. I can make more money, fuck more women, create a band, get signed, and become a rock star in Los Angeles. Alabama? This guy's gonna to want to fuck me, or worse yet, ask me to clean his house, Fuck that. I lived for too long as a caged animal. I need to be free.

My sister, Jamie, calls me one day. I haven't heard from her in a while. I hear from my aunts that she's using drugs a lot. I love Jamie, and I'd do anything for her. She was so abused, and no adult ever stepped in to stop it. I've been away so long. I don't think I've actually seen her since 1979, except for that one day at her wedding. Before that, I hadn't seen her since she took off with her boyfriend in 1977 – they were gone before I entered my first mental hospital in late 1977. And then I was in Leroy's Boys Home from 1977-1978, and she was living her life either on the streets at sixteen, or with him. I've never wondered why she never visited me or wrote me any letters. She's more damaged than anyone I've ever known.

She thinks sexual abuse is love. She equates my mother's sociopathic control with motherly love. I remember the sweet, innocent little girl, but I don't really know this drug addict they tell me she has become.

I still don't understand drug and alcohol addiction. And there's many people who still argue that alcohol isn't a drug. From my vantage point, alcohol is the worst of them all. I understand my perspective is not everyone's, but I can only draw conclusions from my experience as a child. They taught us in school that drugs were bad, bad, bad. And I believed everything I was taught. I view drug use as a waste of time. It leads nowhere, and you crave something that's elusive and gives nothing back. I had plenty of family experience to watch and draw from. But this was my sister Jamie. I really loved her, and I felt tremendous compassion for her. God gave her nothing.

When Jamie was three years old, my mother did not have her strapped into a seat belt. Fortunately, I was barely twelve months old, so I received the drive comfortably buckled into a child's car seat. My mother was a horrible driver, and on this day, sometime in 1966, she was rocketing to her destination on the freeway. She had no regard for the safety of others, let alone the safety she was responsible for providing to her first-born child – Jamie. So as my mother barreled her through traffic on the freeway, doing 90 miles an hour, she careened out of control, and collided with the guard rail in the center median. Jamie was thrown from the passenger seat into the windshield. Luckily, I was buckled into a car seat, so I emerged unscathed. Thank you, Mom. But my poor sister –she flew into the windshield, cracking her head open, with glass shattering and cutting her, and in that instant, her eyes were severely damaged, and crossed forever. There was no fix. My mother was responsible for Jamie's eye damage and leaving her with a permanent disability. My sister was forever changed by my mother's reckless disregard for her safety. Jamie's eyes would forever require glasses, and of course, as she grew up, the kids were cruel.

She never knew her real father. She was born out of a bottle on a one night stand my mother had when she was sixteen, while my father was in the Air Force. This guy apparently never responded to my mom when she told him she was pregnant. Of course, I don't trust my mother's stories, so maybe he tried, maybe not. Bottom line is that Jamie was born after my mother had met my father, and they were having a relationship. He went off to the Air Force, and my mother was still going to have her fun, hence, Jamie's birth.

Jamie calls and wants to borrow my truck. I have two cars, and I want to help her. She says she just needs it for one week. She's going to come over on Wednesday, and we agree that she'll bring it back the following Wednesday. I give her my address, and hope she wants to spend some time with me. Maybe my older sister will take me to lunch? I'm not asking for anything in return for letting her have my truck, but it would be nice to see her and hear how she's doing. On the phone, she doesn't offer any lunch or dinner, and she tells me she's in a hurry, but we'll get together soon. A friend of hers drives up to my apartment building and Jamie gets out. We hug for a second, and before I hear an answer to my question, "How are you," she asks for the keys, gets in, and drives away.

I don't hear from her the whole week, and I don't want to bug her. I call her on Wednesday, and she answers with a quick, "I can't talk right now, but I'll get you the car back as soon as I can." She hangs up on me. I'm concerned, but more concerned that I'm not mad. I don't understand myself. I loved her very much and still, I couldn't protect her. I remember the sweet little girl who was my sister. Now, I don't think I know this Jamie very well. Whatever.

She calls me in the middle of the next week, and says if I want my car back, she'll bring it to me, but I have to understand there's some things missing. I don't understand. She says someone stole my rims, and other parts, and on top of all that, my windshield is missing. Ok, just bring the car back, Jamie. We agree that I'll meet her outside where I live, and she calls me before she leaves. She states emphatically that she feels responsible for the missing parts to my car, and she wants time to get them back. I'm confused, but I tell her to at least come by so we can talk about it. She does drive to my house, and I see my truck in the exact condition that she told me it was in but worse. It's missing the rims, it's scratched everywhere, and she drives up without a windshield. Unfortunately, just before she drives up, I receive a call from a friend who offers me $500 to show him my cock, and possibly let him suck it. I've got to get over there. Now.

While I'm fascinated seeing my sister with that look of horror in her eyes, driving in my see-through truck – I let her drive off without stopping this debacle before it gets worse. She convinces me she's going to hunt down the missing items and be back soon. And I don't see her or hear from her for the next month.

In about four weeks, I begin getting tickets for my abandoned "frame" of what was once a truck. They state that my frame is about to be towed at my expense, and that my truck has piled up over $300 worth of parking tickets on 15th Street and Henderson Avenue.

I'm a little afraid of that area. My life expectancy drops considerably anywhere north of 10th Street (so says the fearless narcissist). And west of Cherry. You have to see the area to recognize its murderous charm. People kill each other every day in this part of Long Beach. And they leave the bodies on the streets. Jamie likes bikers and guys on parole. When she ran away from home at fourteen to save herself from our mother and father, her boyfriend shot her in the face with a bb gun. But she stayed with him, bore my nephew by him, and married him. She has a hole in her cheek, I actually peeked through it once. Anyway, I'm a tough guy, so I'm going down there to see what the fuck she's done to my truck.

I arrive at the corner of 15th and Henderson, and there's my truck. Well, it used to be my truck. Its frame rests comfortably on the ground. There are no wheels or tires anymore. All of the windows are missing, including side mirrors. The inside is completely bare, no seats, no radio, no dashboard, no nothing. There's at least twenty parking tickets taped to the right fender. Long Beach just keeps piling on the tickets without towing it? At this point, I'm thinking should I open the hood, and of course I do. There's nothing there either. No engine, no transmission, no hoses, belts, radiator, nada, zilch. They've taken everything from my poor truck. I still don't understand. But now I'm fucking pissed. I do have an address for Jamie right here. I see stairs that lead up to the second floor apartment that is hers. I bang on the door, loudly. I'm ready to show them what happens when you fuck with Doug Probst. Especially when I've been generous.

I hear a loud male voice shout back, "Who's banging on the door?"

I shout back, "It's Doug, Jamie's brother!"

I hear rustling around, and the door flies open. I'm greeted by the biggest, dirtiest, scary looking white man I've ever seen in my life. He stares at me. This is weird. Shockingly, he says to me in a friendly voice, "Well, come on in, Doug. We're friends of Jamie's. She's not here right now. But you must be her brother. She's told us about you. Come on in, brother." I hesitate for a second, but I cannot show fear here. I walk through the door.

As I walk in, the first thing I notice is a carburetor out in the open sitting on a stool. The stool is next to a huge white man with a swastika tattooed to his cheek. He's also cleaning the barrel of a shotgun as our eyes meet. I'm no longer angry, I'm now consumed with fear for my life. The funny thing is these guys treat me very nicely. The guy ramming the stick in and out of the shotgun barrel, points to the carburetor sitting on the stool and proudly exclaims, "We found your carburetor for you, Doug. We're gonna get your car parts and put it back together for you. It fucking sucks what they did to your car."

Since I know danger when I'm in it, I meekly reply, "You know what? Thank you so much for what you're trying to do for me. I really appreciate it. Can you let Jamie know that I came by looking for her?"

"Yeah, Doug, we will. If you want to wait for her, she's coming back in an hour."

I tell them I've got to get going. And I walk out the front door. As I take all the tickets off the truck, and get into my Datsun, I breathe a sigh of relief. I feel like I've escaped with my life. I feel better when my car starts, and I'm on my way out of there. On my drive home, I start pondering what is going on with Jamie. Do I really know my sister? I can never hate her, even if she sold the parts to my car for drugs. I remember how painful it was to be Jamie. I still love her with all my heart.

2 4

My Adult Film Family

Autumn 1983...

Too many people are educated beyond their intelligence. Here I am, in your world for a mere sixteen months, and I'm meeting more people with degrees who don't know shit. I've been in many social situations conversing with college educated people who don't know history, who can't tell the difference between a continent and a country, and don't care about anything of substance. They know nothing about real life. Priests are perfect to them, religion is celebrated, and everyone worships Mother's Day. And they follow some god they were taught to believe in. They love Christmas to the point of mass insanity. There's people dying everywhere, and yet when Christmas comes around, it's time to celebrate the world's largest marketing scam again. The government lies, people lie, AIDS is killing thousands of people and yet all anyone cares about is what happened last night on "Dallas." They believe cops are perfect, the USA is perfect, that black people were better off as slaves, and a whole lot of other shit that I know from experience not to be true. I don't have any education, and yet I seem to know a lot more about how the real world works than these trust fund babies. A lot of formally educated people lack this deductive reasoning; in particular, the people who love a God they can't see and hate the Gay person right in front of them.

October 1983

My morning ritual of reading two to three newspapers, cover to cover, is now taking up two to three hours of every day. One section I love to read, are the obituaries. I love reading about the deceased person's life, what they accomplished, how many children they had, and how they died.

The obituary I read this morning went like this:

"Steve, a thirty-eight-year-old male died after a long illness. He loved hiking and camping. Steve had hundreds of friends and will be missed by many. The funeral service will be held at Our lady of the Rosary Parish, 14815 S. Paramount Blvd. in the city of Paramount. His two sisters, mother and father request that all donations made in Steve's name to be sent to the Salvation Army or any Christian organization of your choice."

There was no mention of his partner Jack, or that he was gay, or that he actually died of AIDS. I know this because I knew Steve. He was a good friend. I remember when he detected a purplish spot on his leg in 1982, and he spoke about it to Mike Dewitt and me in my apartment. He was concerned that he had this "Gay Cancer" and like many of my gay friends, didn't know what to do. I felt anxious and worried because I instantly knew Steve had this new disease.

Straight friends would tell me their brother died of pneumonia. I'd ask, "How old was he?"

"Twenty-two."

Twenty-two-year-old men don't die from pneumonia.

I'd already lost over thirty friends to this ghoulish "Gay Cancer" or "gay pneumonia," and I was getting tired of making friends with people who were going to die. Steve partied hard. He was always inviting me to a party where everyone was sure to be dancing, drugging, and fucking their brains out. I always declined. He never got upset, and I looked forward to our conversations. Steve was an intellectual. And now he was going to die. I felt sadness and anger as his immune system collapsed and his body became racked with pain. It was slow and it hurt to not know what to do for him.

I watched helplessly as Steve developed infection after infection and wasted away until he gasped that last breath and died in October 1983. During his life, Steve's family had turned their back on him because he was gay. They were Catholic and had despised him for being a "homosexual." They labeled Steve a "sinner," and disregarded those of us who attended to him when they would not. Now, his family wouldn't let us in the hospital during the last weeks of his life, as he was dying. In addition, they controlled how his death would be reported, and who could see him on the day he died. I remember how Steve's lover, Jack, cried and begged the hospital staff to allow him to visit Steve. He wanted to hold Steve's hand, as all couples would. He was turned away at Steve's "Christian" family's request. No donation was requested for AIDS research, or for any gay related causes, only for "Christian" organizations.

As 1984 approaches, I'm alarmed by the increasingly strange shift in the way certain obituaries were reported in the Los Angeles Times, and the Long Beach Press-Telegram. Dead men were reportedly dying after a long bout with "pneumonia" or "skin cancer." These men were unusually similar in their age groups, mostly between thirty-three and forty-two. They hardly ever leave wives or children, and remarkably, parents are usually the ones reporting their son's deaths. I realize these men are actually dying of AIDS, but the newspapers are concealing the truth. So now men are dying of a disease that isn't happening, according to the newspapers. What the fuck? Reporters, mortuaries and families are hiding the truth from the public. This is a new kind of conspiracy. It's a conspiracy of shame.

It's a conspiracy that will only contribute to more people getting infected, and more people dying. But they don't care, they only feel embarrassed. So, because you feel embarrassed about a dying person's diagnosis, you lie and spread misinformation that will lead to more death. It's your world, not mine. I can't relate to you fucking hypocrites. My gay friends are dying. I don't have any medical knowledge, but it's becoming clear to me that AIDS may not be a government conspiracy. It looks to me like gay people just got unlucky. A virus landed in their world, and they're spreading it through anal sex with each other. Your world not only doesn't give a shit, but you also actually hope they die.

I was born into a dishonest world. I didn't ask to be born, and I certainly wasn't born a dishonest baby. Your world has lied to me from the moment I was born. I wanted to believe in something. I still want to believe in something, now that I'm in charge of my life. But inside or outside, it doesn't seem matter.

The game's rigged. I was only eleven years old when you determined I wasn't fit to live in your society. Maybe my parents were right — I'm no good. Fuck that. Fuck it. I've been out sixteen months and I haven't been arrested once. I don't commit crimes, even though I guess prostitution's a crime. I've got talents. I believe in me. I've got dreams, and they'll come true.

1984

I don't know where the idea came from, but my friend Randy and I suddenly decide we want to get jobs. He says he knows of a job at a company called Dial Precision in Torrance. They're hiring now. It's a company that makes small precision parts for aircraft. Randy is an idiot, but for some reason, I'm interested in this job. I have no idea why, but I think it has something to do with my need to be a part of this world.

I'm supposed to have a job. If I get a "real" job, Laura's dad might start to like me. He's a loudmouth who lost an eye years ago in bar fight; but I'd still appreciate his approval. He hates me. I'm eighteen and Laura's fifteen. I have a hard time seeing anything from anyone else's point of view, especially when I want something badly. I want to continue fucking Laura very badly. She's my girlfriend. Anyway, I go to Dial Precision in Torrance, and learn the company needs people who can run manual lathes. I have no idea how to run a manual lathe, but I guess they believe I can do it, because they hire me after the first interview, almost the same day. So now I'm standing in front of a manual lathe.

They tell me I need to cut grooves into parts that will be used on airplanes made by Boeing. I'll have to hold "high tolerance" levels. What the hell does that mean? I'm told it's mathematical. The highest math I learned was fractions. Anyway, I don't understand any of this, but they show me how to use the lathe and work the controls.

When I finish, and the lathe spits out my part, there is a "part inspector" who sits at the right end of my lathe, and she inspects the part. She's there to make sure I've done my job correctly. They tell me that she's an illegal alien, whatever that means. How is a human being illegal? She's hot — she can't speak English, but after I start the job, it's not long until I fuck her. She didn't speak English, and I didn't speak Spanish. But we didn't need to. We both spoke the international language of lust.

The job sucks. I learn how to run the lathe, and I begin to meet my quota of 600 parts a day. All for $6.92 an hour. I was making $6.92 a minute before this job. I still see John Thompson and a few regular clients once in a while. But John is not pleased when I show up smelling like a machine shop. He lets me know, but we still rendezvous, and I'm able to supplement my low wages with his regular $500 to $1000 a month.

The machine shop at Dial Precision is filled with lathes, milling machines, and cutting tools. I don't know anything about these machines. I just followed the training instructions and learned how to use my lathe. It sucks to drive here from Long Beach. I have to get up at 5 a.m., to be at work by 6:30 a.m. Every day it's the same routine. Get up, shower, dress in my work clothes, get into my car, and drive to work. I work for eight hours, and then I drive home — dirty, smelly, and tired. It's synchronized, autopilot, symbolic sameness. I've joined the people I write songs about. I sit in a sea of cars on the freeway, one of thousands driving en masse to get nowhere. People choose to do this for their entire lives. That's unfathomable to me. A low paying job is what I've wanted to avoid. And now I have one, and I'm keeping it. I don't know why I do the things I do. I don't like this job, but I never miss a day of work. I show up on time, and I never get reprimanded for anything. I may not be the top parts cutter, but I'm a working stiff.

At the same time, I decide to move. It was an ADHD moment based on a client's promise of free rent. Call it a spur of the moment decision without Ritalin to help me decide. I call a client named Carlos from the Advocate Ad. He's a sweet older Mexican guy who lives in San Pedro. I used to fuck him all the time. Carlos couldn't get enough of my cock up his ass for $500 a fuck. He didn't have a lot of money, so I didn't see him often. The last time I spoke to him, he was kicking out his roommate. Carlos has an old two-bedroom Victorian style house on 2nd street in San Pedro. He's thrilled to hear from me when I call. I ask if the room is for rent, and he gleefully says yes. I ask for how much, and he tells me he wants $500 a month. My business side immediately wants to negotiate one ass fucking a month for the rent. Instinctively, I know he's gonna beg for more.

Carlos also has two assholes he calls sons, two daughters, and an ex-wife who's a loony old mean ass lady. Of course, none of them suspect he's gay. Carlos' nine-year-old grandson Luis is very close to Grandpa Carlos. Grandpa Carlos is kind and compassionate to him. He's the opposite of Luis' father. I love seeing Carlos with Luis – they are bonded.

Moving to San Pedro was a good move logistically, but Carlos and I fought a lot. He wanted me to fuck him all the time without a condom. I don't want shit all over my dick, and fucking a fat, sixty-five-year-old man takes a lot of work on my part. I need straight and bisexual male porn for a while before I can perform. I fuck Laura all the time in my room at Carlos' house. Of course, he was nice to her, but even she realized that Carlos was jealous. It was a burden I carried for being desired by both sexes. Laura was young, so I enjoyed teaching her so many sexual positions.

1984 wasn't the epic year for me like it may have been for you. Your world enjoyed the Macintosh, the LA Olympics, and everyone rediscovered George Orwell. I spent 1984 working every day. I was out of the Shawn Mayotte limelight. I performed on very few musical sessions. My musical career didn't progress much this whole year. But I kept my job and ran my lathe efficiently. I still posed for nude photo shoots, and I still entertained clients on an occasional basis, and I was still horny all the time. But I got up every day and got down and dirty working for a machine shop.

While being with and fucking Laura all the time, I was still seeing young men, my clients and surrogate fathers John Thompson, Joe Lauro, and Arthur Travis. I went to parties with my fellow adult film stars and serviced escorting clients I met through my ad in the

Advocate.

Many of my fellow adult film stars were addicted to drugs or had AIDS. Jim Rideout, better known as Kurt Marshall, was one of the most beautiful young men to ever get fucked in an adult film. He was confident, and with good reason. He was smart, charming and very intelligent. Jim had charisma. I remember seeing him at a party and I could tell we were both attracted to each other. I liked him, not only for his beauty, but we could also converse about anything. He had a broad range of knowledge, and he wasn't ashamed of being gay. We chatted about using our porn fame as a vehicle to fight for gay rights.

Jim was overconfident. He was younger than me, yet he didn't miss a chance to let me know he was more popular than anyone. He was so charming and intelligent; he was cute even when he bragged. The next time I saw Jim, he was strung out on meth. He could barely speak. His self-confidence made him think he was omnipotent and ruined his career. Jim's drug use was the catalyst for him doing things he would never have done had he been sober. He went into rehab and got sober, but it was too late. I cried when he told me he had AIDS. I loved him and visited him in the hospital when he was dying. He was still cheerful knowing he was about to die, but our conversation was unsettling since I didn't know how to comfort someone who seemed comfortable dying. He passed in 1986. He was twenty-two years old. Kurt Marshall (Jim Rideout) was the 66th person I knew who had died of AIDS. I cursed that thing that calls itself God, and moved on, waiting to get the call from who'd be next.

Jon King was another friend I knew from the Industry. His real name was Jon Gaines. He was a sweet, nice guy who had been taken advantage of by Bill Higgins and hated him. We all hated Bill. Bill was a piece of shit who took advantage of young men by demanding they get fucked in the ass on camera with no condom, or he wouldn't pay them. Bill and his movie production staff were like the audiences of the Roman Colosseum screaming for their performers to die. Most of us were homeless and we needed the money. So many of my friends felt they had no choice. And so they died. Fuck Bill Higgins. In my opinion, he was a murderer.

When Jon would complain about Bill, I'd try to talk him into performing for YMAC Studios. He never made the move because what he really needed was someone who would listen. I saw myself in Jon, both of us trying to survive in a world we didn't belong to. We both had parents who didn't give a shit about us, and we were both lonely. Jon put his body and soul into his performances, and he felt he wasn't appreciated for it. The audiences appreciated him as his name got bigger and bigger. I loved him and was happy to see him finding peace even when he knew he was dying of AIDS. Jon died in 1994. He was the 126th person I knew who died of AIDS.

One guy I'd see at parties who turned me off was Nick Iacona, better known as Joey Stefano, the most famous bottom of all time. Nick could be likable, but it was mostly an act to get whatever he wanted. And he obtained a lot. But it was mostly drugs. He had the attitude of an addict. He thought he was more powerful than the drugs.

He bragged a lot, and sometimes I'd see him at parties and wondered how he could brag when he'd be so strung out, he looked like death itself. He was a typical drug addict. While his ship was sinking, he'd still imagine he wouldn't drown. If he was on death row, Nick would brag about being the most popular guy on death row. And then it happened. He was found dead from an overdose of cocaine and heroin mixed together in what's known as a "speedball." I hope you finally found the peace you needed, Nick.

25

Still La Principale of Ocean Blvd

Throughout 1984 I see new Music Superstars emerging. The world I grew up in is changing. Everyone wants to forget the 1970's. The musical styles are evolving; or are they devolving? I like Howard Jones and singular songs like Thomas Dolby's "She Blinded Me with Science" – but most of these new Musical Artists spend more time creating elaborate hairstyles and costumes, rather than actually making great music without machines. Prince is still my idol. Everything he writes and produces is imaginative and created manually. He also incorporates every style of music I love into each song. The albums Dirty Mind and Controversy are masterpieces, and I play them over in my car. I blast Prince in my car all the time. There's one other new musical Artist that I'm intrigued with. Even though I've never been fascinated with Female Recording Artists – mostly because they just sing and don't write songs (except Joni Mitchell and Chryssie Hynde), there is something about this new Female Recording Artist that intrigues me. I first saw her on American Bandstand.

I just happened to be watching it and this cute young smiling girl was hopping around, all dressed in black, lip synching a song called "Holiday." It was a mediocre tune, and even though she wasn't a great singer, there was something captivating about her. I thought her name "Madonna" was silly, but I was truly intrigued. She was sexy and projected confidence. She smiled the whole time, even during the interview with Dick after the song ended. I kept watching to hear her speak. I'm ready to hear infantile meanderings, but I was wrong. She kept that smile going while answering basic questions, never missing a beat. But it was her answer to Dick Clark's final question that I've never forgotten.

He asked her what she wanted out of the rest of her career, and she stated with a smile: "To rule the world." That's the answer a real artist gives. That's the answer a leader gives. I think the Music Industry should take notice of this Madonna. She exhibits the confidence that a true Artist must have to stay on top and build a community, not just have "fans."

Of course, I'm really into her because I want to fuck her. She's got a great body, she's confident, and I love that smile. She exudes sex. We'd make a great match. We'd be fuck buddies. Madonna, my fuck buddy. I look up her astrological sign, and of course, she's a Leo. A Leo is the perfect match for an Aries like me. We're two huge egos fucking their brains out to see who can fuck better than the other. I jack off to that thought.

After almost a year of working for $7 an hour at a machine shop, I decided to quit. I'm not seeing my clients as regularly and I'm afraid of losing them. I decide to risk it. I just ask for my last check and walk out. It's now February 1985, I've moved back to Long Beach and I'm curious if I can still make money just walking down Ocean Blvd. I move to an apartment at 4th Street and Redondo Avenue which is only a mile away from the ocean. One day, I decide to put on my trusty white shorts that I used in my last photo shoot with Kent, and walk shirtless and tanned down to Ocean Blvd. I start walking westward so anyone still cruising can slow down and see me. To my shock and surprise, within minutes, cars in both directions are slowing down, cruising me with lust in their eyes.

I was mesmerized by a gorgeous black woman driving a white 1984 E Class Mercedes. She was driving alongside me for a minute before she pulled over to chat. I was attracted to dark women and had tasted the African American sexual fire twice already. I immediately walked over to her car and her face shouted money to me. As she rolled down the passenger window, I leaned in and heard her speak.

"You're cute. And you have a sexy body. I don't normally do this, but are you for sale?"

"Yes, I am, my dear."

"I used to cruise Ocean Blvd. when it was bustling with young men, but it's slowed down. I didn't think this would be my lucky day. I have an office in Belmont Shore, but I'd rather take you home with me. How much?"

"$300." I was stunned at how fast I blurted out my price. I made it up on the spot.

"Well, jump in. Let's take a ride to my house. I don't know what it is about you, but you've got me thinking horny thoughts."

I'm right there with you honey.

She asks me my name and I tell her, "I'm Shawn. Nice to meet you. What's yours?"

"I'm Jacqueline. You can call me Jackie. I live in Naples near my office. It's not far."

I'm very familiar with Naples. It's where the uber rich in Long Beach live. It's the Lido Isle of LA County.

We reach her mansion and get out to greet her butler. He's nice to me and seems to know that a tan shirtless twenty-year-old white boy isn't here to discuss the Dow Jones report with Jackie. I have no coat for him to hang up, so he leads me into the spacious living room where sitting before me is a beautiful black Steinway piano. I immediately jump on it and start playing and singing "You are the sunshine of my life" by Stevie Wonder. Jackie looks stunned.

"Wow! You've got talent Shawn. Maybe you could give my sons' lessons."

"I'd love to." I respond with visions of more money coming my way in the near future.

She hands me a glass of red wine and sits down next to me on the beautiful round sofa rich people love to own. She wastes no time laying down three-hundred-dollar bills on the glass coffee table in front of me. She's horny. I don't reach for it, but hesitantly I lean over and kiss her. Sensuously, she opens her mouth, and we lock tongues together, flickering them back and forth while our hands are groping each other's bodies. She reaches for my erection which is throbbing forcefully, straining to be released from my white shorts. In fact, I'm so hard, the head of my cock shows itself as it pushes itself out of the loose white surfer shorts, I'm wearing.

"My God, Shawn. You've got a gorgeous cock. I want you inside me, but I need to shower first. My two sons are upstairs, and I'd like for you to meet them and entertain them with their nanny while I prepare. Is that ok with you?"

I love children and follow her upstairs to meet them. In one room, I see what looks like a nine or ten-year-old boy laying on his bed reading a magazine. She introduces him as Marcus, her eldest child. In the other room down the hall, I hear music blaring from inside. I immediately recognize the song as Madonna's "Like a Virgin."

I walk down the hall, and I'm greeted by a small, but effervescent, effeminate little but not small black boy with a huge smile on his face. "What's your name?" He asks the question with no fear or hesitation.

"I'm Shawn. What's yours?"

"My name is Louis, but you can call me Louise."

Louise is a great name for him. Now think I get it. He keeps replaying Madonna's video "Like a Virgin" and that's either a coincidence, or he named himself after his favorite musical diva.

His bedroom is enormous with high walls and vaulted ceilings. Boudoir windows adorned with white silky curtains gave his room an exquisite luxurious final touch.

"How old are you Louise?"

"I'm seven."

"You like Madonna, don't you?"

"I love Madonna!" He exclaims loudly as he strikes a pose and struggles to put on his shiny new go go boots. I ask him if he needs help.

"No, I can get put my boots on myself. Do you like them?"

"I love them! They're shiny and fit you perfectly." Louise then proceeds to dance around the tv singing "Like a Virgin" with Madonna, never missing a word or a pose. He grabbed my hand and asked me to dance with him, and I happily obliged.

As we danced to the video, Louise noticed my long hair. He froze in a half turn mid pose and told me to sit down. I sat down on the chair in the middle of his room. He then proceeded to feel my hair and asked if I'd let him braid my hair.

"No, I can't braid it now, but maybe next time. It's not long enough." My hair was bare-ly shoulder length. I thought to myself, "Most black women don't like long hair on white boys, so if his mother is gonna be a regular customer, I've got to keep it short."

Just then, Louise's older brother Marcus walked in. Without hesitation, he blurted out:

"I know my brother's a homo, but I love him. When the kids try to pick on him, I sock 'em in the mouth." I loved hearing that!

Just then, I heard Jackie yell from down the hall, "Come here, Shawn!"

As I sauntered down the long corridor, I heard the housekeeper shut both boys' bed-room doors. I entered her bedroom and was greeted by a sexy, olive skinned, nude, gor-geous black woman standing in front of me. I could feel my cock straining to break free from my shorts.
She could see my erection pulsating outward, and she came over and started stroking me.

She couldn't hold back her excitement.

"You have a big beautiful white penis. Can I suck it?"

"Yes, you may."

For the next hour, Jackie and I were having incredible sex. We both came and relaxed to chat.
Jackie laid back and told me she needed what I gave her. She also complimented me on how I treated her boys. "I can tell you're not homophobic. You loved Louis just as he is. He's the love of my life. People think I'm a bad mother because he's gay. I hate them. I hate those religious folks who want to convert him. And Marcus protects him. They're both beautiful kids." She was right. They were two beautiful children.

26

Famous Clientele

1985 – 1986, West Hollywood, Pasadena

I've now had the pleasure of fucking over 50 women since I re-entered your world. I've fucked twice as many men, and though I love many of them, it's mostly business. I've learned a lot about women. Confident girls fuck like I do, they're aggressive without being pushy, they get into it without reservation, and they aren't afraid to talk dirty or eat my asshole. I'm always "rim ready." Confident girls don't analyze, feel guilty, or lay there like a statue. Confident women have ideas of their own and aren't afraid to let themselves enjoy fucking. I don't understand the others. I've been in bed with girls filled with Catholic guilt, and to get in, I've got to get the cross out. They cry, they're hesitant, and they question themselves while we're in bed. Sometimes, when I look down at one of these girls' faces, I want to scream "You're already in bed with me, quit whining and fuck." But the cross can be a major obstacle. Somehow, I usually found a way to get it out.

I can tell Madonna would fuck me, matching thrust for thrust, and I'm sure she swallows. Madonna's got that "You know I'm a good fuck" look on her face. She's building an audience selling her sexuality to teenage girls. Laura and all her friends now, dress like Madonna. I see them everywhere, young Madonna wanna be's. This is no minor thing. In the 70s all of our female recording artists were sold to us as chaste virginal singers who longed to for love. Olivia Newton John, (Who I loved) Debby Boone (Who I didn't), and Helen Reddy were just three of the numerous safe country singers that were selling millions of records.

Of course, there were female singers who used sex to sell their songs: Cher, Chaka Khan, Donna Summer, Dale Bozzio, and others, but no one was prepared for the sexual influence Madonna would have on the world. She was the demarcation point between sexuality deemed inappropriate for female recording artists, and a complete sexual revolution. She literally gave young girls the permission to fuck. And they obliged. Sex was no longer understated. Girls could feel good about being sexually active. I saw it and took advantage of it. Thank you, Madonna. In my opinion it started with one video. After Holiday, she released "Lucky Star" which was good, but it was a masterpiece of a song called "Borderline" that changed everything. Or I should say the song and video together. This was a brilliant use of a great song combined with a stunning video that made every girl relate to her.

The video places her in a lower-class neighborhood where she is the girlfriend of a cute tough guy. They're dancing, and a rich photographer notices her. He hands her his card, inviting her to call him for a photo shoot that could make her famous. The boyfriend is jealous, and Madonna brushes him off, meeting up with the photographer at a later time. She has many pictures taken at the photographer's home, and in the video, we see how now she has outgrown her neighborhood. She tries to come back but is rejected by the boyfriend who she previously rejected. Madonna now realizes her mistake. She has lost her roots and taken for granted the very people who love her for just begin her and challenges the photographer to withstand her volatility by spray painting his car. He proceeds to throw her out, and now she's back in the neighborhood, humbled and hoping her former boyfriend and street friends will accept her. They do, and all is well. I recognize the brilliance of this right away. The song is very well written, with an emotionally compelling keyboard track, supporting modern sounding synthesizers, combined with a danceable drum track. The lyrics are reflecting her feeling that she gives all her love, and the lover is not making a choice, and is pushing her to the "Borderline."

This great song combined with a video that shows her having two choices (The rich vs. the street kid) gives young girls a new heroine. And from what I see everywhere I go; they're aspiring to be like Madonna. This is brilliant marketing, and I realize that videos used correctly in conjunction with a great song are the modern tool in helping to build a following. And I follow her along with the rest of the world.

In 1985, your world suddenly discovered AIDS. It was because a famous actor named Rock Hudson admitted he had it. Now, someone famous had it. Someone from the "general population" had it, as if gay tax paying Americans weren't part of the general population. But AIDS didn't bring out the best in people, it brought out the worst. Especially in Christians. Instead of leading with love, they condemned and judged people with AIDS as devils cursing them, spending more energy blaming the victims than fighting the disease. They hated, so I hated them back. I never liked them anyway, selling life after death like it's a product. I'd send letters to the Long Beach Press Telegram to combat the hate filled Christians who blamed AIDS on "gays" who were reaping God's wrath for their lifestyle. I'd joke that I have ascension robes and rapture dildos for sale when they're ready to rapture. Of course, the Press Telegram didn't print my letters. But I still hated them. They're hypocrites and sell snake oil to the gullible. Life after death is a great product; no one ever comes back to complain.

In September of 1985, I put a second advertisement in the Advocate. I use the same wording: "Long Beach Fox 8 ½ " cut" and immediately I start getting calls.

I got many calls from famous people, but two that stand out the most were Robert Reed and Dack Rambo.

On a warm September day, I heard the phone ring and said hello. On the other end I heard the voice of Mike Brady, the father of the television family "The Brady's." It was so distinctive; I couldn't help but ask him if this was Robert Reed. He confirmed it and added that he was interested in meeting me. So, Mike Brady was gay? The All-American Dad liked young men. Nothing new here.

Robert asked me to meet him at a gay bar in Pasadena. I never thought of Pasadena as a gay enclave, but I quickly learned it was as kinky as Long Beach, just on a smaller scale. I met him at a bar called "The Boulevard Bar", located on Foothill Blvd. As soon as I walked in, all eyes were on me, but I quickly spotted Mr. Brady at the far end of the bar. He greeted me with a warm handshake and a friendly smile. I could tell he was in the closet. He wasn't real outgoing, but he was a good conversationalist.

He talked about his upbringing and asked me about mine. He was from the Midwest and talked about how he got into acting with the blessings of his family. I kept my story short telling him my childhood was not good, but I'm having fun now and left it at that. He asked me to call him Bob but seemed embarrassed. He was a mixture of confidence and insecurity. We went to a motel and I fucked him in his ass. He really enjoyed being fucked hard. We hardly had any conversation. He was quiet, even while I fucked him.

He enjoyed being fucked, and I held myself back from coming until after he came. He good looks added strength to my erection. Once I came in his ass, he was very generous with me. We negotiated a price of $500 over the phone, but I walked out with $1,000 dollars. Later, when I heard he had AIDS, I called him because I wanted him to know someone cared. He was still in the closet and it wasn't a subject he felt comfortable talking about. He gave me a large wad of cash because he wanted me to keep his sexuality a secret. He asked me to promise him to never tell anyone he was gay. I was sure many people knew already, but he didn't have to ask me. It was no one's business, and I would never out anybody without their permission. He was a very private person.

Dack Rambo was a special person. Because Dack and I became close friends, he wasn't just a "trick." He was a kindhearted person who confided in me, allowing himself to be vulnerable. We became very close and I want to remember him with these thoughts. I miss him terribly and my love for him has never died. We had fun in bed that first night, but sex was not the most important aspect of our first meeting. Dack shared an intimate bond that I'll cherish forever. I'd like to share the memorial tribute to him that you can find on The AIDS Memorial Website. For you Dack:

I still remember the sleek elegance of his Porsche when I saw it parked outside Numbers restaurant in West Hollywood. I remember feeling relaxed when I climbed into the passenger seat, knowing we were headed to a fancy hotel to be together on the Sunset Strip. It was a night of curiosity and fun. It was the night I met Dack Rambo.

In the mid-1980s I was a personal escort. I ran an advertisement in a National Gay Mens Magazine, "The Advocate". It read "Long Beach Fox 5' 10" slim muscular build, 8 ½ cut". I received hundreds of calls and met men from all walks of life. I met Politicians, Priests. Actors, Electricians, Makeup Artists, Movie Moguls, Military men, and many others. Most of them I remember fondly, and there are others I wish I could forget.

One man I'll never forget was Dack. When I got the call, I had never heard of him. Having been a hustler, prostitute, escort, personal counselor, or whatever you'd call me, I could assess people very quickly. My ability to keep a roof over my head depended on it. Listening to Dack on the phone for the first time, I heard an intelligent, kind and cocky guy who was also a bit naïve'. He wanted to see me, we negotiated a price, and I immediately drove from my apartment in Long Beach to meet him at Numbers in West Hollywood.

Upon arrival, I noticed how handsome this man was. And yet, he was paying me for sex. He sure didn't have to pay anyone, but I'd met many men and women who lived their lives this way. I didn't know who he was, but there was never a dull moment in our conversation. He told me he was an actor on the television series Dallas. I had never seen one episode. I thought of myself as an intellectual whore and a silly television series like Dallas didn't interest me.

But Dack was an intellectual too. On that first night we laughed about how he wanted to do Shakespeare, but he needed to pay his bills. I learned a lot about him that first night.

He was a hard-working actor who had been in the business since he was a kid. Though I had lost many friends to AIDS, I learned about another kind of loss from Dack. He was still visibly upset by the death of his identical twin brother Orman. Orman had died in a car accident in the late 1960s. Dack and I bonded over loss.

The sex that night took a back seat to conversation. Though we were burning rubber in bed, neither one of us could stop talking. We were both bisexual and we both felt the world didn't understand us. I knew we had a bond. He was so nice, I felt guilty about asking for payment. I fell asleep forgetting about it. Still, the bottom line for me was payment, and to my pleasant surprise, I woke up with more money on the nightstand than we initially agreed upon. The man knew the direct path to my heart — generosity and kindness. I had a love affair with those two attributes in those days.

That night sealed the deal on a friendship that lasted until he died of AIDS in 1994. Although Dack called me only a few times to have dinner together before he told the world he was HIV positive, I was his listener, his dinner companion, and his partner in loss. We always met at the French Quarter restaurant on Santa Monica Blvd. and though often he had tears in his eyes, he also laughed and smiled through the pain. That's what we do. When we're going through hell, we keep going because it's the only way out.

Dack, when others as famous as you hid their diagnosis, you bravely shared yours with the world. You changed the world by being honest. You were kind and you made me feel special when we were together. The world was cruel to you when it took Orman away. It was cruel again when you were diagnosed with HIV. But you left a legacy of courage and a body of work that we can all re-experience thanks to today's technology. And the moments we laughed about life I will always cherish. Though AIDS stole you from us, I'll always remember your love for acting, your trust in me. and your love for your brother. Thank you for being my friend.

Me with my mother Peggy, and father Kurt

From left to right
My sister Jamie, me & my mother Peggy

Jamie and me

1976
Me playing Piano

Me at 5 yrs old

Me at 12 years old

Me and Jamie

5043 Carfax Avenue Lakewood CA 90713
At my mom's house – new owners 2021

Los Padrinos Juvenile Hall
Court Entrance

Los Padrinos Juvenile Hall Walls
High walls barbed wire

Rancho San Antonio Boy's Home

Sylmar Juvenile Hall 2020
High Red Walls with barbed wire

June 1982
My first photo shoot

1982
7 Up & Cummin - My first movie

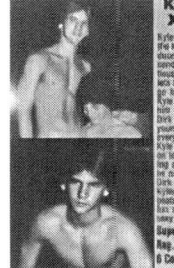

Robbie Leonetti Adult Film Star
John Movido

YMAC Films - 1983
Hot, High & Horny

143

Doug and Rick best friends

My Ocean Blvd white pants

December 1985
In Touch Cover Photo

1985
2nd photo shoot

1985
2nd photo shoot

1988
3rd photo shoot

Darren and me

Hustler corner 2020 Boulevard of Boys
Broadway & Pacific Long Beach

My first aprtment
Ocean & Bonito Long Beach

Falcon Bar 2020
Long Beach, CA

Broadway Mine Shaft Bar
Mine Shaft Bar 2020

Ripples Bar 2020
Long Beach Ripples club

Hyatt Regency Hotel
Pianist

145

Circus Books 2020
Santa Monica Blvd.

Hollywood - Hustler Corner
Santa Monica & Highland Ave

At The Rage

Vaseline Alley behind Circus Books
West Hollywood CA

APLA Center 2o2o
Kingsley Drive Los Angeles CA

Director of West Coast A & R
1981-87 Arista Records
Ritch Esra Publisher Music Business Registry

146

My drummer
Eric Kretz later joined Stone Temple Pilots

Musician party
Eric Kretz, Kelly, Tom

Dan Palotta Me Ritch Esra
Dan Palotta Founder of AIDS RIDE

Me Terry, Music Artist Manager Ben Malave A & R
Party 1991

Me, Shilah Morrow, Myles Mangram
Shilah is An Artist Manager at 14 Inch Fringe & Myles is a Music Business Attorney

Rehearsing with Joe
Me long hair and my favorite checkered shorts

In Valley Center Studios 1993
Me and Chili, world class bass player

Joe Cantrell, Clyde, Neal
Josh's 3rd birthday party

Me with bandmate Joe Cantrell

Porterhouse Bistro 2003
Ritch Esra, Me, Rosemary Butler

In pool smiling
Josh 1991

Venice Beach Apartment 1992
Josh and me

1993 West Hollywood
Josh and me

Saddleback trail
Josh's first horseback ride

Venice Beach Apartment 1992
Josh reading the newspaper upside down

John Michael Cox - The first openly Gay Rock Photographer/journalist.
Rock Music contributions to Mandate Personal Photographer to HAIR co-creator Gerome Ragni.
New York rep. for In Touch magazine.

27

Darren and James

I still have no relationship to you and your world's rules, so I've never taken the time to understand it. I don't want to understand it. I just want to do what I want to do. Make music, make money, and fuck 'em all. That's still my mission after this machine shop venture. My path hasn't changed. I exist for no good reason.

I was employed at Dial Precision for exactly one year. I've gotten so tired of Kent brow beating me to meet this rich guy from New York I finally agree to it. I've got contradictory feelings about wealth. I'm impressed by it, but it doesn't impress me if you're a wealthy ass-hole. Someone once said that money will take you anywhere you want to go, but it doesn't replace you as the driver. I know I'll be rich one day, and I'll still remember the little kindnesses and courtesies that matter more than money. But money still matters. I'm interested in meeting this rich New Yorker. He's a big shot on Wall Street. Kent says he's obsessed with me and I would benefit greatly from knowing him. It's starting to become an everyday thing; wealthy men obsessing over me. I don't think about it deeply, but I wonder if this is what people refer to as "taking it for granted."

Even though I leave my job, I have plenty of opportunities available to me to make money. Billy Preston calls me to jam with him, and of course I respond, and he lays out his interest in playing on a tour together. I jam with him at his house on Waveview Entrada in Malibu. I hate the winding roads, but it's worth it when I get there. I also still see John Thompson regularly, along with many other wealthy clients, and I get offers to play the keys, the guitar, and the bass on many recording sessions. I recognize that my efforts to get my music recorded is lagging behind my sexual addictions.

In 1985, I place an advertisement in Music Connection magazine looking for a singer and musicians to form an R&B/Pop/Rock group similar to the "System" and Prince. It read:

"Musician/songwriter Doug Probst is forming a new band. I'm infusing all styles of music into one group; examples include: Peter Gabriel, Prince, The System, and Steely Dan. Phone: xxx-xxxx"

I also state I'm only interested in serious people. I get the quacks and bad players, but I finally receive a phone call from a guy named Darren. He says he wants to form the same type of musical group. Darren sounds very intelligent, lives in Inglewood, and his name is Darren. He sounds black to me – just what I want. I never have to worry about playing music with black guys. They just do it. My experience with black musicians is that they're most likely to be more innately musical than white ones.

They don't have to learn it. I wish more white musicians had the talent level that black musicians do – but they don't. On a Saturday, Darren arrives at my house and knocks on my front door. I open it and I'm greeted by a tall, good looking, young black guy who is smiling for a second, and then the smile turns to a gaping stare. He extends his hand to me and warmly says:

"It's nice to meet you, Doug. I've been interested in forming a band just like your ad stated."

He continues to stare intently, and I'm not sure what that means. Is he gay? I'm more interested in getting started on creating music together. I invite Darren in, and he sits down on my couch, still gawking at me. He's a tall guy, not real muscular, and this is one time I'm not sure about a person's sexual preference. He knows my name is Doug, and I like his intelligence and interest in my musical abilities. We get to work fast, he is skilled at drum programming, he can sing, and we share similar tastes in music. We also agree to look for other musicians to complete our band. I feel I have a partner. He's very intelligent, and musically versatile. We immediately start writing songs. And to make this long story short: We do find band members that share our tastes in music, a guitar player named Terry, and a funky bass player named Greg Ross. We start rehearsing, and very soon we have four or five good songs that I've written and completed with Darren's help.

We tape our sessions and listen back often. We're very good. We're developing our songs and continue to rehearse. Darren and I get closer as friends, and he moves in with me. Now Darren and me are roommates. I'm curious about his life, and I grow to love him. He's a sweet, intelligent, trustworthy, talented guy. Finally, he sits down with me one day and opens up. Darren tells me part of the reason for his fascination with me is not just because of my musicianship and songwriting ability, but also because from the second I opened the door and he saw my face, he realized he had just met Shawn Mayotte.

Darren: "You're Shawn Mayotte."

Me: "Yeah, I am, so how do you know about that part of my life?"

Darren says he was in his mother and father's bedroom one day and looked under their bed. He found some magazines, and one of them was wrapped tightly, but had obviously been previewed before. The cover was not visible due to the wrapping, and he was curious about this, and because his father had a furious temper, he opened it carefully. It was a gay porno magazine with Shawn Mayotte nudes. He could tell that I was what his father was obsessing over because he had always suspected his father was bisexual. Darren said his Dad looked at young blonde, white boys often when they were together. He was afraid to ask his father about this, and I knew why. I'd been over to Darren's family's house, and although his mother wasn't the nicest person, his father wouldn't even come out to meet me when I visited once.

I met Darren's sisters and mother, but I now wonder what kind of reaction his father would've had if Darren had introduced us.

When I ask Darren what he thought of me, he said he thought I was hot! My room-mate, singer and co-writer in our band is gay. And yet, he's never once made a sexual move on me. I haven't discovered him fondling me when I'm sleeping (I've experienced that un-pleasantness before), and I've never felt uncomfortable around him. I respect him even more. I relate to having a father who futilely attempts to hide his sexual attractions. Why the fuck do they do this? I don't know because I hide what I'm ashamed of also. If I knew, I might not do it too. At least I'm not sexually attracted to children. That separates me from my dad's sickness. But for now, I don't really give Darren's dad's obsession with me another thought. I'm not surprised. He's another Shawn Mayotte fan.

I'm beginning to realize I've got more than I thought. I need to use my fame to do something charitable for the world. I want to see every child on the planet have enough food to eat. That's always been something I've wanted to solve — world hunger. I constantly hear celebrities tell their fans' things like: "For every album of mine you buy; I'll donate $1 to "such and such" charity. How can I do something wonderful for the world using my Shawn Mayotte fame? Maybe I could start a charity, "Plant a tree every time someone buys a photo of me." I don't really care about trees. Maybe it should be more specific. "Every time you cum jacking off to my pictures, a child eats." That doesn't sound right. I don't know how to keep track of how many times a day someone cums anyway, so I forget about it. Darren and I bonded like brothers, and that's never changed. He also introduced me to a creative, talented man who would become one of my best friends ever. James Hajdukiewicz.

I'll never forget when his creativity with scissors raised my self-esteem 1000%. After he cut and styled my hair, I felt like a king. As I walked down Hollywood Blvd., I noticed more people staring at me than ever before.

I met James in 1985. Darren and I were booked to play at a club, and I wanted a new hairstyle that reflected that year. Darren told me about his friend James who was one of the top hairstylists and makeup artists in the world. I was skeptical but Darren was also creative and smart, so I trusted him. He introduced me to James and I instantly felt that I was in the presence of greatness.

James' personality was playful, helpful with a strong work ethic. The most significant life lesson I learned from watching James, was that talent was overrated. His talent was ev-ident. He had no peers, and he was responsible for making some of the biggest stars in the world look beautiful for their entertainment videos and modeling catalogues. But he never bragged or took a break. He worked day and night. He wasn't a talker. James was a doer.

James and I became very close. We were attracted to each other and we both loved smoking weed. James was five years older than me, but he partied like a rock star. He was such a committed workaholic; he could get high and suck a dick while he was styling and coloring my hair. And it didn't matter if I was there, and he was sucking his friend, or if he wanted me to kick back and enjoy his warm mouth.

James was such a huge part of my life when he died of AIDS in 1995. I wrote a song about him. Years later, I found a picture of James and I together and although the memories made me emotional, I decided to write a memorial tribute to him I that I want to share. (You can also find it on The AIDS Memorial).

FOR JAMES:

I was digging through my old pictures and I found this one of my friend James Haj-dukiewicz and I from 1986. James was one of the world's top hair and make-up artists of the 1980's. I miss him, but his impact on me is still palpable today.

His work graced the covers of Cosmopolitan, Vogue, Glamour, and many other fashion magazines. He was the lead makeup artist for the 1984 movie Krushgroove and classic 1980s music videos Sex Cymbal, Dancing on the Ceiling, and many others. He was also the hairstylist and makeup artist to many of the world's top models and Recording Artists of the 1980's, including Prince, Sheila E. Lionel Richie and Billy Preston. James was also the hairstylist and makeup artist for many of the singers who performed in the USA for Africa We are the World video.

He was also a dear friend who would always take the time to "re-style" my hair for whatever band I was playing in. I wrote so many different styles of music that I was creating new bands every month. This picture is of me with the "punk" hairstyle and makeup James had created for me.

I was immediately struck by James' creativity. He had dolls hanging from the ceiling in his apartment, many of them "painted" with James' amazing makeup (Some of them bloody). It was like walking into Disneyland's Haunted Mansion. Many of his clients would call him in the middle of the night and James would rush over and make them beautiful just in time for a photo shoot.In addition to being one of the most Artistic hairstylists I've ever known, James was also an accomplished classical pianist. With all this talent, it was surprising to me what little ego he had. He was ready to jump on stage to help out when a band member couldn't work, and I have fond memories of James taking over an instrument with ease and playing out the set on stage as if he was in the band.

My favorite memories of James were when we hung out together. James would always create my hairstyles in his apartment on Kenmore in East Hollywood, and we had many memorable conversations. We shared joints, laughs, and many wonderful times in his apartment. One thing about James that always stuck with me: His principles.

No matter what famous client he was working with, James refused to gossip. He was privy to a lot of private information that could have harmed many of his client's careers, but you were not gonna hear about it from James. He was trustworthy.

I knew that if he could hold his tongue with regards to his famous client's shenanigans, he could be trusted with my secrets. James was a true friend.

He was styling my hair the night he told me he was diagnosed HIV positive. We were at his apartment in 1992 watching the Republican National Convention on his television. It was a horror show with Pat Buchanan declaring war on America, spewing hate for people who were different than him, reframing it to shape his 1812 view of "family values."

While I was shouting my disgust at the TV, all James would say is "This doesn't sound like family values to me." He was sweet and gentle, and although he did not understand bigotry, he wasn't fooled by Pat's verbal diarrhea.

James got very sick in 1994 and went home to Pittsburgh to be with his family. He died there in 1995. I still remember his words to all of us at his bedside: "Don't feel sorry for me, I've lived a great life. I've done everything I've wanted to do, and everything's going to be fine." I cried and cried, but I turned my tears into a song about him.

James, thank you for sharing your life with me. I was delighted to be invited into your world, and I wish I could hold you and tell you how much you meant to everyone around you; especially me. You knew this life is not a dress rehearsal and you impacted the world more in 35 years than most people do in a 100. I loved you. Rest in peace James. You are not forgotten.

28

Maybe I'm Lovable

1985 turns out to be a transitional year for me. Joe L, a married Insurance Broker from Brea, is in love with me. He is a sweet man, and I empathize with his situation. I'm his therapist and he pays me for listening to him. His wife is cold and detached. He gets no sex from her, they haven't done it in fifteen years. They have two sons. He can't relate to young women, and he's finding himself attracted to young men. I've always wanted to know how someone "finds themselves" doing anything? Isn't it a choice? I've never "found" myself in an alley… I chose to be there. Anyway, I like him. He's kind to me, always complimentary, and although he's a bit cheap compared to my other clients, he's another father figure to me. He also loves hearing me play the piano and guitar.

I first met Joe way back in 1982, when he came to my beachfront apartment to meet Rick Crawford.

Rick is my friend and hustles just like me. He's very good looking, one of the only guys that can compete with me for clients. He looks like a young Jack Wagner. I was letting Rick live with me at the time, and Joe knocked on my front door expecting to meet Rick. I answered the door, and when Joe asked for Rick, I said, "Will I do?" I know it's not cool to steal a client, but I didn't think Joe would fall so hard for me. I figured it would be a singular event. I'd make my money, tell Rick, and he's call Joe and be back to business with him. I never expected Joe to be more emotional than sexual.

These days, Joe travels to my apartment once a week, and is never late, nor does he ever cancel. We'll go out to dinner, come back to my apartment where he listens to me play the piano. He closes his eyes, enraptured by what my fingers on the keys are doing. This is a man who loses himself in music. I love being the person who is giving him his musical escape. He also loves to hear me play my songs on the guitar. Sometimes I entertain him on the rocks at the far west end of Long Beach. I strum the guitar, sometimes making the songs up on the spot, and we look out onto the water, feeling the cool sea breeze together, as I sing and play. He immerses himself in the experience. In between songs, we talk about how I can write songs and get them recorded by artists and still work to pay my rent. I'm not making as much money escorting, as I've narrowed down the ones I see to a few VIP's, Of course, I like to keep my options open. If the price is right…

Joe tells me I could obtain a California Real Estate License and sell Real Estate while I'm writing songs. I don't know anything about Real Estate, I'm only nineteen years old, I didn't even graduate from high school, but he suggests the idea to me as if it's the solution. I don't like to sell anything except myself. Joe says I need to take the California Real Estate Exam to get my license. I'm just a vagabond who writes music and wants to fuck all the time. But he keeps throwing dollar amounts in my face. I forgot about that part. I want money as much as I want to fuck. I listen to one of my surrogate dads. I've only spoken to my biological father five times since I was released to the streets. Once, when I was seventeen and living on my own, he wanted to claim that I was living with him for tax purposes. The second time was when he gave me a porno tape for my eighteenth birthday. I forgot he called to get it back because Ginger Lynn was in it. That was the fourth.

The fifth time was when I had all of my musical equipment, most of my clothes, and my Datsun Z car stolen in front of Darren's friend James' house in Hollywood. I was getting my hair cut by James, and I had my Yamaha DX-7 keyboards, my guitars, and my $4,000 Linn drum machine in the car parked outside of James' apartment. In addition to my musical equipment, I also had the majority of my washable clothes stuffed into a laundry bag because I was heading to the Laundromat after the session. My Z was stuffed to the point I could barely fit into the driver seat.

When I came out of James' apartment, and saw an empty space in front of the curb where my car was. The voice in my head pounced on the occasion, and immediately I was paralyzed by the palpable sound of it reveling in my calamity. It gleefully reminded me how stupid I am — how I was facing life with nothing now, because I had no car insurance. So, this was my fault. Everything is my fault. I didn't buy insurance because….I don't know why…fuck you…I can't explain it. Does it matter? Some motherfuckers stole my car and got everything I worked for, including my musical instruments, the car, and most of my clothes. This is a war in my head. How the fuck is that my fault? No matter what, it is. Now, in an instant, I have no car, no musical instruments, and no clothes. And they're all gone forever.

James is horrified, but he's got another client to make beautiful for their music video. Though he's glad I paid him for my haircut because most of Darren's friends expect freebies, he has to move fast. He'll give me a ride home, but that doesn't solve much. Maybe at home I can cry. I want to cry, but I shut off that mechanism a long time ago. But I still need to find a solution. The only person I think of calling is Joe Lauro. He's so loving, he won't question why I don't have insurance. And that's even though he's a car insurance salesman! John Thompson would lecture me and be disappointed.

I've got to call Joe now. I use James' phone, and Joe answers immediately. He listens to me describe my predicament, and rushes out of his office in Orange County, driving 50 miles to Hollywood, and picks me up. He realizes how life altering this catastrophe is, and angrily exclaims his hatred of thieves.

"God, I hate thieves! When they do things like this, they steal more than property. They steal hope. Those people never think about how their actions affect so many lives."

Yeah, I know. I'm the one with nothing. I have a home, but since Jamie stole my truck, the only transportation I had was my Datsun Z. Now, I have no car. And no musical instruments – no tools to work. I'm thankful I still have my eight-and-a-half-inch tool, but I'm no good for sessions or my band if I have no instruments or a car.

After Joe has finished his anti-thieve tirade, he tells me I should call my father. I'm shocked that he'd even suggest this.

"My father's not going to help me. That's crazy to think that he would. "

Joe says he'd help, but he can't give me enough money to purchase a car. I have no credit, and no verifiable income. The two wealthiest men I know, I'm hesitant to call because I get money from them all the time. They are my regular job, but it's the wrong time to ask. I don't know what to do, and I'm scared.

Joe says to me, "He's your father! He hasn't been there for you one time in your whole life. Even he has to know you've been on your own since you were twelve years old, and you've never asked him for a dime. He should be able to see that. He's your father. He'll understand."

Excuse me? You obviously don't know my father. I adamantly refuse to call my father. I know him. You don't. Joe insisted, and "threatened" to call my dad himself if I didn't. Go right ahead. Joe said he would call him from his office the next day. And he did. I told him to call me immediately after he spoke to my father. And he did.

I answered the phone. "Hello?"

"It's Joe."

"Did you talk to my dad?"

Joe is silent.

"Joe?"

Joe says, while crying, "I've never spoken to a colder individual in my entire life."

"I told you. What did he say?"

"I introduced myself, and I said I was a close friend of your son, and he said nothing, which made me feel uncomfortable."

"Yeah, that's how he is. Go on…"

"I told him that your car was stolen and said you had worked very hard to buy that car on your own; and you also had your musical instruments stolen."

And…

"I don't even want to repeat what he said. Doug, I know this man left you to rot in Boys' Homes, I know he's never helped you in any way, I also know he makes a good living as an Engineer at Borg Warner Corporation. So, I was shocked at what he said."

"What did he say?" I'm still shocked to hear that he actually spoke to my dad.

"He said, and I quote: "Doug needs to learn to live within his means. And it's obvious from what you've told me, that he doesn't do that. So, no, I'm not helping him. If Doug has problems, he has to learn how to figure them out on his own. Don't call me again.""

"He said a lot more in your conversation than I've ever heard him say in one of ours. I hate to say I told you so, but I told you so."

Joe starts crying again, and now I'm uncomfortable. I don't even know why I feel uncomfortable around a man who's crying for me. I just know I need to calm him down. I fucking need help. In the last year, I've started to spend a lot of money rather than saving it like I did the very first year I was on my own. I didn't think this kind of catastrophe would happen to me; all in five minutes. I thought car insurance was a scam – what the fuck do I know, maybe there's a reason for it. The rates they quoted me were outrageous, but maybe I should have had it. I'm an idiot. Carless, instrumentless, and clothesless.

I know I need to call people. Joe has convinced me to make those calls, and he's convinced me to obtain a California Real Estate License. I don't need convincing to know I need to buy musical equipment. Without a car, or musical equipment, I'm worthless. I do remember the whole point of going back in time to tell the story of my car being stolen. That was to let you know about the fourth time I spoke to my father. And I actually didn't speak to him. I've always known there's no point to having a conversation with him. Now it's time for me to call people who might help.

Fortunately, help arrives from my gay dads. But I have to buy a car with all cash. My cash reserves have been dwindling since I've become accustomed to earning money quickly. I've spent a lot on nice clothes, food, musical equipment, and other vices. But I need a car. Nobody walks in LA. I don't want payments, and I wouldn't qualify for a loan anyway. What job description would I give them, Professional Prostitute? Pleasure delivery service? And I don't have any paycheck stubs. That's your world. I buy a Ford Escort after combining $4,000 I have stashed away, along with another $3,500 from John Thompson, Joe Lauro, and my newest mentor, Arthur Travis. Arthur is the man Kent's been hounding me to meet for a long time. He's that big shot Wall Street tycoon who is in love with everything Shawn Mayotte. I finally meet him at Kent's house, and he's cute like a giddy child.

"On my God, it's such a thrill to meet you Shawn. Please, is there anything I can do for you?"

Of course, there is. That's what I'm here for, so, you can do for me. I know I've got what you want, so I'll gladly make that trade. Arthur only wants personal pictures for himself the first time we meet. That's why we're meeting at Kent's house. They are pictures of the same – me, naked, cock hard, standing up, sitting down, etc. – and this personal photo session for George is worth it. George hands me $2,000 when we're done. Now I'm the giddy one.

This is also the time when Joe Lauro convinces me to study for my California Real Estate License. I've left Dial Precision, the machine shop, and I want to be able to have income and continue to pursue getting my songs recorded. It's a confusing time for me. It's 1985. I've left a menial job that had no purpose, I'm now studying for a Real Estate License that mirrors my stupidity in making the choice to operate a lathe for money. I have a couple of rich dads who now greet me with thousands; but my destiny is in the hands of a psychologically disturbed twenty-year-old fraud: me.

Whatever you want to call me: Doug Probst, Shawn Mayotte, Dirk, Perfect dick, Asshole, musician, narcissist, nice guy, tantrum thrower, Dreamer, Caged Animal with more rage inside than your world can fathom — whoever I am, I'm just wandering around, listening to men who care because I look good. I believe some of them really do care, but what do I know? I'm fucking lost.

It's weird. I'm twenty years old. Kent keeps hounding me for another photo shoot. Arthur Travis has appeared and I'm now a few thousand dollars richer every three weeks when he travels to Los Angeles for our monthly meeting at the Roosevelt Hotel. I finally know why Kent also hounded me to meet George. He expected a "finder's fee." Fuck you, Kent. You can take your finder's fee and shove it up your ass. I'm the one you're using to make ten times the money you've paid me, you greedy piece of shit. I'm a piece of meat to you. I don't mind being a piece of meat to men like John Thompson or Arthur Travis (aka Travis) because they value me and treat me with respect. You're a bottom feeder.

I follow Joe L.'s advice and I study for my California Real Estate License. It's 1985 and the only requirement to get a License to sell Real Estate is to pass a 200-question test. I have no idea what's on this test. Like I said before, I only reached the 7th grade in your world, so I'm a bit unprepared. But I like the challenge. I decide to study. Studying for the Real Estate exam consists of obtaining 100 practice tests and taking them over and over until I achieve at least 85%. They're tests with questions that appear on the official State test. They're mixed up, so I need to take these tests multiple times. I also buy the California Real Estate book of…California Real Estate. I like to read and learn about almost anything, so this isn't a chore for me.

Laura's really helpful to me in this new endeavor of mine. She goes to the library with me and helps correct my practice tests. I'm apprehensive and I worry this will all be in vain. These tests have many geometry questions, which baffle me. (The highest level of math I know is fractions.) I just keep plugging along, taking practice test after practice test. Laura and Joe L. are extremely encouraging to me. Joe L. comes to the library with me on many occasions. I continue on until I finally start passing many of the practice tests. I'm gaining confidence as I surpass my own expectations and begin to score 90% on every practice test. They're getting excited for me. I don't want to analyze too much, but it's fascinating how Joe L. (who is in love with me), and Laura (who is also in love with me), are sitting side by side at a circular table in the Long Beach Public Library. I wonder what they're really in love with, though. I'm an older guy to Laura, and I'm a younger man to Joe. It's a great day to be me.

I nervously walk into the room where they're conducting the California Real Estate License Exam. It's an old classroom that has a musty smell, as if it's rarely been cleaned. The chairs are scrunched together, and they sit behind large tables.

There is about a hundred people in this classroom with me. Randy's lover, Chris is also taking his Real Estate License Exam. Chris manages properties and has been involved with Real Estate much longer than I have, so I expect he'll pass. I sit down at my seat and listen to the instructor give the obligatory speech about not cheating, wishing us good luck, and to use the materials provided to us. It's all kind of a blah blah sound, like when Charlie Brown's parents talked in those Peanuts cartoons. I'm ready to go. It cost me money and time to get here, so I'm very prepared. I become confident as I realize the practice tests are paying off. At about 30 questions in, I'm becoming certain I'll pass. I've become familiar with many questions, and I know what an easement is, and what encumbered means. Even the math questions are not intimidating. I've done my homework, and I feel good. The time is still slow, but I'm the third one to finish the test. I look back and see a flustered look on Chris's face. I feel sorry for him, but at the same time, I don't really like him — I've caught him in many lies, but now I wonder if he'll pass. It's more important that I pass, but since my brain changes course in a nanosecond, I walk out of the class, barely hearing from the instructor that we'll have our results sent to us in two weeks.

Everything is fucking slow. I'm on my way out the door to go fuck Laura until she's sore. The only reason I do things that matter to your world, is to fake my way through, so I can do what really matters to me: Fuck, make money instantly, and sometimes play my piano and guitar. Fuck everything else. I'm not interested in what your world offers in forms of relaxation. I got mine.

Two weeks later, I get my results. I passed! Apparently, I'm one of only three people out of 101 others who passed the California Real Estate Exam. I wonder if it was the first three of us who turned in our test. Joe L. tells me that Chris failed. I do feel bad for him. No matter how much I don't like someone, I don't wish failure upon them. I always hope they change for the better. But I think about their flaws a lot. I've got a few of my own. I just brush those off. I guess it's easier to concentrate on the flaws other people have, rather than examine my own. I passed your world's Real Estate Exam without attending high school. It's definitely your world that's flawed.

As 1985 ends, Laura and I are fighting regularly. I can't help it if she's a lying bitch. I can't control Laura, and it's eating me up inside. Everywhere we go, there we are: fighting. I'd love to beat the shit out of her, but I won't, because I'd never hit a girl. But it still crosses my mind.

I caught her lying to me, and then her best friend Stefanie (who I fucked) tipped me off that Laura was at a motel and had stayed the night there fucking her brains out with another guy. As Stefanie tells me about it, I feel a strange physical paradox coming over me. I feel jealously enraged and yet intensely sexually excited at the same time. How can this be? I don't know, all I know is my dick's getting hard, and yet I'm fucking pissed because my grandiose self-image has been destroyed, as all things superficial eventually do. I ask Stefanie for details: Did she suck his dick? Did he eat her out? And while she tells me, I'm thinking of jacking off. I'm sure Stefanie knows, as I've fucked around with her. You see, it's okay that I fuck Laura's girlfriends, but it's not ok that she fucks other guys. Well, maybe if I could watch.

What the fuck is wrong with me? I don't know... Isn't something wrong with all of us? I'm the narcissist here. How can I be aroused and jealous at the same time? Stefanie's already fucked me, but I'm supposed to be angry about this. And I am. Laura really fucked up. I've got to get to that motel and teach Laura a lesson. I'm not sure what lesson I'm teaching, but I'm not gonna be disrespected on this level by anyone, especially my girlfriend whose cherry I popped.

Stefanie gives me the address of the motel where Laura is. This proves she's spent the night there. I've tried since last night to get on the phone, and she has not answered. How dare she lie to me, and actually stay in a motel overnight? Not only is she risking our relationship, she's also underage, and I'm sure her parents are worried and angry. She's fifteen years old. Her one-eyed father already challenged me to a fight on his front lawn; I only backed off because I felt sorry for him. He had his right eyeball cut out in a barroom fight in his younger years. I guess you're never too old to be stupid. It's easy to deduce why Laura has "issues." Her parents are clueless. Still, they have the power. And they exercise it.

I break down the door to Laura's motel room, grab her by the hair, and drag her on the floor out the broken door to my car. I yell at her while she cries in the car. I race to her house and open the passenger door and push her to her front lawn. She's crying that she's sorry and begs me to take her back. But her mother runs out into the yard, snatches Laura and tries valiantly to take her inside their house. Of course, I'm feeling vindicated and omnipotent. I start my car and rev the engine loudly. I'm racing to my apartment. I feel uneasy but proud of myself for not giving in. Soon, I hear banging at my door. It's Laura!

She's screaming that she's sorry. I'm so filled with my own self-righteousness, there's no room in my heart for compassion. She screams to no avail. As I tell her to go home, I peek through the door and see blood on her wrists. To me, it's not much blood, and I seriously doubt she's really trying to kill herself. I mock her. It feels good to be angry. I'm justified. She lied to me. How dare she think I'd feel sorry for her. I don't feel any compassion. Again, I'm justified, and again, I got fucked by your world. I trusted her, and she lied to me. Your world has always lied to me. Where was the compassion when I was getting beat in the face by my child raping father? Why didn't your world "step in" and save me from getting beat up by the Crips in Los Padrinos Juvenile Hall? Where was my share of your world's compassion when I was getting raped by George at Sunrise Community Youth Home?

I'm justified in feeling nothing for Laura. But then I hear another voice. It's her friend, an older girl who has come to Laura's rescue. She's yelling at me through the door, calling me a "heartless piece of shit." I open the door and tell her to fuck off. She grabs Laura and hurriedly takes her away, all the time looking back at me hatefully, as if I'm the devil. Unexpectedly, I begin to feel disconnected from my anger. Her words reverberate in my head. I don't like this feeling. I instinctively know what's coming next: Demoralizing paralytic guilt.

I don't know the girl's name, but her words affected me. Slowly, almost imperceptibly, I realize what I've done. I neglected to help a scared little girl when she needed me the most. I did the very thing that's been done to me over and over. She was screaming out to me: "Help me, I need you, I'm sorry." Everything gets dark. I can't think, and I begin to quiver. I shake and start to lose my balance. I lose my balance and go down to the floor. I'm looking up from the carpet. What happened? I fell from my rightness perch.

The world is spinning. Guilt has seized my heart, mind, and soul. The voice pounces: You're no fucking good. Why don't you just repeat after me? I'm no fucking good. I'm no fucking good. I'm so bad, I'd let a fifteen-year-old girl die because I'm mad at her. I'm no good! I've got no right to live. I should die for how I've treated her. I'm more than wrong. It was wrong for me to be born.

I look outside for Laura and she's gone. Fuck it, I've got to get to her. I've got to tell her I'm sorry. So fucking sorry. I race over to her house. Her friend's car is out in front. Great! At least I know she's there. I slam on my brakes in front of Laura's house. As soon as I exit my vehicle, I see her one-eyed father struggling to break free from the grip of two women: His wife and the girl who brought Laura to their house. He's yelling at me. As bad as I feel, I immediately revert into combat mode. Her father stares at me coldly. I stare right back, "mad dogging" him. I'm always a sucker for a mad dogger. The more he stares, the more I feel provoked. Then it occurs to me: I'm mad dogging a blind man. How lame is it to believe you're being stared down by a blind grandpa? I quickly come to my guilt-ridden senses, and I beg Laura to come outside so I can help her. I can see she wants to come to me from the window, but she's being held back by her sister, Sheri. I'm helpless.

How could I have done this to the poor girl? I'm self-righteous and it's backfired on me. I take shit too far. And this is always the end result. I'm tumbling from my rightness perch fast. I'm crying like a baby. I'm no good. I could have saved Laura from heartache and pain, but I chose to hammer the nail right through her heart. Now I'm the one needing mercy. I park down the street from her parents' house that first night and cry myself to sleep in my car. It's funny how my shiny car means nothing at this moment. As much as I love my money and possessions, they can't fill this hole in my heart. I'd give everything away if I could another chance to help Laura when she was cutting herself. My God! Where are you now? Maybe I'm doomed because I've said I don't believe in God. But tonight, I'm on knees promising that fucker anything to have Laura back in my arms. I'm not only dishonorable and weak, but I'm also a hypocrite. I hurt.

I drive back to Laura's house the next day, only to find the house empty. I go home and call a friend of mine who knows the family. He tells me they've placed Laura into a Psychiatric Hospital on Paramount Blvd, La Casa Mental Health. She's not getting out of there for a while. I feel horrible hearing this, as I can relate. I was placed into Mental Hospitals by my parents too. I've been there, and now I'm the reason a frightened young girl is in one. None of this is part of my plan. What the fuck is my plan? I'm so disoriented by my emotions that I forget everything I'm supposed to do to make a living.

I don't report to my Real Estate Office: Bay Cities Realty on Long Beach Blvd. I don't return phone calls to musicians. I don't return calls to investors. I'm paralyzed. I park my car out in front of La Casa every night during the month of September 1985. I cry and play the radio, contemplating how I can break her out of there. It seems like on the radio every night I hear "You give good love" by this new singer named Whitney Houston. The song is a constant reminder of the fairytale love Laura and I have. Every night, the same routine: I park on Paramount Blvd., turn off the car, but keep the radio on, and they play "You give good love." I'm an emotional wreck. I'm a fucking mess. But I always have been. I just know how to hide it.

After a week of this, I slowly realize I'm getting nowhere. Crying about a situation I have no control over isn't getting me anywhere. But it doesn't stop me. I still obsess over it. It hurts to know what a bastard I really am. It hurts not to have Laura to say I love you too. It hurts to be me. So, what else is new?

One morning I wake up. I mean, I really wake up from this nightmare. What the fuck am I doing? I'm a talented musician. I'm attractive and young. I'm desired by both men and women. I can find someone else. I'm twenty years old and I've already played music with Billy Preston. I'm better than nearly every musician I've come into contact with. I don't give a fuck if you call this ego or whatever, this is ridiculous. I'm pussy-whipped on a little girl.

Maybe I don't have to buy into the voice. Fuck the voice in my head.

29

Becoming a Centerfold

At the same time, Kent tells me that my nude photos will appear next month in a men's magazine called In Touch. It'll be their 'end of the year Christmas edition' and I'll be the centerfold. That's exciting! I wonder what opportunities being a nude centerfold will lead to. I'm happy to hear this. I wonder if any of the men who are now my colleagues at Bay Cities Realty are in the closet. I'll find out next month when the Christmas issue of In Touch magazine arrives in the bookstores.

During this time, I also attend a football game at Jordan High School in North Long Beach. I hear a familiar voice a couple of rows above us. I turn around and see Laura sitting there with her friends, Stephanie, and the one that hates me. I don't know how to feel, as I still feel a bit guilty, and I don't know if Laura hates me now. I notice a big smile appear on Laura's face as we lock eyes. She's happy to see me. Is this some kind of hypnotizing hold I have over girls? Naw, she's just as lonely and screwed up as I am. Seeing her grin at me makes me feel good inside. I'm happy she's looking at me with love and lust again. I vacillate between gratitude and dismissive. I know I should be grateful, but my arrogance will have none of it. She still wants me. And I still want her. Until I don't. But just like two dysfunctional people, we decided to get back together.

Finally, when the Christmas issue of In Touch magazine has been released. I walk into a bookstore, proceed over to the dirty magazine section, and voila! Oh my God. I usually hear other people say that when I drop my pants, but now I'm being heard loudly in this store "Oh my God."

I'm staring at myself with angst and bewilderment. I'm proud to see myself on the cover of a magazine, but I'm insecure at the same time. On the outside I show happiness, but on the inside I'm very critical. My hair is too dark, my chest reveals a scar I wear from working out so heavily, and I don't have a smile on my face. I also don't like the pose they chose. But someone decided I looked good enough to sell the magazine by gracing its cover. I'm grateful.

I was unprepared psychologically to handle the fame that came with being a centerfold.

There was a strange dichotomy about it. I didn't think it was a big deal, but I couldn't help basking in the glory of being treated like the king riding my golden chariot waving at my adoring fans.

Everywhere I traveled during 1986, I was recognized by someone who'd seen this issue of In Touch Magazine. I was an overnight star in San Francisco and Los Angeles. I visited San Francisco in the spring of 1986 and as I strolled down Castro Street, men were asking me to autograph their copy of The December 1985 issue of In Touch. I was flattered and of course I signed. I had no idea how much I meant to them. When I came back to Los Angeles, I wanted to sign copies for my friends who were dying of AIDS.

These were not sad moments. I loved my men, and it gave me great pleasure to bring them happiness before they died. I felt somewhat ashamed of being famous for my nakedness, but those thoughts were quickly dismissed when I saw the joy men were receiving from seeing me. I fought every shameful feeling with all the self-esteem I could muster without medication. I loved walking into Adult Film Stores and seeing myself displayed in places like Circus Books in West Hollywood or Mission News in San Francisco.

It felt good to know that I was bringing happiness to men and women. I wanted to be known for my music, but this was satisfying in its own peculiar way.

When I came down from my high of being recognized for my cock and body, life showed up and I had to deal with reality. I kept making money through escorting, meeting, and pleasuring many famous clients. It was my job, but I started loving it.

And no one in the straight world knows.

3 0

My 21st Birthday Party

On January 20th, 1986, I get a phone call from my mother. It's surprising to hear her voice on the other end of a telephone line. She doesn't sound drunk. That's surprising, and to get a phone call from her is very unusual. I never hear from her. Maybe she's finally stopped drinking. She tells me that she wants to have a party for my twenty-first birthday at her house. She sounds excited about this. I'm mildly amused, but deep down inside, I crave attention from her. She called me. And she doesn't ask for money? I'm shocked, but I'm also happy. It's been a while since I've talked to her. I don't know how many chances I'll have to spend with my mother, and my birthday is two months away, April 1st. Maybe she's finally getting herself together. Maybe she wants to apologize for her bad choices and create some happiness. Maybe I finally have a mom.

I'm completely uninterested in selling real estate. I walk into the office of Bay Cities Realty and sit down at my desk. I'm completely baffled as to what I'm supposed to do. I'm a cynical prostitute who's supposed to be a happy salesman. This is unreal. I have no idea how to turn my cynicism into salesmanship. I don't want to be here. But I'm an automaton. Just what I've always dreamed of: Wearing a yellow vest and representing Century 21. Fuck that. Are there any rebellious real estate offices that have rock stars working there?

I want a different job, but the applications always ask about my former "occupation." Does beauty need a resume'?

I tell my colleagues at the Bay Cities Realty that I have a birthday party coming up. There's a new guy named Tim Santa I'd like to impress. He just got his license, so he's even more of a newbie than I am. I want to invite Tim and my other Real Estate cronies to my birthday party. I'm not sure who I want to impress more — my real estate buddies, or my mother and Robert's friends. But I want to have my new professional friends enjoy my party. My mother hasn't showed this much interest in me in a long time, and I want so badly to believe that this party is something that will be fun and sane. I choose to trust her.

I choose to keep my gay family separate. I don't know how to invite my gay friends to a party where the majority of people attending would judge them. It wouldn't just be my mother, Robert and his gangster friends, my real estate friends, my Lakewood friends, everybody at the party would treat them with scorn. I guess my mother's love is still more important to me than revealing who my true friends are. I make a list of all my friends that I'm going to invite.

Terry, my real estate office friend, Laura, and her friends, and also other girls I've had sex with, but I'm friends with first. There's so many. I make sure I only invite the girls I know who won't cause trouble. Of course, most of the girls I've gone out with aren't mentally unstable. I'm starting to figure out that the one I continue to be obsessed with is the liar, cheater, and the most mentally unstable: Laura. There could be 100 stable, calm, compassionate, trustworthy women in one room, and I'll be attracted to the only mentally unstable, vindictive, lying, cheating backstabber there. Go figure.

They arrive along with my other friends and began to drink and commiserate. The party progressed and then digressed. Soon, there was loud screaming from the backyard. Many of us rushed outside only to find my mother's boyfriend Robert stabbing another man in the pool. There were two other Norwalk gangsters who were assisting in attempting to murder this man, and the pool was turning red as if someone had their leg bitten off by a shark.

I don't remember the three men who jumped in, but one was a real estate colleague, and they wrestled the knife away from Robert, pulled the man out and began CPR. Robert and his friends ran away, jumped into his truck and sped off. But that wasn't the end of the circus.

My mother had drank herself into a stupor and began calling me a faggot in front of my friends. My girlfriend Laura had cornered my friend Terry N. and was heard begging him to fuck her. Alcohol is literally a motherfucker. My mother heard her, broke down the bathroom door, grabbed Laura by her blond hair and dragged her into the shower, turning on cold water to "sober her up."

By this time, the Lakewood Sheriff's had been called and a police helicopter was loudly hovering over the roof of the house. About seven cop cars rolled up in front of my mother's house and they began shouting through bullhorns "Everyone come out with your hands on clasped together on top of your heads."

I came out followed by my real estate colleagues and the rest of the guests who weren't inebriated. To say I was embarrassed is the understatement of the century. We were ordered by shotgun wielding deputies to drop to our knees with our hands still clasped together on our heads. On my left side. I was next to Tim Santa, a new agent in my office, and on my right side was Ken Friedlander, one of the old timers. Both of them were wearing suits and expensive ties and they looked very uncomfortable on their knees.

This was more than I could bear. Embarrassed, I said to both of them, "This has never happened before, I'm so sorry about this you guys."

A Lakewood Sheriff's deputy with a shotgun pointed at our heads overheard me and laughed out loud replying: "Bullshit. We get called to this house at least twice a month. Peggy and Robert are notorious in Lakewood. We've had this house under surveillance many times due to the criminal activity that goes on here."

That was the final demarcation point for me. I made the decision then and there to never speak to my mother again. I wrote her a six-page letter, mostly filled with "Fuck yous" and vowed she'd never hear from me again. I didn't hear from her either.

Three girls true lifelong friends

It was in 1986 that I met a girl who was to become my closest friend for life: Krista

166

Petty. I met her in the Cerritos Mall, and we became instant friends. She was younger than me, but she had also been thrown out onto the street by her mother. I offered to let her live with me, but she was determined to make it on her own. That impressed me. Not only was she gorgeous, but she was also an independent thinker and doer. Just like me. We had so much in common it was scary. My two favorite Elton John songs "Harmony" and "Someone saved my life tonight" were also her favorite Elton songs. I loved it when she'd come to my apartment in Long Beach and I'd play the piano for her. She would look at me as if my piano playing made all her troubles disappear for a while. We also loved the same recording artists such as Prince and Elton. Our friendship is still going strong. I still see her off and on today. It's a relationship I cherish with all my heart.

I was also friends with the mother of a girl I had lusted after since grade school in Bellflower: Grace Reid. I became friends with her mother, Barbara Reid, after I was on my own. Barbara was like the mother I never had. She would come to my apartment and listen to my hatred for my parents with love and compassion. But I really wanted to meet Grace. Grace visited me once in San Pedro, and I could barely contain myself from not kissing her and doing more because she was so hot. She treated me with love too, and listened to me play her my songs, replying: "I can't wait to come see you in concert Doug. You're gonna be huge." I loved her for believing in me. I still love her and see her today when we can.

Later, I met a lovely girl named Marcela Tovar. I met her in a class at Los Angeles City College when we both were studying Psychology. We were attracted to each other physically, but she had tender, deep emotions that I sensed, and I couldn't help but love her. She and I made love, but our friendship was stronger. When she had trouble at home, I helped her move into her first apartment. It was wonderful to see her enjoy her independence. Marcy is one of the most special people I've ever known. We watched both of our first-born sons grow up. Later, when I started chasing a drug more than I chased her, she still supported me and loved me, hoping that I'd change. It took a long time, and she's never stopped loving me – even the unlovable Doug whom I know still exists, but I work on him every day. Marcy, please know that I will always love you as one of the greatest friends I've ever had, and I'm always here for you, just as I was in the beginning.

It was also around this time I heard that my friend Little Richard had ran his car into a tree on Sunset Blvd. He was seriously injured and was in the hospital. I hadn't seen him in a while, so off I went, bringing along a card and a little piano cupcake.

I spent a fair amount of time with Little Richie, so I knew how brash and annoyingly outrageous he could be. But even I wasn't prepared for what I was about to see.

When I entered Little Richie's room, I noticed his right leg being held up in a harness with a cast on it. But I also noticed the bed was moving. I walked in and said, "Hey Richie!" and immediately noticed he was masturbating furiously. And he wasn't gonna allow me to interrupt.

"Put the card on the table. I'm about to cum!" He shouted.

I looked at the TV and I saw a blond man fucking a black man in the ass in beautiful color. The blond man was ramming the other guy hard and he pulled his cock out, exploding at the same time Little Richie did. He then asked me to wipe him up. I didn't mind. So, I wiped the cum off of Little Richard's cock and made sure he was all cleaned up and we had a great visit.

31

Embracing Life and Death

Although January 1987 starts off with the usual butcher's bill listing how many more of my friends have lost their lives to AIDS, I begin to make decisions that enhance and enrich my life. Although I still feel like an outsider in your world, these past couple of years I've come to realize I may not be the problem after all. The experience of my twenty-first birthday party taught me a lot. My mother was responsible for the mayhem, not me. Since living on my own, I haven't been arrested or locked up. Maybe I'm making good choices on my own. Maybe it wasn't me that was a threat to society. I've proven to myself that when I'm in charge of my own life, I don't end up in custody. And better choices lead to higher self-esteem.

I decide to volunteer down at AIDS Project Los Angeles. I had been there at its inception in 1983, but I didn't stay. I'm a newbie at volunteering my time at any organization, so I don't know what to expect. I'm very surprised at how overwhelmed APLA is, and how much they desperately need volunteers.

It was simultaneously heartwarming and heartbreaking. Comforting, feeding and nursing dying men was sad but gratifying. The buddy program was critical in these early days. We helped clients with AIDS complete daily tasks, we interacted with them, motivating them to participate in games and social activities. Sometimes I just sat and held their hands, to let them know someone cared. I volunteered to take meals into the hospital rooms of AIDS patients when the hospital staff were too frightened to be near them, and left trays outside the door.

One volunteer I had the pleasure to meet and who made a profound impression on me was Elizabeth Taylor. She wasn't as big a deal to me as it would have been had I bagged groceries next to Paul McCartney, but I knew she was a big deal. She was funny and down to earth. Many times, I was fortunate to bag and deliver groceries with her. I could see how starstruck the men were to know Liz Taylor bring food into their homes. Some of these men were blind and suffered from multiple infections, but they lit up when they knew Liz was in their home. She treated every person the same and I saw her express sincere love to men who desperately needed to know people cared about them.

The medicine was so pathetically crude and useless. Pentamidine and Isoprinosine, were keeping people alive for a week or two. And of course, all the hucksters were out there selling vitamin anti-aids formulas that did nothing but let you die with vitamin enriched blood. The most pathetic part of this was that doctors were giving this shit to their dying patients. That's all they had. There was no rush on the government's part to research new life saving therapies and it angered me. The government acted like my parents. It was republican, ignorant, bigoted and hateful. It lied. But It was what I didn't see that angered me the most. I didn't see any government programs being initiated to help people with AIDS.

Of course, many things angered me. A lot of the time, just being angry made me feel good. Anger without a plan to eradicate what's making you angry serves no one. I was learning.

Sometimes when an APLA worker finally convinced a government disability worker that AIDS was a disability, by the time they were convinced and approved, the person with AIDS had already died. I saw this happen over and over.

I heard about a group called ACT UP started by my hero Larry Kramer. Larry was an American playwright, author, and film producer, who, because of witnessing the deaths of so many friends from AIDS, became a public health advocate, and LGBT rights activist.

In 1978, Larry Kramer introduced a controversial and confrontational style of writing in his novel Faggots, which earned emphatic denunciations from elements within the gay community. Larry's portrayal of what he characterized as shallow, promiscuous gay relationships in the 1970s alienated his own people. Larry presciently predicted AIDS two years before it arrived in New York City and began killing his friends. He shouts loudly his frustration with what he sees as the sex obsessive NYC gay community, "If we don't stop fucking all the time, we're gonna fuck ourselves to death."

He co-founded the Gay Men's Health Crisis (GMHC), which has become the world's largest private organization assisting people living with AIDS. Larry grew frustrated with bureaucratic paralysis and the apathy of gay men to the AIDS crisis and wished to engage in further action than the social services GMHC provided.

In 1983 he wrote one of the greatest essays on AIDS in history: 1,112 and counting. I remember reading it in The New York Native. He threw hand grenades while everyone else lobbed softballs. He wrote: "I am sick of guys who moan that giving up careless sex until this blows over is worse than death. How can they value life so little and cocks and asses so much? Come with me, guys, while I visit a few of our friends in Intensive Care at NYU. Notice the looks in their eyes, guys. They'd give up sex forever if you could promise them life."

That line hit me the hardest. It was exactly how I felt while watching my friends die. I didn't know what to do, but Larry did. From then on, I followed everything he did.

He expressed his frustration by writing a play titled The Normal Heart, produced at The Public Theater in New York City in 1985.

His political activism continued with the founding of the AIDS Coalition to Unleash Power (ACT UP) in 1987, an influential direct action protest organization with the aim of gaining more public action to fight the AIDS crisis. I was angry but still living mostly for myself. ACT UP was an angry plan of action. ACT UP stood up. They have been widely credited with changing public health policy and the perception of people living with AIDS, and with raising awareness of HIV and AIDS-related diseases.

They wanted research and medicine that would save men's lives, and they weren't putting up with the government's indifference to the plight of gay men anymore.

I wondered how they were going to change things, but I trusted that Larry Kramer cared enough to do it. I already knew that it's passion that matters more than any other virtue except courage. There's no stopping you if you combine both for your cause. If you don't give a fuck, then you might as well kill yourself, because no one else gives a fuck either.

3 2

Transition

In early 1987, I received another call from Kent (Kurt Detrick) about doing another photo shoot. Escorting was much more lucrative. I was making a ton of money seeing Arthur Travis every two weeks, so it didn't interest me. When Kent said that he would pay me $1000 and introduce me to more wealthy benefactors, I listened.

When he sees me, he's surprised to see how much muscle I've amassed since our last session.

He really likes my transition from smooth twink in 1983, to centerfold stud in 1985, to muscle man in 1987.

1987 is a transitional year for me. I'm starting to like myself. I start a relationship with a psychologist who listens to me, encourages me to self-examine, and slowly I realize I have intrinsic self-worth. I don't mean to insinuate that suddenly I've had a self-esteem transplant, but I do work on myself to feel better about me.

I also begin to write introspective music that's therapeutic, including a piano ballad that expressed my hurt feelings that my mother didn't remember or care enough to break the silence between us and at least send me a card to wish me a happy twenty-third birthday. Even a phone call from her would've softened my heart, but that call never came. I had written the song on my upright Kawai piano in my Long Beach apartment.

I now had a really nice apartment on Redondo Avenue near 4th Street. It's a spacious one bedroom and I fill it with real plants and some antique furniture. I love looking out onto Redondo Avenue from my balcony. I can walk to the beach, yet I still live in a big city atmosphere. And my Kawai piano was all I needed to comfort me when I was down.

I was very influenced by the master power ballad writers/producers like David Foster, Michael Masser, Tom Kelly and many others who wrote for Chicago, Whitney Houston, Heart, Peabo Bryson, etc.

I think the one that captured my attention the most was "I want to know what love is" by Mick Jones and Foreigner. I was blown away by that song's sincere beauty and sentiment. I could relate to the lyrics. I want to know what love is too. And not just from a woman. I want to know what love is, period. It was also masterfully produced. "You're the inspiration" by Chicago was another one I couldn't get enough of. 'Through the fire" written by David Foster & Will Jennings and sung by Chaka Khan was a masterpiece I obsessed over.

With most of these songs, I connected with the music more than the lyrics. I would say to people, "It's the music business, not the speech business." Although it's still true, looking back on it, at that time in my life, the pain of my childhood was so deeply disturbing, I disconnected myself from it just to make it through from day to day.

I learned how to play most of them on my piano, so I could be ready to play them at a piano bar gig. It seemed like every day, a new Foster or Masser ballad was being played on the radio, so it was time I wrote mine.

I began it with an intro that used single notes instead of chords. This was different for me, and it musically conveyed how hurt I was by my mother's inattention to me. It was an intro of pain. I then began writing chords that complimented the intro and within minutes I had a good opening, but no lyrics. I then closed my eyes, dug deep and the chorus flew out of my mouth while playing, and I knew I had something worthwhile. "When was the last time you told me that you loved me?". I expanded on this and knew I had a powerful hook line. After I completed the lyrics and melody, I knew I was ready to record this in a professional recording studio.

I remember calling many recording studios to get their hourly rates. I had the money, but I also wanted a great engineer, and I needed control. That's me. I want control, especially when it's my song. This is life or death to me. If I don't have control, something else will, and I don't trust anything. I couldn't figure out why, but this is the way I am.

I finally settled on a recording studio in the Motown building at 6464 Sunset Blvd. in Hollywood. The people who managed the studio were great. I immediately felt they sensed what I desired. They had the Yamaha Grand Piano I needed, they had the 24-track board I needed and an engineer with good ears.

Maybe the reason for their talents was because it was an official Motown recording studio. Standing in the middle of the lobby, I saw all of the gold and platinum records. There was Marvin Gaye's "I heard it through the grapevine" next to The Supremes "next to Smoky Robinson's "Tears of a Clown" next to The Jackson 5's "I want you back" next to Stevie Wonder's "Superstition." I was immediately humbled. I was standing in the same lobby my musical heroes had, and I knew I was standing on the shoulders of giants. This was the first black owned record company started by two fearless black men: Barry Gordy and Smoky Robinson. They had so much talent on their label, they competed with the Beatles for the most gold records in the 1960s.

Standing there, I remembered how much I loved the songs. I remember, how, while watching "Soul Train" as a child, although I saw the color of the musicians making this incredible music, the color of their skin didn't mean anything to me. They were incredibly talented, and I'd never understand why people divided other people by race, especially when it came to music. Radio stations were segregated, and I wanted to hear all the songs.

I wanted to be as great as they were, but my ego told me I was already as great. I hadn't learned yet that the beginning of true greatness is getting out of my own way.

The whole floor had four or five recording studios all owned by Motown.

The third day I was there, recording my piano part, while singing the melody over the keys, I heard a voice over the loudspeaker saying someone wanted to speak with me immediately. It yanked me out of my therapeutic musical trance, and then came a knock on the studio door. It was the engineer telling me that some black guy who was recording in the studio next door to ours wanted to speak to me.

33

Reliant Atkins: Recording My Song at Motown

I immediately walked out of the room and was met in the studio's front area by a warm, friendly black man who stuck out his hand and said, "Hi, my name's Reliant Atkins. I was listening to your song through the wall to the studio next door where I'm recording my album for Motown Records and I loved what I heard!" I had a very good feeling about the man I was meeting.

Reliant proceeded to tell me how he and his studio musicians had heard my piano playing along with the song, and they were all in agreement about how good everything was. He told me he was interested in pitching it to the Motown execs because he wanted to record it and place it on his album. He then said he thought it was so good, he wanted it to be his single. Suffice it to say, I liked what I was hearing.

I told him I was very interested in hearing his voice. I had written the music and the melody but lyrically I had only written the chorus:

"When was the last time you told me that you loved me?
When was the last time I knew you'd be there?
When was the last time you picked up that phone and you called me?
I'm sorry but I don't remember, it's funny how I don't remember
But when was the last time you told me that you cared?"

In addition, because I wrote it about my mother, I had no idea what words to use for the verse and middle bridge melodies. I was writing songs that I hoped would be hits for other recording artists. My goal was to be a professional songwriter. But this song was personal. What artist would want to record a song about MY mother? Especially when it's not some "My mother loves me this I know" crapola – it's you fucking cunt, how could you ignore me...

Reliant assured me that we could make the song universal. He pointed out to me that the chorus could be heard as a song for lovers. He said he wanted the song, and we'd be traveling to Barry Gordy's house to get it signed to Tamla/Motown/Stone Diamond Music so he could record it. He wanted to write the lyrics with me. I already had full melody for the whole song. I knew immediately I needed his help to finish the lyrics. And I loved that he made me aware that I could write a personal song and still make it universal.

Reliant was gay. He reminded me of my friend Sylvester and a new recording artist named Jermaine Stewart who had just released an infectious pop single entitled "You don't have to take your clothes off."

Sylvester was well known internationally for his hit song "You make me feel mighty real." I met him at the Revolver Bar in West in Hollywood when he was becoming famous. He was attracted to me, and I loved his song, and the more we talked, I admired him for being real. He was fearless and proud of being gay. Later, when he was in and out of the hospital with AIDS. I would see him from time to time, and even as his health and good looks deteriorated, he never lost his sense of humor or his will to fight the disease. He was from Los Angeles County like me so we could joke about Watts and South Central because I grew up in the LA County Probation System with the Grape Street Watts Crip gang that ruled his neighborhood in the 1970s and 1980s. Although Syl died the next year in 1988, I still miss him very much. Syl was a powerful voice for many gay people. He was ahead of his time and made us all feel mighty real whenever we were around him or heard his music. Rest in peace Sylvester. You're not forgotten.

Of course, I still hadn't heard Reliant sing, and I wanted to hear him sing immediately before I agreed to anything. The minute he opened his mouth, I knew he was one of the most amazing singers I'd ever heard. He had a voice that was capable of sounding male or female accurately. His falsetto was staggeringly beautiful, but his masculine voice had more power and more emotive expression than Peabo Bryson. He had the perfect voice for my song! And he was signed to Motown Records. This was almost too perfect.

He worked fast. Reliant wanted to take me to his house so he could grab some clothes and head on up to one of the Gordy's houses in the Mount Olympus section of Los Angeles. Actually, I needed to drive him, because he didn't have a car. I really liked how down to earth he was. As I drove him home, I noticed the neighborhood was turning sinister, and he warned me about it. Reliant lived in an area of Los Angeles known as Baldwin Village, affectionately known as "The Jungle."

He turned on Coliseum Street at La Brea Avenue and I immediately noticed there was only one way in and one way out. He told me to keep my head low, and I saw why. People were staring at me. I sensed my life expectancy was lowering by the second every few feet we traveled. I realized this as we drove in. The color red was everywhere. I wondered, is this a "Blood" neighborhood? I remember I could never find a "Blood," but there were so many Crips. Maybe it was because they were scared to admit and there were so few of them. Reliant explained to me that they were even more deadly than the Crips because they had to kill or be killed. So, I asked, why the fuck do you live here, Reliant? He explained it's all he can afford, but it was all gonna change now that he has the record deal, because Motown was funding everything — his record, his publicity and his tour, and he knew his star was about to shine bright. Also, he told me my song would help make that happen.

I really began to respect him because at his apartment, he shows me that the Atkins family had a record deal with Warner Bros. in the late 1970s. There's Reliant smiling away on the top right.

Reliant played me a few songs from their album. It was his voice that carried the songs as, in my opinion, they were second rate stabs at disco.

He was not ashamed of being gay, but as many unashamed gay men did in the 1980s, he didn't carry flags or run around demanding attention for being gay either. He just lived his life. You either accepted him or not. I respected him for that too.

We left his house and headed up to the Gwen Gordy's Mt. Olympus home. Mount Olympus is a very wealthy LA enclave, just east and north of Laurel Canyon. It has a population of mostly rich entertainment industry titans, recording artists and actors. I love the gates. They proudly declare "Welcome poor people." I have a love/hate relationship with pretentiousness. I like to think I'm not pretentious, but I crave belonging to that club. I know I belong. For now, I'm just a 'temporarily embarrassed millionaire.'

We pass through the entrance and he directs me straight to the Gordy home. Reliant tells me Gwen has already heard the song, and she loves it and wants to sign it to their publishing company. I've never been in this situation before, it's like a dream come true, but I truly know what I'm doing, and I don't want to blow it. The voice in my head immediately senses it's the perfect time to pounce.

You know you can't write great songs. This isn't real. And if they do sign the song, you'll sign it away, giving them full rights, and they'll fuck you out of whatever money you should get, because you're an impatient idiot with no lawyer.

When we entered the home, I saw the expensive furniture, the ostentatious courtyards, and the enormous pool outside the French doors, and I could see through the "den" area. I know wealth, I've been in a hundred of these homes before, but this is the first time I'd been in one based on my songwriting ability, not because of my outside shell.

All I'd experienced from wealthy people was their desire to pay me for use of my body. There's nothing wrong with that. I presented myself that way to them, and they pounced on the opportunity. Still, inside me, I wanted to be paid for my other talents. And I finally am.

I also immediately noticed there was a platoon of people running around. It reminded me of "One Flew Over the Cuckoo's Nest." I saw a man smoking crack from a pipe in the corner of the living room. He then proceeded to walk around crookedly, scrunching his mouth together, with a crazed look on his face. And then I recognized him. It's Marvin Gaye's son. I had heard he was retarded, but now I see it up close. Reliant whispers to me that he's not retarded, he's "cerebrally challenged." I feel bad for him. I never heard that before, he just looks retarded to me. I loved his father, Marvin, not just for his singing, but because he wrote songs that were personal and told his feelings about the times, we were living in. "What's Going On" is one of the greatest songs ever written. Marvin wasn't just a singer; he was an artist. His father was a piece of shit. I can't imagine being so cold as to shoot my own son, but I can imagine my father shooting me.

Others were prancing around the living room as Gwen Gordy greeted us and leads us into a quieter office area. She sits behind a desk and hands me a contract. I acted like I was reading it comprehensively, but in reality, I was just skimming it over.

I saw how they wanted to own the publishing rights to the song for ten years, but I was assured they will be using it as much as possible, including being one of Reliant's singles. Gwen tells me he's their new Motown Artist and they'll be promoting him heavily. She also let me know they're going to put a lot of money into producing the song magnificently. I told her that I really admire David Foster and Gene Page styles of production and she understands. She assured me they have staff producers who would produce it and bring its potential to the listener in a way that would make it a hit.

I was skeptical, and I told her I wanted to give them my ideas on how I think it should be produced. Surprisingly, she agrees. I sign the contract, with a $5,000 advance, so I leave with thoughts of my first hit song in my head, and lots of royalty checks buying swimming pools and chaise lounges for years to come.

I met the producers back at the Motown Studio Reliant is recording in, and they listen to me as I break down my production thoughts for them. I have to give them credit for not treating me like a songwriting idiot. Apparently, my songwriting skills had impressed them, and they were eager to get to work on it.

Reliant and I also had to complete the lyrics, which took us a total of one day in his house. We turned it into a love song, with one lover feeling lonely because the other had neglected him. It worked beautifully. He was ready to go back into the studio with Motown producers to completer the finished product,

I was apprehensive, but when I heard their finished production of my song, I have to admit, I was stunned. I listened to the opening, wanting to hear my string arrangement, and even though they kept it intact note for note, they used an acoustic guitar instead of piano/strings. At first it was a shock, but soon I realized how brilliant it was. It turned what could have been heard as a bombastic opening into a soft, organic emotional opening which is exactly what the song called for.

They also added a distorted guitar "hard rock" opening to the middle bridge: "Maybe we should just stop pretending, we could have a love never ending...I can see it in your eyes!"

Reliant's voice was spectacular. He opens our melody with his beautiful falsetto: "Early in the morning, I'm watching the raindrops fall, you're lying next to me, yet I'm still alone."

He hit the chorus with his incredible baritone (his vocal range is outstanding), and during that middle bring, he displayed both his gorgeous falsetto and masculine "Peabo Bryson" vocal. The producers liked my piano playing enough to leave it in as the foundation for the song, and they did add the string arrangement as the song faded out.

I was astounded! They worked hard, and made my song spectacularly radio ready.

I knew right then and there, though I could write good songs, I did not have the production skills (or the voice) to make them spectacular. Everyone had equal value in creating a masterpiece.

After I received a cassette copy of the song, Reliant said he'd be in touch about the tour he was about to embark on, and so we didn't stay in contact as much as I would have wanted to. I lazily left it alone to the Gordy's to make the song get on the charts, not realizing that if I wanted it to be as big as it could be, I needed to stay in touch with on a daily basis. I was lazy and naïve'. The story of my twenty-three-year-old life. More on this later.

I wanted to play music live on stage. My music. I couldn't sing for shit, but I'd try and find a way. I'd been playing music with Darren Abner and our band for a couple of years, but everyone was a flake, and I didn't want Darren singing songs about my sister getting raped. I don't want to hold back anymore. So, what do I do?

At this point, I'm at a crossroads in my life. I've finished my latest photo shoot with Kent. It's the same old thing. I pose, get hard, flex my muscles, pee, lay out in the sun stroking my dick until I shoot gobs of cum, while he shoots a lot of pictures. All this time, I'm thinking about getting a job playing piano or starting a band. But I also want to stay connected to my longtime gay adult film star friends who are still alive.

3 4

Pleasure Delivery Server

In 1987, I applied for a job as a bus boy at the new Hyatt Regency Hotel in Long Beach. There is a connection, I just don't see it yet.

I go into the Hyatt Regency's Restaurant Manager's office to fill out the application, and instantly he tells me: "I've seen you! In fact, I have you in this drawer right here behind me."

I'm a bit puzzled as I watch him open the drawer, and then it hits me like a thunderbolt of lightning. He's pulled out the 1985 Christmas issue of In Touch magazine with me on the cover, and in pictures as the centerfold. He promises me he won't tell any of the other employees (as if I've already got the job), and guess what? I do.

I don't really want to be a busser; I want to play piano here. But again, I don't have the confidence to just apply for that job, so I go in for the lowest position they have to offer. In addition, they already have a piano bar guy.

I learned how to bus tables for three weeks at Clifton's cafeteria. It's hard work. I left because I didn't like being yelled at, and I was making thousands of dollars standing in the bushes. But now, at twenty-three, it's time for me to start playing in public by myself. I need to gain courage. I've played in bands on stage, but I want to play piano in a bar. So, now I'm a bus boy at the new Hyatt Regency hotel in Long Beach, California.

The first thing I realize as I put on my uniform and apron is that bussing tables is still hard friggin work. No one gives a shit about you either. The waiters are all complaining, I'm never fast enough, and the customers sit around until the last minute, and then I'm obligated to clean it all up. The worst is when fifteen people from the country of India come in smelling like ass juice and cologne, eat for hours and leave two dollars. Then my waiter is pissed, I get no money, and we have to spend a half an hour cleaning up after these people. And for seven nights in a row, because they're vacationing in Long Beach. Somebody come save me.

My manager notices my struggles, and he wants to promote me to waiter. I want that too, but I also want to play the piano. We have a meeting in his office, and of course he tries to kiss me and pull down my pants. He's attractive, but now is not the time. I've become an expert at this.

He calms down and tells me there's two reasons he wants me to start waiting tables. The first reason is because of my personality and looks. His words. He's been noticing how many customers look at me with lust (which in his head translates into money), and they think I'm a waiter anyway. The second reason is a bit morbid. John conveys to me that the restaurant is losing waiters to AIDS at an alarming rate. He said that in the last six months alone, four waiters have died. I've only been working here a month, and I can see that Franklin is very sick. Also, it's well known that Charles is near death. He's wasting away right before our eyes. The two of them like to stay upbeat and do their jobs, but they will probably both be dead within a month. Both are only twenty-four years old.

It was serious because the restaurant was losing waiters faster than they could hire them. I really liked these guys, but I'd already learned not to become too close to anyone with AIDS because my heart couldn't take any more breaking when they died. I gladly accepted John's offer to move me up to waiter. I thought it would be a lot less work than being a busboy. I was wrong. It's the same amount of work, I just get to be the center of attention. Perfect job for my ego, but I had to learn and work fast. I learned how to open a bottle of wine with a corkscrew. And I had to practice for an hour before I could do it quickly without breaking the cork and looking like a fool. I must have broken fifty corks inside bottles before I was ready to serve one.

Being Shawn Mayotte the server in a classy hotel restaurant was like being a kid in a candy store — I get to pick whatever I want, whenever I want, as much as I want. It only added fuel to my already overflowing ego. I'm the star of the show, and every night the crowd begs for more. I get at least twenty phone numbers a week from men and women, married and unmarried, young and old, all to call for one reason. Pleasure delivery service. Being a waiter was the second-best occupation for picking up dates I ever had.

Being a waiter also made me a kinder person. I wanted to keep the job, and I've got a temper this hotel doesn't know about. I was still seeing Norman, the expensive but wise psychiatrist from Newport Beach. He gained my trust just by listening without judging. He was making a difference by allowing to figure out where my hostility came from. It may be the anger from my childhood, but if I let loose on some of these rude customers, I'd break out in handcuffs. I already spent half of my life locked up, and my parents are to blame for that. I'm not gonna blow up, sit inside another jail cell, and have only myself to blame. Fuck that. It's important for me to prove I'm not the bad seed.

I was also a room service waiter. I had women at the tables specifically ask for me to deliver their room service meals at night. I'd get to the door, and most would open the door with a see-through bathrobe on and their breasts in my face. I loved it, but it became a bit of a burden. I had to perform on demand. There were many men who offered me money with sexual requests. I fucked a lot of them too. I also had couples wanting me to join them in threesomes, and of course I obliged, but then my manager John found out and he got mad. He was jealous.

He discontinued my room service job and transferred me to banquet waiting which was very hard work. It was during my time as a banquet waiter that I met three guys who became friends. Eric Kretz, Kelly, and Mike. Here they are in all their 80s colorful clothing glory.

3 5

Music or Sex?

Even straight guys were wearing colorful clothes. Everything was so gay in the 80s, nothing was gay anymore. Eric impressed me when we talked. He was a drummer who really appreciated great music. We had lengthy conversations about music and his dream was to have a career drumming in a rock n roll band. This was music to my ears. I was in the same place in my head as Eric. Eric was serious about his ambitions. He listened to me talk about my past as a professional musician. Eric intrigued me. He knew music and wanted to form a full band. I learned that he's from Santa Cruz in Northern California, and both he and his buddy Ernie had come to LA to form a band and get signed to a record label. He and I talked for hours after waiting and cleaning up the banquet tables. Believe me, he's willing to work hard to clean up, even with over forty people at one table. I'm impressed. But that's a drummer for you. They work hard.

One day, I invite Eric to my house so he can hear me play both the piano and guitar. I notice our conversation is extraordinarily comfortable. Eric's a Gemini. Our relationship is starting off just like an Aries-Gemini (both males) relationship should be: breezy and easy. Sleazy comes later. Eric and I start bonding over music.

Now, when I want to show off my musical skills to another musician, my conversation is short. As Eric enters my apartment, I walk straight to my piano. I quickly decide I'm gonna play a recent song I wrote that I think he'll like. It's about my friend Carlos who died of AIDS in 1985. I know my voice isn't great, but I need for Eric to hear the melody. I begin playing the chords on the keys, and very soon Eric is wide eyed with amazement. I know he's feeling my passion as I play. He sat down next to me on the piano bench and tells me "Damn I wish I could play like you. That's incredible. You're the best keyboardist I've heard." I loved hearing that. I want to play the guitar for him too.

He invites me to his house so I can hear him play his drums. He lives near my apartment in Long Beach. When we arrive, I notice his kit is set up in the den. The older houses in Long Beach have large rooms, so he's very lucky to be able to practice inside his home which he shares with a friend. As soon as he hits the high hat with hard 1, soft 2, hard 3, soft 4, I recognize right away his timing is impeccable. And then he adds both the snare and bass drum in perfect time. His playing is just what I need to start a solid band. The drummer is the maestro, and Eric's a maestro who serves the song, doesn't overplay, and knows when to hit hard and hit soft. He's good enough to be in a band with.

Eric also brought his friend Ernie from up north to start a rock n roll band together. I must meet Ernie as he's already Eric's band guy. Before we do that, we agree to play together at least once to see if we're in musical synchronicity.

Eric arrives on time at my apartment, which is important, because most musicians are notoriously late and think that it's cool. They're the ones who never make it. He's on time and sets up his drums in my house quickly. I decide to see how he frames a ballad I just wrote for my friend Carlos who died of AIDS. In fact, I'm going to his funeral this weekend. I think he's the 45th friend I've known intimately who has died of AIDS.

As I start playing my song for Carlos, Eric is noticeably entranced. He listens intently and begins to add subtle percussive nuances. His ear helped make the song more beautiful and he frames it exquisitely. So many rock drummers turn piano music into bombast. As we play the song over and over, we give it more emotion by loving it together. I realized what I wrote about our music sounds like we're both about to cum.

Eric continues to give me high praise for my piano playing.

"I've never heard a better piano player in my life."

I soak it in and my belief in his musical expertise helps to ward off my cynicism.

We start practicing together often. Eric introduces me to Ernie and right away I smell trouble. Ernie's ego is bigger than his talent, and he doesn't see it. He also commands us, wanting to run the show, and he's paranoid while drinking and arguing every time we practice. And he loves guns. He's a nightmare: A gun loving paranoid alcoholic with a temper and an anger problem. What could go wrong? And we're supposed to make music together? I'm also a dictator with a temper and a huge ego. The potential for disaster is obvious.

Two sickies don't make a wellie.

He plays electric guitar proficiently enough that I'm able to deal with him. It's his drinking and constant nitpicking that makes our band practices hard to get through. This guy loves his alcohol and argues over everything.

But he bugs me about how I have to grow my hair long to be in his band. Wtf? No one who is half the musician I am is gonna command me to do anything I don't want to do. Because I want to grow my hair long again, and the girls love it even more than they did in the 70s, I'm letting it grow. Anything that makes it easier to get laid. But Ernie has no idea that my hairstyle in this picture with him on my right has helped make me half a million dollars since I cut it off in 1983. It's the 80s and gay men and many women who pay for sex love the short haired college boy look. Here's Ernie and I in 1987.

We write a few songs together that are half bad. But at least that means they're half good. I still think half good songs might make us stars. I'm naïve. Eric and I just stare at each other during our three-man band practices while Ernie's singing and drinking. He makes up crappy words on the spot. I tell him we need to flesh out the lyrics, so they make a story, and he grudgingly agrees. I am a professional songwriter, so I know what I'm talking about. With him, I want to say, "Shut the fuck up and let me handle the songs," but I'm not interested brawling with him.

We don't even have a name for the band when we land a couple of gigs at small clubs in Long Beach. We also play for friends. I take over the bass and allow Ernie to be the sole guitar player. It's evident right away that we shouldn't be allowing anyone to see us until we have great songs, and more players. Of course, getting rid of Ernie would be a great start. He's not a bad guy, he's just hard to get along with. Eric and I talk privately because he's had enough of Ernie.

Eric is also aware that I'm missing a practice here and there because I'm constantly prowling for women. I'm also partaking in orgies and fulfilling my sexual fantasies. Cocks, pussies and asses are more important to me than this band. I know this band isn't going anywhere, and in my head, my mission is still mostly sexual.

It's simple, Eric is serious, and for different reasons, Ernie and I are not. I'll never forget one gig in a biker bar where there was an avalanche of girls up front. Most of them ugly. Anyway, I was also drinking along with Ernie, and by the end of our set, I was drunk. I continued to order drinks from the bar, and we moved into a booth.

Suddenly, three ladies squeezed into our booth, boxing us in. As the girls positioned themselves to snatch the musician of their choice, the ugliest one latched onto me. After my fifth whisky and coke, and about six beers, I wasn't making jokes anymore, I was dead drunk. All I remember from that point until the next morning, is this chick grabbing me and saying she was taking me home, and my next memory is waking up in a dirty basement in sheets right next to a Harley Davidson motorcycle.

I have no recollection of how I got here or where I am. This woman starts asking me how I like my eggs. I ask her where I am.

"You're in the basement of my farmhouse, honey."

"How did I get here, and what the fuck happened last night?"

"You and Ernie were drunk, and you started to fight so I grabbed you and pushed you out the door into a cab. One of my girlfriends took off in her car and I took you home with me. You don't remember that? Do you remember what happened after that?"

I feel like my head was squished in a vice, and I'm dizzy and I throw up.

"No, I don't remember anything. So, what happened when we got here?"

I'm looking into the face of death. There's nothing wrong with being ugly, but this chick's overdoing it. This is a woman with jagged scars covering her face and has only four teeth. She's also sporting and a massive tattoo of SWP (Supreme White Power) on her throat. She's got chopped red hair and she resembles a hooker with a meth addiction who just got laid. Shit!! Please, don't tell me I fucked you?

"You were a tiger last night. You fucked me for an hour, but you only like to do it doggie style. You don't like to kiss either. I tried to kiss you, but you kept flipping me over. You pounded me hard and I came ten times. You've got a big, nice white dick, babe. Just rest and eat some eggs. I made coffee for you too. Eric drove your car home to his house, and I gave him this address. Call him and he'll pick you up. But please don't leave so soon. I wanna cuddle."

I gotta get the fuck outta here.

"I'd love to cuddle, honey, but I have to get home and get to work."

She looks devastated. There are two shotguns leaning against a wooden wall. I look up and there's about six inches between my head and the door I can escape through. I'm really in a basement. Fuck. I gotta call Eric.

Buttuglyness is sad but she gives her phone to dial Eric. It's a rotary phone so I pray that I dial every number correctly or I have to start All over again. I hate these fucking phones.

Eric answers on the first ring. I'm rescued.

I can't say the same for our band. Eric pulls me aside at the Hyatt and asks me how I'd feel if he left our band to pursue another one. He is so nice. Without missing a beat, my ego puts my ambition in its place.

"Of course, you can. You're good enough to be in any band. You'd improve on whatever they have already."

Eric tells me one last time that he'd rather form a band with me, but I know I'll meet someone even better and I'll get there faster anyway. Underneath my bravado, I sense I'm losing a great bandmate who understands and appreciates my talent, but so has a hundred musicians already, and I know a thousand more will in the future. I've got nothing to worry about. Plus, I'm getting laid tonight with a hot chick I met in the mall last week.

Eric still wants me to accompany him on band auditions. That's very high praise for me. He trusts my musical acumen so much that he won't join a band without my input. Wow. I'm honored.

I go with Eric on three auditions for him. The first one is a band that sounds like Metallica on steroids with a cookie monster lead singer. It was easy to give him a thumbs down on that one. The second band is a three-member band a la Rush or Triumph; in fact, they sounded a lot like Triumph. The lead singer could almost reach Rik Emmet's high notes. They played us a couple of their songs and liked Eric's drumming, but I told Eric that though this band was ok, they'd never make it with a lead singer who was "almost" as good as a great lead singer. This is the music business, and a band is only as good as its lead singer. He or she must be spectacular.

Suffice it to say, Eric settles on a band that I approve of. Sadly, I was too busy chasing girls while Eric was busy with his career and we lost touch.

Later, in 1990, I'm reading a story in Music Connection magazine about a new band named Stone Temple Pilots that's getting rave reviews everywhere they play. Their drummer is Eric. I'm very happy for him, and I know I'll be famous soon too. I vow to not look him up until I achieve the same level of professional success. I keep my word on this one.

36

Tim Kramer

In the mid-1980s, music was changing again. We had gone through the punk/new wave movement only to hear Recording Artists who were considered on the edge in the early 80s like Tears for Fears, become mainstream and have huge hits like "Shout" and "Everybody wants to rule the world." Rock sucked. All the organic, genuine hard rock bands from the 70s had either split up (Led Zep, Bad Co.) or were churning out less than stellar records that were never going to be like who they grew up listening to: AC/DC, The Who, Led Zeppelin or Queen. They were all poser bands.

I was also a movie goer. Oh, how I loved my movies, but I'm intensely critical of most movies because I can't stand unrealistic fantasy shit meant to mesmerize twelve-year olds that end up being $150 million blockbusters. To me, that says most adults think like children too. I preferred movies that were intense, dramatic, and had realistic storylines with powerful dialogue; and I loved older classics like "Sunset Blvd." and "Grand Hotel." I loved "Scarface" in 1982, mostly because of the screenplay, written by Oliver Stone and the direction by Brian DePalma. I felt validated, really digging it, when most critics dismissed it as "obscene." That's me: obscene and loving it. I also loved the performances, especially Al Pacino's swagger.

One movie I loved that left me speechless and traumatized was Oliver Stone's "Platoon." While the rest of the country was loving "Top Gun" because of their brainwashed obsession with American heroes, I fell in love with this realistic portrayal of a young man's true front-line adventures in Vietnam. I had to see it a few times to really appreciate it. I've never stopped loving Platoon and Tom Berenger's performance as Sgt. Barnes still makes me sit in awe to this day. Top Gun which was as banal as watching socks hang from a clothesline. Platoon appealed to liberal thinkers while Top Gun appealed to conservative thinkers. Just my "never to be humble" opinion.

In 1987, I attended an HIV positive support group. I was there supporting my friend Danny who had AIDS and was near death. The leader of the group was Doug Cooper, (Tim

Kramer) one of the biggest gay adult film stars of the 1980s whom I had met years ago when we were starting our escorting businesses in Hollywood.

I was overjoyed to see Doug again, and I knew this would be good for Danny. Doug was compassionate and told everyone they only had to share if they wanted to. Danny was emaciated and began crying. He knew he was going to die soon. He opened by stating that he would try in the short time that he remained on earth that he would forget about his pain and be of service whoever needed his help. Doug put his hand in Danny's and told him he was selfless and heroic to think of others. Doug's empathy for Danny was palpable and it made

Listening and watching Doug's passion for helping men in distress was oddly sexually arousing for me. He didn't say much, and he didn't have to. He listened with compassion.

When the group ended, Doug and I took Danny to his house together. We had that unexpressed sexual feeling that was leading us into a night of passion. He invited me in, and I complimented him.

"You made a difference in Danny's life today. And I noticed you didn't speak much in your HIV + group. You listened to him, and that's just what he needed." I was intrigued. Doug's answer still reverberates in my head today: "I'd rather have a heart without words than words without a heart."

We moved closer and Doug's cherry lips met mine. We started off with very soft, slow kisses as both our hands moved down each other's chest. Our hands began exploring our belt buckles as we slowly unzipped each other's pants. Doug was extremely aroused as I felt his large cock starting to pulsate in my hand. He pulled my cock out and began sensuously stroking me until I was hard.

We kissed and it felt natural. Doug was simultaneously sexual and sensual.

This felt like love to me, but did I really understand what love felt like? The climax to our beginning was thrilling, but we knew we were friends, not lovers.

Doug and I knew we weren't interested in falling in love or having that kind of relationship. We were close friends. He and I both had lucrative escorting businesses and we didn't compete. We didn't play the zero-sum game. We both knew there was enough out there for everybody to profit. We didn't compete; we cooperated. We loved each other as friends. He impacted my life so deeply.

For you Doug:

Doug Cooper was known as Tim Kramer, one of the biggest Gay Adult Film Stars of the 1980's. I met Doug through a mutual acquaintance. We quickly became friends.

Doug was a smart and compassionate person. Since I was only posing for photo shoots and he was very successful performing in Gay Adult Films, I thought of him as a "Star". He was always humble and treated everyone with kindness and respect. I learned a lot just from being around him.

Doug and I not only shared first names; we also ran escort services in Hollywood. I didn't see it as competition because there seemed to be enough clients for everybody. Also, my foray into the escort service business was lucrative but brief.

Doug was smart, and he knew the value of the "Tim Kramer" brand. I remember when he told me about a solar installation company he wanted to invest in, and though I saw the potential, he saw the future. When he was diagnosed HIV+, he started an AIDS support group and began promoting safe sex. He truly cared about others. He became very ill in 1991 and passed away in 1992.

Doug, you taught me how to stay strong and care for others even when we're in pain. I know your star shined bright and brief, but you made a difference in many people's lives, including mine. If you were here today, you'd be thrilled to see that you were right: Solar was the future. I cried when you died, but I know you're in heaven making it a happier place for others. You taught me a lot about life and thinking ahead.

I'd like to end this tribute to Doug with a line from one of my favorite songs by the Waterboys that describes my feelings about him and his vision:

"I saw the crescent, but you saw the whole of the moon."

Rest in Peace Doug. You're not forgotten.

37

Songwriting Partners/Vanity: Denise Matthews

Although I was building confidence day to day, I still felt like an outsider. One reason was because I was working with musicians who connected to shallow music and wanted the easy "hit." I did too, but I was also writing songs about myself that were visceral and told the truth. Two of these musicians were Tina and Mike Ray. I don't remember Tina's last name, but I met her through an ad in Music Connection magazine in 1985. I was looking for a female singer to write songs for, and Tina answered my ad.

When I met her, I was blown away by her looks and her voice. Tina was a sex bomb. She had a beautiful face, huge breasts, and a voice that sounded like Alyson Moyet of "Yaz." Yet she still sounded uniquely like herself. Using Madonna as my guide to how to build a successful female recording artist career, Tina had every combination we needed to make a superstar. She was also willing to write songs with me. I thought I was on my way to building a music career with my first discovery.

I was jacking off thinking about her at home. Damn, I wanted to see and suck on those breasts. Every time I came, I had written a new sweaty, sex drenched song for her. They were good, raunchy and still retained that mainstream hit vibe that could launch her career. And I was willing to let her write her own lyrics as long as she stayed within the sex prism, I was focused on for her. I was totally unprepared for her response to hearing the songs I wrote for her.

"I'd never sing those songs!" she shouted at me in my apartment. "I'm a Christian. I don't want to be known for degrading myself. I will never lower myself to singing those songs for my career. I want a wholesome image. I'll still write songs with you because you are a phenomenal songwriter, Doug. But I'll never sing sexual songs."

A Christian who wants a career in the sex obsessed music industry? That's like a black person wanting to join the Ku Klux Klan. The music industry is rebellion to me. It's sex, drugs, and rock n roll. This is the fucking 1980's. I'm Shawn Mayotte — I do porn, I fuck men and women and I'm an atheist. Not a good match for you. I wouldn't even know how to

186

write Christian songs. I write anti-christian songs. I asked her how she felt about gay people and she gave the wrong answer.

"Homosexuality is a sin." I should have known this twat would say this. She's from Iowa after all. Now I don't like her. Can't get a hard on for a prude.

I told her how I felt, and we argued about it until I gave up and we agreed to just be a songwriting team.

We write a few songs and she's a good lyric writer for my ballads. The one we feel strongest about, "No More Cryin'", we record at Tina's friend Mike Ray's home recording studio. After we finish the recording, we all feel strongly that it's a hit. Tina and I decide to enter it in the Los Angeles Songwriter's showcase, run by Dale Kawashima who had his own Music Publishing Company. He had a roulette wheel, and all of us amateur songwriters put cassettes into his wheel, which he spun and listened to the song the wheel landed on. He was critical, but I felt he gave many songs way too much time. I would shut off some of these songs much earlier than he did. As he gave a song his thumbs up, the song moved to the next level. Dale really loved "No more Cryin'", in fact he kept choosing it over every song it battled. Then came the final round. It was our song against a hit songwriter, Diane Warren, and I knew it was tough because her song was, of course, very good.

I had met Diane before, and though she was a successful songwriter, she was very down to earth. I asked her about her first hit "Rhythm of the Night," which was a number one hit for Debarge, and she said, "That song bought me my first house in Studio City." She said this in a very humble manner. I want my songwriting to buy multiple houses too. I just need to write better choruses. I don't want to work where I have to listen to the mechanical choruses of cash registers at a fast-food place, I want to work where I'm writing musical, spiritual and hooky choruses that are played on the radio around the world.

In the end, Dale listened to "No more Cryin'" and Diane's song more than four times back-to-back saying it was very difficult to choose. But, alas, he chose Diane's song. I can't remember which song it was, but it became another hit for her. I was heartbroken. Tina took it better than me, but then again, my songs are personal, and I consider them my babies. I still can't believe I kept working with her after she said homosexuality is a sin. Now I want to flash her my dick. I don't wanna fuck her anymore, but I'd love to fuck a guy in his ass in front of her just because I can. Tina don't sermonize to me. I can preach a better sermon with my life than my lips.

I quickly become good friends with Mike Ray, who Tina introduced me to. He has a recording studio in his house. He's a real nice guy, who, although divorced, still sees his two sons often, and pays his child support on time. I have the utmost respect for him for being a great dad. I've always said I could never be friends with a man who doesn't love his kids, even if he's not with the mother. If you can't connect with your own flesh and blood, how can you ever connect with me?

Mike's house with my Yamaha DX-7 and Roland Juno-106 piled on top of his recording console. 1986.

Mike Ray was a good bass player, but he wanted to produce a "hit" song rather than make music that was timeless. At that time, I also fell into that category. Mike loved my keyboard and guitar playing, and we connected over many things, especially the value of children. Mike introduced me to another talented musician, Durand Gist

Durand was an extremely talented songwriter. We wrote many songs together. The first one we wrote "Your face is international" had tremendous potential to be a hit. But none of us followed through the way we should have. Mike had no knowledge about how to get a song recorded, and I was too busy fucking everything that wasn't nailed down. But we had a lot of fun and created some good music.

Mike also preached, but it didn't bother me because he was still a regular, rational guy. He and picked up on girls together. Overall, he was a trustworthy guy who I looked up to, but he also followed me, because he believed in my talent.

Mike's favorite band of all time was Styx. Not a bad band at all, I like a couple of Styx's albums, but Mike praised them as much better than the Beatles. And Tammy wouldn't know great music if it hit her in the head. I remember arguing with them when Tammy claimed Expose' was just as good as the Beatles. I was dumbfounded. Together they couldn't grasp what was so great about "Eleanor Rigby" even after I broke it down to them in no uncertain terms. I felt like the meat in an imbecile sandwich. I realized how little they knew and shut my mouth after that. Have you ever noticed that the less people know, the more stubbornly they know it?

I was writing a lot of very personal songs that they'd never understand. I wrote one called "Father Francis goes down" about a priest who loves to suck young boys' cocks. I also wrote a song about my sister's sexual abuse at the hands of my father called "The Truth." I was getting down to the heart of my pain and I wasn't gonna hide it anymore. No more running away. I was no longer a stranger to myself.

Mike also introduced me to Denise Matthews, better known to the world as "Vanity". She was the leader of the musical group Vanity 6, created by Prince. I had lusted after her for years, so I was horny and cocky when we met. She was everything I'd seen in her music videos. Tall, olive skinned and gorgeous. I was attracted to people of mixed races, and she fit that bill.

Denise was attracted to me too. It was obvious the way she scanned my body like radar. Mike and her lived in different apartments in a building called "The Grand" on Sepulveda Blvd. in Sherman Oaks. It was the trendiest place to live if you were in the Music Industry. Janet Jackson lived there, Bobbly Blotzer from the rock group Ratt had an apartment there, and many famous music titans had full blown 64 track recording studios in The Grand.

Denise and I went to the Cat n Fiddle club on Sunset Bl, in Hollywood on our first date. We shared our experiences in the music industry. She was brutally honest about how she felt victimized and taken advantage of by record company executives. It was a familiar story. I was heartened to hear my hero Prince had treated her well. She loved him but said many people had stopped talking to her because they felt Denise partied too much. That night, I found out how much of an understatement that was.

We were drinking heavily at the Cat, and both of us were bored, so she suggested calling her "connection" and pick up some crack to take home with us. Hollywood at this time was overrun with Crack. There were dealers up and down every street. Driving north on La Brea Blvd. or east on Sunset could get you killed in the crossfire between warring black and latino gangs battling for customers. The drug was so popular that you couldn't drive on streets like Yucca where the famous Capitol Records building sits, unless you were a buyer. Crack was selling like quarter pounders and the dealers were open for business 24/7. It was just like a drive thru fast-food restaurant. Hearing her mention a connection made me feel safe. I didn't want to buy crack on the street. We drove to her dealer's house in the Hollywood Hills and bought $800 of crack cocaine. We took the crack back to Denise's apartment at The Grand and the fun began.

I was so horny knowing I was gonna smoke crack and have sex with Denise, that I nearly orgasmed during my first hit. She took a long sensual hit, and my cock became rock hard watching her fall back on the couch and open her dress. She wanted me to feel her breasts, but I wanted to take a hit first. I hit that pipe long and slow, and the sexual intensity overpowered any rationale there was to stop right there. I stood up with her face at my crotch, Denise unzipped my jeans, and took my erection deep into her mouth.

She deep throated me, and that hasn't been easy for many women. She praised my size and ordered me to get down between her legs and eat her out. I must have eaten her for an hour, and she orgasmed 10 times.

We fucked like animals in heat, and I didn't want to stop. At some point, Denise said she wanted to get more cocaine and her dealer would deliver to her house if we bought at least a thousand dollars' worth. I was stuck on the drug and her and gave her my ok. We dialed his number, and he was there in 30 minutes.

When he got there, he gave us the dope, Denise kissed him on the cheek and ran off to her bedroom to get that hit. The dealer was a 300-pound black man who grabbed me by the arm and warned me to keep an eye on her. He told me in confidence that Denise was becoming one of his most addicted customers, and he'd rather see her in rehab than passed out on the floor, scarred from pipe burns and smelling like she hadn't taken a shower in a week. I was still high, but I listened. He said Denise would smoke crack for days, staying awake sometimes for almost two weeks. He liked her, but he'd seen this before. He told me about customers who started out with million-dollar homes and ended up in a tent smoking crack on Skid Row. I never forgot his final words to me: "You can live in Beverly Hills and still have skid row between your ears."

Denise scared me because she couldn't stop herself from smoking crack. After I was exhausted, she kept going. People in the Grand knew she was smoking after a week up, because the lights were still on in her apartment. I hung out with Denise a few more times after this first night, but I had to stop being around her. I was a Vanity addict, and she was a crack addict. Later, I heard she got sober through religion and I was happy for her. Being addicted to Jesus Christ is a better plan than being addicted to cocaine. When she died young, I was crushed, but I'll always remember her laughter and warm smile. The world was alternately kind and cruel to her, as it has been to me. I had some crack experiences that were traumatic, and I eventually hurt some people like all addicts do. But Denise got it together before she died. I hope she's still a sex shooter in heaven. Rest in peace Denise. You're not forgotten.

I started to frequent the clubs in Hollywood, West Hollywood, East Hollywood and Downtown Los Angeles. In addition to the Sunset Strip Club scene in West Hollywood, there's a lot of clubs in the Hollywood and Downtown LA areas that feature live music that wasn't played by mainstream or silly hard rock artists. There was the Anticlub in East Hollywood on Melrose, the Palace on Hollywood Blvd., Al's Bar and El Cid in Downtown LA, Egg Salad on 9th and Bonnie Brae, and The Mint on Pico for funk and soul.

I remember going to The Anticlub one night in 1986 and seeing this band that played their set with nonstop, frenetic energy. It was like watching four manic escapees from an insane asylum. I was intrigued because the bass player was phenomenal, and though they didn't really have songs, they didn't care, they were playing for the love of music. I asked someone who they were, and they told me they were the "Red Hot Chili Peppers." I thought that name was silly, but it certainly was appropriate.

Music was exciting again. The late 80s were a time of change, and music was undergoing a metamorphosis. Instead of the "new wave" and British bands that dominated the early to mid-80s, I was now witnessing more angry and experimental bands such as The Sonic Youth, Jane's Addiction, Suicidal Tendencies, Live Nude, The Exotic Birds, The Misfits and many others.

On the other side of town, I was witnessing a resurgence of singer-songwriters. The person who made the biggest impression on me was a girl named Tori Amos. I'll never forget watching her play the piano and becoming entranced within seconds. She sat sideways on the piano bench, but that oddness was just the beginning. She sang personal songs that kept all of us spellbound while she performed. Her red hair and cute young face were an innocent mask that when she stripped it away, she revealed an old soul, a tender heart, and a spirit of courage that astounded us all. I was mesmerized and I took her home with me, and I started writing more personal songs on my piano.

38

David Geffen

In the spring of 1987, I was strolling along the Sunset strip when a musician acquaintance of mine mentioned there was a great band playing at the Roxy. This was one of the few people whose musical opinion mattered to me, so I decided to check them out. I obtained a ticket from my friend Joe the scalper, and after an hour outside, I walked into the Roxy not knowing what I was about to witness.

I noticed the audience first. They were tribal. This was not just a band. I could feel the electrifying fanatical devotion to this band as I made my way through the crowd.

I made it just in time to see them perform the first song from the set. I power emanating from the stage as the guitar player pounded out the opening chords to this song is hard to describe. It was venomous. Both the lead guitar player and snarling lead singer combined sophisticated guitar power chords with honest, visceral lyrics. This band was real. They were in our faces, thrusting their music onto us, making sure we believed in them as much as they believed in themselves. The band's name was Guns 'N Roses.

Seeing them helped me make up my mind to grow my hair long again. I had already started to let it grow and it grew fast.

I loved my long hair. I was more than grateful it wasn't falling out. Since I was five years old, I worshipped men in rock bands with long hair. My earliest memories are filled with me growing my hair long and playing in a rock band.

The first song I heard from Guns n Roses was called "It's so easy." It was pure venom. In a relentless manner, the song clubbed us over the head with nasty chords and lyrics such as "Turn around bitch I gotta use for you." I related to the lyrics and loved the simple but still sophisticated power chords that drove this song' intensity. This was the first time I had become completely entranced with a band in a long time. I also became mesmerized with all the long-haired boys around me. Besides, in every music video on MTV, the former early 80's coiffed, short haired lead singers of bands were now sporting a darker, more menacing look with long hair. Bono of U2 in "With or without you," Michael Hutchence of INXS in "I need you tonight" showed me hair was no longer going up, it was coming down.

Later, in 1989, while hanging out at the Rainbow, I saw Axl Rose, Guns n' Roses' leads singer throw a glass at a girlfriend of mine who was tending bar. It infuriated me, so I called him out.

"Throw the fucking glass at me you pussy, and they'll be putting pins in your neck to hold it up after I'm through with you." I have enough anger inside me to kill him.

Being the king of world, he wasn't used to this. He stared at me with seriousness, and I knew he was no poser. He was ready to fight. I stared back at him and mocked his real name.

"C'mon, Bill Bailey, if you feel froggish, leap." I was ready to go to blows.

We stared at each other, both of us being accustomed to people backing down from us, and we both walked away. Later, I learned about his childhood and how his stepfather fucked him up the ass when he was three. I now felt a kinship with him. Still, if my real name was Bill Bailey, I'd change it too.

I also began playing my personal songs live. I played "The Truth," the song about my sister's sexual abuse, and I had quite a few girls crying during the song, and they told me privately they were also sexually abused. I wrote this with the thought that I could become a deeper Elton John. I'd write piano ballads that contained personally painful lyrics. My personal audience grew, and my idea was working, but of course I was inconsistent. I canceled gigs at the Coconut Teazer and Al's Bar downtown. I was still busy chasing after short term remedies to my own childhood pain at that time.

By the summer of 1987, I knew I had to do something drastic to make an impact. I wasn't satisfied with the long run, I wanted to get a record deal now. I was still insecure. Both of my parents were selling their homes at this time in 1987, and while both of them knew I had a real estate license, neither one bothered to contact me to sell their homes for them. This hurt immensely. I remember calling my dad up and reminding him I was an agent and would love to help him sell his home.

I'll never forget his response: "I already found a real estate agent and we already have my home on the market." He expressed it to me as if I asked him what temperature it was outside. And then, he had to go because he had a meeting with her.

Though I held it in, that really stung. I know that was the beginning of the end of our relationship. I didn't understand how a man who left me to fend for myself at age thirteen and had done nothing to help me in all these years since 1978 could justify this. It hurt.

And to top it off, my sister told my mother was selling her house in Lakewood and found an agent already. That stung too.

So, I proclaim to myself, it's time to get noticed in the music industry. For most people that would mean creating an unforgettable act on stage or writing an outrageously provocative song. Not me. On autopilot, without a second thought, I decide I'm going to meet David Geffen and through my looks, brains, and force of personality, he'll understand me and listen to my music.

Although record company executives have never been heroes of mine, there are three that have always stood tall among the "hangers on" to musicians. They are Ahmet Ertegun, Clive Davis, and David Geffen.

These three men were like rock stars to me. They knew how to get great recording artists heard by the masses, and they knew how to make musicians successful. They cared about music. Especially Ahmet. He and his brother Nesuhi genuinely loved R & B music and they were determined to record black artists so the world could enjoy their music too.

Two Jews and two Turks made us fall in love with rock n roll.

Clive was known as a song man. He was a genius at putting the right song with the right artist to give them a hit. Being a song person first, I really related to him. But the man I was most impressed with was David Geffen. I was most impressed with him because he had the Midas touch. No matter what he did, he profited from his decisions. In 1987, money is still my master and I'm still most impressed with those who make a lot of it. David created Asylum records with Elliot Roberts in 1970, and then started Geffen Records in 1980. He signed many of my favorite artists to both labels. He believed in people when no one else would. He signed the Eagles, Jackson Browne, Joni Mitchell, and Linda Ronstadt.

As his label grew, so did his net worth. I was impressed with his story also.

David wanted to be in the movie business, so he got a job working in the mail room at the William Morris Talent Agency. They required a bachelor's degree, which he didn't have. To get hired he lied and told them he had a B. A. from UCLA. He came to the mail room every morning and searched for that letter from UCLA denying his claim to a B.A. It came one day, and he threw it away so his bosses at William Morris never saw it. To me, that was a rebellious and courageous act of defiance. He wanted in and found his own way. Fuck a degree. I'm the same way. I don't need formal schooling to teach me what I already know. I could play Bach and Beethoven by ear when I was five. I didn't need any university to teach me that.

David's a hustler like me. And he's gay and he likes young, muscular blonde men. I'm going to go to his office on Sunset Blvd. and meet him no matter what. He'll see me, and the rest will be history.

I have no doubt I will make my big "break" on my terms.

It's a warm summer day in 1987 when I shower and get squeaky clean. I put on my best casual but sexy clothes that I know will get David's interest. I come prepared.

I drive to Sunset and Doheny, where Geffen Records is located. I park and build up confidence by staring at myself in my rearview mirror making sure every hair is in place and every muscle is accentuated by a tight-fitting shirt with casual shorts to show off my legs.

I strut casually into the building and although inside I'm nervous, on the outside I exude fearlessness. In fact, I over act the part just to get my way. I waltz into Geffen Records, the most successful record company in the world in 1987, with Elton John, Peter Gabriel, Guns n Roses, Whitesnake, Aerosmith, Neil Young, Sammy Hagar, and Gene Loves Jezebel on their roster like I own it. And I do own it at this moment.

The front office has gold records adorning the walls and expensive office furniture everywhere. The three people sitting in the front area, including the "secretary" all look at me as if I'm from Mars. The lady at the front desk finally asks me who I am and how she can help me.

"I'm here to see David."

"David?" As if there are other David's here at David Geffens' record company.

"David. David Geffen. I'm here to see David."

An effeminate gay man coming down the stairs is profusely salivating, while staring at me, lustily, on a cellular level. But he's a nobody. I'm here to see David.

"Does he know you?" the secretary person asks me.

"Of course, he does."

"Ok. I'll ring his office."

She gets on the phone with someone, and after a couple of minutes, a classic 1930's phone on a cabinet across the room started ringing.
She told me to pick up the receiver.
I walked over to the phone and picked it up. David was clearly the person on the other end.

"Who are you?" He asked in a squirrelly, Brooklyn accented voice.

"I'm Doug."

"And you're here to see me?"

"Yes."

It was obvious that he had time to play games on the phone, but I didn't. I told him I was here to see him and that was it. He stopped playing games and eased my worries by telling me he was impressed.

"You came walking into my company, demanding to see me, claiming I knew you. I can see you're a very good-looking blonde boy. You've got balls. I'm impressed. Why don't I give you my address and you drive to my house tomorrow night?"

I don't know how he can see me, cause I can't see him, but I take down his address in Malibu, and tell him tomorrow evening will be fine. Nothing is more important than meeting with the most powerful man in the music business at his home.
I call David the next day to let him know I'm leaving from Long Beach and this "Lurch" sounding voice answers his home phone with "Geffen residence." Lurch passes the phone to David and we decide on an 8 p.m. arrival time. I drive to David's house on Pacific Coast Highway in Malibu the next evening. I've seen a lot of wealth in my years as an escort, but this house is the apex. It sits on a swath of sandy beach in the most expensive zip code in California.
I have to park on PCH which is somewhat dangerous, but I'm gonna live forever so I'm not worried.
David's butler greets me at the door with David quickly rushing up behind him. I notice David moves at a frenetic pace. He is a doer who doesn't waste time. I've got a million questions I want to ask him, and although I want to lie to myself and imagine he wants to hear my music, I know his agenda with me is sex.
We sit down on his couch. David asks me why I sought him out. I tell him I'm a songwriter and musician, so my goal was not just to trick with him. He doesn't seem to care. He's very intent on having sex. I start asking questions.

"It's fascinating for me to be in David Geffen's house. I've admired you since I was a child. I pay attention to all thing's music, including who recorded what, who wrote what song, what label my favorite artists are on, and who runs the label, etc. And then I read the background of every person involved."

David starts telling me about his life. He doesn't realize I already know all about his upbringing except a couple of things that I desperately want to know.

"I was born in Brooklyn, New York," he says, "And I learned a lot about business from my mother, Batya."

I already know this. His mother Batya owned a clothing store and she bartered with customers every day and David watched and soaked up how to make self-beneficial deals as a child.

David talks for a while and I listen intently. I ask about Elton, my hero, and David immediately talks about him vituperatively.

"Elton's an asshole." He declares loudly. I want to know why.

"I gave him money, and it was never enough. And then he didn't deliver. He cost me money and argued with me about it."

It sounds like two queens having a catfight.

David then proceeded to disparage most of my heroes. He called Joni Mitchell a little bitch, he said Don Henley was a pompous asshole, said he and Marlo Thomas were in love, and finally called John Lennon a queer who slept with guys but didn't want people to know about it. I don't know if he thought he was impressing me, but if that's what he was thinking, he was out of touch with how his overinflated ego was ruining my night. I think he underestimated my intelligence, but his endless successful decisions would make anyone think they're smarter than everyone else — especially someone he sees only as a prostitute.

David then pulled out two Quaaludes from his pocket and attempted to "2 Q" me. I'd been "2 Q'd" before and although the sexual euphoria produced by Quaaludes was something I'll never forget, it frightened me a bit and I turned him down. A bit ruffled, he then pulled out a huge baggie of pot. It was at least a pound, and he offered to smoke it with me. I didn't want to be stoned with him either.

He enjoyed talking about himself. He allowed me to ask a ton of questions, and then he got bored and used a remote control to turn a television on that emerged from a stone wall – it was ostentatious and more like something from The Addams Family. On came Whitesnake, who I didn't like, but David praised them stating to me that they were selling 42,000 units a week. He talked about them as if they were his children and he was proud of them for getting all "A's". I loved Guns n Roses and he said they'd be the biggest seller he'd ever have. Of course, he was proved right over the years. David's never wrong.

I asked him what his father did for a living, and he became visibly agitated and told me his father, Abraham, was an unemployed bum who never worked a day in his life. His hostility towards his father was palpable. I could relate. But David had had enough of small talk.

He finally said, "You're trying to figure out how I did all this? How I became successful?"

What could I say except "Yes."

David was bored with talking. I told him I had a tape of my music that I wanted him to listen to. He took it and placed it near his stereo. And then we moved to the bedroom.

I wasn't horny, but I knew I could perform. That's what I was there for, and even though we hadn't negotiated a price, I figured with David's wealth, I'd at least walk out of there with a thousand dollars.

I'd made much more and barely had sex with less wealthy men.

We move together to his bedroom, and I realize I'm just not into having sex with him. But since that's never stopped me before (especially when I'm getting paid), we remove our clothes and quickly get down to business. The business of sex.

After getting naked and emerging from the shower with a good six inch hard on, David applied the good old cock ring on his dick. It didn't turn me off, but it reminded me of how mechanical sex is to some gay men. I don't know why the fuck I went to that place with him because I still liked him even though he bragged all night. It was slightly annoying, but he had all the right in the world to brag.

We both tried to kiss, but it was an uneasy kiss. We put our penises together and stroked them. I was keeping a hard on, but David was noticing my lack of enthusiasm. He was still very turned on by me, so he stayed hard. But we both sensed something lacking. It was mostly me. David tried, but I just couldn't get into it like usual.

I think the night was overwhelmingly intellectual and it took away from the sex. Who the fuck knows what it was? We eventually got through it without the fanfare, climaxed together, and we both fell asleep in his bed.

At 5:30 a.m. the next morning, David shook me awake. He said he had to go to work and basically kicked me out of bed. My first thought was, "You're worth $250 million dollars, you don't have to go to work," and then it dawned on me. This is exactly why he's worth $250 million dollars. Because he's this self-disciplined to get himself out of bed and go to work. This is who he is. Disciplined. He needs no one to tell him what to do, help him, and he lets no one take him off the course he's on.

He drops five $100 dollar bills on the nightstand next to my head, and proceeds to tell me, "I'll bet this is the most money you've ever gotten for hustling eh?" For the first time his ego had turned him into an idiot in front of me. The most I've ever gotten? You're delusional. My inner voice was telling me:

Arthur Travis gave me $22,000 for doing nothing, and I've made thousands many times over for less. In fact, I'll see George (Travis), next week, put on boxing gloves and stand up for two hours with a hard on while he rolls around on the floor and walk out with $3,000 or more. David, come on, you're so cheap that you actually think I'm impressed with $500? I've gotten $500 taped to a door without having to do shit. At 17, I made $500 just for letting people feel my dick through my pants standing in the bushes at night.

I still like David, but he has no idea how stupid that comment was. Still, we plan on another night together.

The next night I came over, it was the same thing. We talked for hours, he bragged for 90% of the time I was there, he offered me drugs and I refused, and then we had lousy sex. David's not an addict, although I'd say he's addicted to money and trying to outsmart people. And I can't find much fault in that. Money may not buy happiness, but it sure rents a lot of fun. And it also makes misery a lot easier to live with. When he dies, he won't be able to take it with him though. Hearses don't come with luggage racks.

This second night I stayed over, he handed me another $500 in the morning, but I could tell this was probably the end of our relationship. I wasn't performing live and packing 5,000 people a night to my show, and his "boys" that I heard about are a dime a dozen. He did promise me he'd listen to my tape and turn it over to Eddie Rosenblatt. I knew my tape wasn't my best because it was a mishmash of my personal songs and the best of Mike Ray, Tina and I. Which is sort of like listening to the best of Total Ceolo. We sucked and I knew it. Oh well, I made a thousand dollars in two nights and I had a David Geffen story to tell later in life. There you go.

I called him once after this, and he answered in his New York accent. "It's just not working, Doug. You're a nice guy, but I don't think you're gay. I wish you luck with your music, but it just isn't working between us." David didn't lie to himself or me. He moved on, so I had to.

39

My Father: The Reckoning

1987 is coming to a close. I don't speak to my mother anymore, I'm still searching for something to define myself by, and I wake up every day wondering what the hell I'm gonna do with my life. On a cold December day, I decide to go the Spotlight Bar on Selma Avenue in the middle of the gritty, dangerous, crack infested part of Hollywood.

The Spotlight is a sleazy, old style hustler bar where the investors and entrepreneurs are both severely damaged, so there's always a fight inside or LAPD arresting someone on the sidewalk outside. I came here a few times and met some sweet poor investors. I let them have a discount just because they were so sweet. But I like to see the drama here too. It's good for $100 and a laugh.

Tonight, however, is no laughing matter at the Spotlight. I park my car and walk over but I see something ominous. The LAPD have two guys — one black and one white — pinned up against the side of the bar. As I look closer, the four cops pull out their batons and start beating on these guys. The two young men are already handcuffed so it's an egregious, horrific sight. A group of gay guys are shouting at the cops to leave them alone. I don't know what happened, but I know better than to get too close to the LAPD. I've seen them beat the shit out of my black friends, they've roughed me up just for being in South Central to play music, and they always fuck with gay guys.

No matter how much the gay guys yell, the cops keep beating the two men. And they beat them bad before putting them into the back of the patrol car, handcuffed and bloody. The Hollywood/Wilcox Police Station on Fountain and Wilcox in the heart of the shithole known as Hollywood is no joke either. These guys are in for more beatings at the hands of the cops and the inmates. I wouldn't be surprised if they are killed. And no one will tell, and no one will know, and so no one will care. Another day in LA.

In January 1988, I buy a 1962 Chevy Nova that's still all original with only 44,000 miles on it from a little old lady for $2,000. I feel like the coolest guy in town everywhere I drive. And of course, I drive it to Hollywood to cruise down Sunset Blvd. with the rest of the hood people to show off my ride.

In late February I cruise in my 62 Nova to Hollywood looking for girls or whatever mischief I can get into on a Friday night. On the offramp from the Hollywood Freeway to Sunset Blvd. I notice a small Porsche 914 stuck in the lane next to me. The offramp is jam packed with twenty-year olds going to Hollywood for every reason you can think of.

As I look over, I see an incredibly beautiful and sexy latin female driver with a not so sexy female passenger. I'm fascinated with the driver. She also stares at me and I immediately plan in a nanosecond to say something that leads to meeting her.

"Hey beautiful, what's your name?" I ask confidently.

"Mindy. Hi." She giggles, but her eyes say she's more mature than what she's selling me.

She's fucking hot. She's my type — latin with an Italian look. She knows how to flirt with ease. But she also exudes intelligence and sex from her car that instantly arouses everything inside of me.

I want Mindy's phone number and she gives it to me. I don't think words can do justice to describe how attracted to her I was. It was like nothing I had felt before. I was mesmerized.

She was beautiful inside and out. She gave her heart to me, but I was absorbed with myself, I didn't appreciate it.

Mindy and I started a relationship that was youthful and bold, sexual and fiery. I don't want to mythologize our relationship, but there was something spiritual about it. We had so much in common it was scary. When Mindy would listen to me play the piano and sing my songs. While I was performing my latest song for her on my upright piano in my apartment, she'd cry. She was really moved by my music and I loved and appreciated her deeply for that. I was twenty-two and she was eighteen, so it wasn't like either one of us had a lot of life experience.

Mindy was savvy and knew when to offer her opinion and when to keep quiet. I lacked impulse control, so I was always opening my mouth and though I did know a lot, I was also putting my foot in my mouth often. This only increased my insecurities which doubled our relationship squabbling. I would never back down.

In addition, I brought in a lot of money, and spent a lot on her which we both enjoyed.

I wanted to introduce her to my father as I wasn't on speaking terms with my mother. I rarely spoke to my father either, but that's not the point. I was proud of Mindy's intelligence, charisma and looks, so, as a young man still seeking his father's approval, I was waiting for a chance to introduce them.

That chance came with an unexpected phone call from my father in May of 1988. He called to ask me to pick him up from LAX Airport. I was thrilled to hear from him, and immediately said I'd be there, no problem. I decided to bring Mindy with me on the day I picked him up. I drove up in my 1962 Chevy Nova at the exact time, hoping he'd remark on the excellent condition of a classic car that would remind him of his youth. He said nothing about the car and proceeded to hand me his bags and climbed him. He acted a bit taken aback seeing Mindy. But he was socially awkward, and I understood how hard it was for him to even say hi.

I introduced her to him as he settled in the back seat. He paid no attention to the beautiful girl I had just introduced him to as the new love of my life. He barely shook her hand. I knew how self-absorbed he was, but I thought he could at least charm my lovely new princess. Instead of acknowledging her, my father proceeded to tap me on the shoulder every time he saw a girl on the street as if I should see this. It was akin to driving with Terry N. "Look at that one" – "Don't miss that one" – he even said, "Look at the breasts on that one." Even Terry N. wouldn't do that with my new girlfriend in the car. But my father was oblivious. I was embarrassed.

As I cruised back home, I worried that she's cursed my father. But, to my pleasant surprise, Mindy was saying nothing. Of course, it could be the calm before the storm. Her observational skills were better than NASA's and my father's atrocious behavior was so blatant, she couldn't have missed it. Impatiently, I had to bring it up.

"Did you notice what my father was doing while we were driving?" I asked.

She replied, "Yeah. He was staring at every girl he saw and then pointed them out to you like he was impressing you or something."

"That was fucked of him to do that. It would have been more comfortable if he'd gotten to know you and asked you about yourself."

"No big deal. He's a typical man. He can't control himself when there's girls around. It didn't bother me."

I was flabbergasted at her response. She was ten times more mature than girls her age.

"That's just him being a man."

Long story short, I drove my dad home, and I hoped he'd offer to buy us lunch or pay for gas, but he didn't. Oh well.

The second incident involving my father that Mindy witnessed, began before I met her.

In early 1988, my father called me to come over to his house. I was overjoyed. I raced over there in the knick knack of time, and we both sat down on his couch. I could tell he was serious about something. It was hard for him to talk to anybody, he was the most volatile and insecure man I'd ever met, and he started the conversation as awkwardly as a gay man cheerleading for a Mississippi college football team.

He pulled his shitty old acoustic guitar out from behind a chair and asked me if I remembered it.

"Of course, I do," I answered.

"I'd like you to take it home with you and put new strings on it for me."

My first thought was he has no idea how shitty that guitar is. The neck's warped and he frets are not in alignment which means no matter what kind of strings I replace those crappy nylon strings with, it will never stay in tune. It's as useless as a Christian doctor in a science lab. But I dare not tell him that. Instead, I lie.

"I'd be happy to do that for you. Do you still want nylon strings because nylon strings aren't good for much."

He didn't answer so I wasn't worried about whatever type of strings I chose.

Of course, that was only a week before my car was stolen with everything I owned inside, right in front of James' house in Hollywood. Although I lost every single musical instrument I owned and paid for myself, his guitar was at my home, safely tucked away in the closet.

At this same time, I was finally willing to make life decisions. I knew my heart and soul were inexplicably intertwined with music and I wanted to have a career in the music industry. I was playing out, but because of my weak vocals and unwillingness to put up with other personalities in a band, I decided to attend a music school and obtain a degree in music.

Of course, not only did I not understand the difference between a legitimate school and a fake one, but I also perused ads in music connection magazine for Music Industry schools where I could learn the many facets of working in the music industry. When it came to legitimate schools, like Long Beach State University, LB City College, UCLA or USC I didn't even consider enrolling. I knew I was smarter than any teacher or student in any of these schools, but I was afraid to enroll because I thought I'd fail. I'd love to see a psychiatrist to help me figure out why that was my thought process throughout my life.

I found a school called Trebas Music Institute located on Sunset Blvd. In Hollywood CA. It was expensive! They wanted over $3000 per semester, and they required two years of attendance before they I could graduate with a certificate in one of my chosen music majors.

For the first time in my life, I screwed on my courage tight enough to ask my father for help.

It was at the same meeting between us in his house when he was asking me to string and fix his guitar. I brought up this subject and showed him the ad for the school. I told him I'd pay for part of the cost of the school, but that I couldn't afford the whole thing, so I asked him if he'd please help me. His first response was said to me with so much anxiety, his lips were literally trembling.

"I can't afford this!" he exclaimed.

Now this was coming from a man who made $60,000 annually and had paid off his townhouse which he just sold for a profit. $60,000 a year in 1988 is akin to making $250,000 a year today. But, according to his math, he couldn't afford to help me.

I persisted. "Can we at least work something out? You know how good I am at music, and I'd love to work in the industry. I'll fix your guitar for you, and once I get a job in the industry, maybe I can start paying you back?"

"I don't think so, Doug. I have my own problems. If you had fixed my guitar for me like I asked you too, maybe I can help you with a few hundred dollars to start out with." (This is coming from a man whose own father offered to pay for his full tuition to college, notwithstanding that I had seen a bank statement with over $77,000 in my father's checking account.)

I had accepted his cheap ways years ago, but I was hoping my sincere desire for a career in the music industry would change his mind.

Suffice it to say, I eagerly took on the job of re-stringing his shitty guitar and told him I'd have it ready for him within a month. That's what I told him.

Realistically, this guitar wasn't worth 50 cents. In 1988, I owned five guitars, and had

already bought, played and sold over 19 acoustic, electric and combo acoustic/electric guitars just since 1982. So, I wasn't going to waste my time "fixing" this unfixable piece of shit.
I had a grand idea which I was sure would make him happy and maybe happy enough to
chip in for my schooling fees.

I decided to trash the guitar and buy him a brand-new acoustic guitar for him. I've
got to spend money to get money, right? Also, I thought it was a nice gesture. I'm actually
helping my old man by gifting him with a new acoustic guitar.

The day I decide to bring his new Yamaha acoustic guitar to his house, I also decide to
bring Mindy along with me. Mindy and I are practically inseparable, and this is her chance
to see my father and I bond over music. Music has always been my father's biggest love,
and even though he can't play a guitar to save his life, this is my chance to show him I cared
enough about him to buy him a new guitar.

We agree on the day that I'm to bring his restrung crap guitar over. When the day
comes. I arrive at his house carrying his new guitar with Mindy at my side. He opens the
door and I sense he's curious about this new guitar he sees.

I'm excited to tell him I bought him this new acoustic guitar. I explain to him that his
guitar was very old and would never stay in tune so I spent $150 to buy him a new Yamaha
acoustic guitar that he'd love and would last a lifetime.

He was not happy. Angrily and without any respect for Mindy's presence, he yells at
me.

"I didn't ask you to buy me a new guitar, I asked you to string the old one. You couldn't
even do that."

Now, I could feel my heart rate increase. I'm feeling the anger rise in me.

"But I bought you a new one because the old guitar was useless. I thought you'd like it."

"Doug, I didn't ask you to do that. You are worthless. You couldn't even follow a simple
request. And yet, you expect me to help you pay for your school."

This motherfucker had just disrespected me in front of Mindy. He was no longer my
father, he was now just another motherfucker who had disrespected me, like the thousands
of assholes he kept me caged with while he fucked little girls and never thought about me
and my pain of needing a father.

You fucked up you fucking piece of shit. Every feeling of anger, of repressed rage, of
open, unhealed wounds that he'd caused, rose up in me in an instant. I had enough. You
punched and beat me my whole life and left me to raise myself among animals and then on
the streets at seventeen. You never once offered to help me, and you have the nerve to lecture me in front of my new girlfriend? And you're a fucking coward, you only hit me when
I was a child. You think it's a good idea to lecture me?

"Everybody has a plan until they get punched in the mouth."
— Mike Tyson

It's my turn motherfucker......
Rage had taken over me and I was under its complete control. I came at him like

lightning.

Within an instant I began punching his face. I was hitting him hard, not letting him get a breath. I had had enough, and I wanted him to suffer. I hit his front teeth with so much power and fury, they flew out of his mouth off into the air like bullets from a gun.

I knew he was a wimp, but I expected a little more competition from him. He couldn't defend himself at all. I threw him off the couch onto the ground and began hitting his face. He was turned sideways, so every punch I threw hit his jaw with ferocity. I could hear his jaw snap, crackle and pop! Blood was pouring from his mouth onto his precious carpet, and I was relishing the sight.

I was going to show him the same kind of mercy he showed me. You fucking walking orifice.

And then faintly, I heard Mindy screaming; "Stop it, Doug! You're gonna kill him! You've done enough damage."

Now she's gonna lecture me too? I was blind. But I did hear her, and suddenly I felt a slight twinge of pity for this pitiful man. He was drowning in his own blood on the carpet. I stopped hitting him and he immediately tried to get up which he couldn't do. I started to feel a vague sense of guilt. And then he opened his mouth speaking to Mindy:

"Get him out of here before I kill him. If he ever shows his face here again, I will murder his ass."

How are you gonna do that when you can't even speak, your eyes are closed, your jaw's broken, and most of your teeth are missing? Fuck you.

He tried to act tough even when he'd been thoroughly beaten, but I expected that. He'd never expressed any emotion except anger and rage. I'd never seen him feel guilty or beg for mercy.

It wasn't like being beaten almost to death was going to change him into a nicer person. He never liked me, and I hated him.

And then suddenly, I began to cry. Without warning, guilt began to rise up in me. I was proud of myself until suddenly I wasn't. With Mindy by my side, wiping at the tears running down my face, I said to her, "I can't believe I just beat up my own father. What the fuck's wrong with me? Oh my god."

She held my hand and wiped the water from my eyes as we walked back to my car.

I also blurted out that I probably just ruined my inheritance. I'm not sure whether I was crying for him or for me. He has money and a will. And where there's a will, I want to be in it.

I called who had become my real dad, Arthur Travis, and he agrees to give me a couple of thousand dollars for the first semester of school. I'll need a Federal School Loan for the rest.

40

Ritch Esra

I entered Trebas Music Institute in June of 1988.

Upon entering Trebas, I didn't know what to expect. Music was my life, but I any attempt to present music in a formal way. What the fuck was I doing at a music school? If you asked me then, I couldn't have answered you. It was another in a long line of ideas where I was looking for hope outside of myself.

At Trebas I felt out of place in the sound engineering and music production classes. There were two of these classes. One was taught by Malcolm Cecil, who co-produced four of my favorite Stevie Wonder records, Innervisions, Music of my mind, Talking Book and Fulfillingness' First Finale', along with two Isley Brothers records and two Billy Preston albums. All of these artists were and still are heroes and icons of mine.

Malcolm was a very nice man who taught with patience. But I soon learned that I was still not interested in nobs on a recording studio board. I learned a lot, but my skill was in playing the instruments and adding production ear candy. I liked the engineering class even less. But I met wonderful people at Trebas. Along with Malcolm, I met Scott Scheer who helped me learn more about music production and we became friends. He eventually helped me produce three of my own songs. The most memorable man I met at Trebas was my Music Business teacher: Ritch Esra.

From the moment I entered his classroom, I felt at home. He produced an effervescent energy that was infectious. He had boundless energy and it was obvious he loved what he taught. But it was more than that.

I felt a deep connection with this man from the moment I walked into his classroom. He was as passionate about music as I was, he genuinely loved teaching us, and from the first day in the class, I knew he could discern musical greatness. I heard him speak about new artists in a way that told me he knew what made them potentially timeless. Tracy Chapman, Guns n Roses, The Indigo Girls, R.E.M., and The Replacements were a few of the artists he would talk about, asking us what made them special. He would challenge us to give him the reasons they appealed to people, and what made them unique. I loved being in his class.

Ritch gave me the feeling that I belonged. It was a new feeling to me. I had never felt like I belonged anywhere except on a street corner. He intrigued me. I wanted to get to know him. It didn't take long before I asked him if he'd like to have dinner with me.

To my surprise, Ritch said yes. I remember we chose to meet at a restaurant on Sunset Blvd. in Hollywood. I don't remember its name, but it was a popular music industry hangout. He was startled when, at dinner, I asked him if he was gay. Ritch was not effeminate, but somehow my gaydar had gone off, and I wanted to know. He was honest with me.

"Yes, I am. How did you know?"

"I'm not sure. I just had a gut feeling. I'm glad you feel comfortable with me to tell me."

From that moment forward, we were very close friends. I loved him, and I knew Ritch's love for me was genuine. We were not attracted to each other physically, but our friendship was deeper than just physical attraction. I could count on Ritch and he could count on me.

We enjoyed each other's company and never stopped talking about music. Ritch was also the West Coast Director of A & R for Arista Records. His boss was Clive Davis. I still thought of A & R people as "wannabes," people who made their living off of artists by hanging around them. It was ironic that by hanging around Ritch, I learned about the skillset of an A & R person, and there was much more than I ever knew.

Although he was older than me and my teacher, he was still a little boy in his heart. A hurt little boy. He wanted people's approval, and he was as naïve' as a seven-year-old kid. I loved that. Sometimes it didn't serve him, but it made him loved and appreciated by everyone everywhere. Ritch was also a Sagittarius and I am an Aries. Two compatible fire signs — the archer and the general. Our astrological signs predestined our lifelong bond.

Ritch also introduced me to Rosemary Butler, a singer I had admired since I was a youngster. I was almost starstruck when I met her, but she was so down to earth, we became immediate friends.

If you've listened to any popular music over the last 50 years, you've heard Rose's voice. And you've also heard the harmonies she's composed for countless hit records such as "Takin' it to the Streets" for the Doobie Brothers, "You love the thunder" for Jackson Browne, and many other hit songs. Rosemary has appeared on more records than any background singer in music history.

She's sang with Boz Scaggs, James Taylor, Warren Zevon, Neil Young, Linda Ronstadt, Bonnie Raitt, Nitty Gritty Dirt Band, Jackson Browne, and Rosanne Cash. Rosemary is that booming voice you hear on Jackson's "Running on Empty" singing "Running Blind...". When I heard that voice, I couldn't get enough.

Ritch, Rosemary and I began a healthy ritual of walking around Hazeltine Park in Sherman Oaks every morning. Sometimes we'd all swim in Ritch's pool too. Rosemary is also a cancer survivor, and we still see spend time together when we can. I love you Rosemary.

I got to know some of my classmates too. Out of the many friends and fellow students I got to know, Benjamin Malavé, Don Miller, Michelle Thompson, Jan Harris and Shilah Morrow will remain forever in my heart.

I bought tickets to the Monsters of Rock show in the summer of 1988. I came to see Van Halen, Metallica, and the Scorpions. To get to those bands, I had to sit through the torturous banal, wannabe rock sounds of Kingdom Come and Dokken. God how I hate musicians who spread bad music. Disingenuous rock poser metal boys disguising themselves as real artists made me mad enough to jump up on stage and kick every ass up there. Or fuck them all in the ass - hard. For anyone who has a visual now, let me help — I did neither.

The worst part of the show was walking back to my 62 Nova and finding that someone had stolen my thousand-dollar Blaupunkt car stereo system. They broke a window and just ripped it out. Of course, I felt stupid for not covering it or removing it. Everyone in the car was too scared of my temper to say anything on the ride home, but I know they were thinking it: Doug's stupid. And the voice in my head pounced. See you stupid dumbshit, you didn't even think of taking the stereo out before you left the car in the open. You can't even impress anyone, cos in the end someone always outsmarts you."

41

Josh's Birth: Back To The Advocate

I wasn't prepared for the next two weeks. I was alone again, but not for long.

I was doing my job, calling all the record stores in the country for the numbers of records sold that week. My job was to give those numbers to my boss, Bud Scoppa, who was a man with integrity. His job was to then give those numbers to George Albert, a man with no integrity. George then manipulated the numbers favoring the record companies who spent the most money on advertising and that's how Cashbox calculated their Hot 100 hits chart.

"Your girlfriend's on the phone."

Mindy called me at my office to tell me she was pregnant with my child.

This was the beginning of a whole new way of thinking about life. Honestly, being a dad didn't scare me. I loved the thought. And I wasn't afraid of the coming reality.

I wasn't prepared for this financially though. I was making $7.92 an hour working as a forklift driver at WEA – Warner/Elektra/Atlantic Records, in the warehouse. Although I had aspirations to move up in this company, I didn't expect to start out with a baby on a forklift driver's salary. It wasn't easy settling for that when I'd made $5,000 cash in less than an hour without breaking a sweat only a year ago

Surprisingly, Mindy summoned the courage to tell her parents we were determined to have this baby even though they recognized we weren't compatible life partners.

During the course of her carrying my baby, we agreed to raise him with the values our baby needed. No matter what differences Mindy and I had, we agreed that our baby came first.

With her parents' support and the medical benefit package I had from working at Warner Brothers, our son, Joshua Probst, was born on February 15, 1990. I was a bit worried that he might not be a boy (Mindy and I both wanted to be surprised), but the first thing I saw when he squirted out was his balls. I yelled in excitement, "He's got balls!"

Mindy and I, even though we had so much in common and dreamed of future together, split up. We were just too young to make it together.

I moved in with Ritch. Joshua was my baby. Nothing was gonna stop me. Ritch was a saint. I placed a crib in the living room of our apartment at 1226 Laurel Avenue in West Hollywood and loved learning how to be a father very quickly. On weekends, I was changing diapers four times a day, making his food, entertaining him, fixing bottles, comforting him late at night, and loving it!

I knew I needed a better job. I couldn't raise a child on $7.92 an hour. I was in a bind — unfamiliar because of the enormity of it, and yet familiar because I've been in that situation before.

So, I went back to what was familiar: Prostitution.

I immediately thought of placing an ad for Shawn Mayotte's escorting services in the Advocate again. At this time, there was another local gay men's magazine that was taking over the Advocate's escort business: Frontiers. I stuck with Old Glory: The Advocate. I wondered if anyone would remember me, and I doubted if it would work. Though you can't fool a whore, a whore can fool himself. I surged ahead with this new job plan anyway.

The response from this advertisement is overwhelming. I answer calls day and night. I'm amazed that people still know who I am. They remember me better than I remember myself. I tell them that I've grown my hair long; they're not expecting to see me with long hair. I'm nervous because I know most older, wealthy gay men and straight women young guys with short, perfectly coiffed hair.

Shawn Mayotte circa 1990:

My answering machine couldn't handle all of the messages. The world remembered me, and it remembered me with lust and respect.

This was a boost to my self-esteem at a time when I needed it the most. I was still working at Warner Brothers, so Ritch fielded some calls for me.

One of the first calls I received was from a man with a very effeminate voice who sounded on the phone like he was already cumming ahead of the party. He was enamored with Shawn Mayotte. I calmed him down and listened to his desire to get fucked in the ass, but he was tough on negotiations. He was an interior decorator in West Hollywood, but this queen was already getting on my nerves and I hadn't even gotten off the phone yet.

We finally came to an agreement, and I drove to his house on Londonderry Drive. Londonderry drive is a street that you can only enter from Sunset Blvd. When I made my turn onto Londonderry, I was happy to see the gorgeous mansions that lined the street. The further I drove, the bigger the houses got, so I knew he had the money — cheap bastard!

To make a long story short, he greeted me with a wet kiss, shoved five $100 dollar bills into my hand, and ran up his beautiful staircase like a damsel in distress eager to be chased, caught and raped. I know this scenario; I've played this game before. I ran after him, we quickly disrobed, and I threw him on the bed as he giggled like a catholic schoolgirl.

To his apparent dismay, I interrupted his fantasy by cleaning and lubing his asshole. I then thrust my penis deep into his anus, pumped him for a few minutes, and promptly shot my cum as he came stroking himself. And with that, what I thought would be a short night, quickly turned into a long one.

He started bitching about how I came too fast. He began pacing around the room, and there's nothing worse than a mad, prancing faggot. I had my money in my pocket, so I put my clothes on, rushed down the stairs before he turned into Kathleen Turner in Serial Mom. I was out and racing down Sunset Blvd in a flash.

Even though I had $500 in my pocket for fifteen minutes of play, it was disappointing. He was an asshole, I wanted good men — regulars who could provide me with a steady pay-check like John Thompson and Arthur Travis did. I want to meet men who are trustworthy and can co-sign for a Camaro. Clearly, this clown wasn't gonna be my benefactor.

I started getting calls from decent people who paid well and weren't bipolar. One guy ran the Ladies Professional Wrestling Association, and he was so proud to show me their new building, still under construction, but he believed they were gonna be huge. I told him it was fake (it wasn't a question) and he laughed and said of course the wrestling was fake. He showed me where they learned all the right moves. He was a sweet man.

As I was building my bank account, I received a call from a man named George Masters. I had never heard of him, but the name sounded familiar, like high society. He spoke eloquently and offered me $1,000 to meet him at the Spotlight Bar in Hollywood. It seemed strange that a man who was so genuinely well-spoken would want to meet at a dive bar.

With thoughts of hundred-dollar bills dancing in my head, I drove to the Spotlight and met George, who was drinking quietly at the bar. I noticed right away how handsome he was. George greeted me with a smile and a firm, friendly handshake. It was like meeting a long-lost brother. The conversation flowed as easily our scotch and sodas did, and soon we had a connection that instinctively told me this was a good man.

He wanted me to leave the bar with him in his Corvette and travel to his hotel room in West Hollywood. I agreed as long as he promised to drive me back, so my car wasn't towed.

As we entered his suite at the Chateau Marmont, I saw clippings on the dining table that revealed who he was. He was George Masters, hairstylist to royalty. I saw praises that called him a "magician," a master transformer, and a Hollywood Legend. He was Marilyn Monroe's personal makeup artist, and his client list included the beautiful Diahann Carroll as well as Bo Derek, Ann Margaret and Marlene Deitrich, but he was best known for trans-forming Dustin Hoffman into Dorothy Michaels in Sydney Pollack's most memorable film, Tootsie.

I was stunned. I was in the same room with the Mozart of hair and makeup. George was passionate and very sexual. George could suck start a B-52. He loved sucking my cock and he took all eight and a half inches down his throat with ease. When I came, he swallowed every last drop. But when it was over, it was over. George masturbated, bear hugged me and said he was taking me back to the Spotlight. I really liked him and was hoping for a little conversation, but with a $1,000, less is more, and I'm good with that.

We exchanged information and I knew we'd get together again. I had found a new friend. George and I got together a few times after our first encounter. Unfortunately, George had acquired an insatiable appetite for cocaine. Cocaine became his primary focus when we were together. I heard later that George died young, at age 63 in 1998. Rest in peace, my dear friend. You're not forgotten.

42

Neal

I ran my ad through the spring of 1990. I began enjoying dinner with doctors, priests and a couple of people with low credit scores. Most were amazed that I was taking care of my son knowing I'd have to do it as a single father. What the fuck? This is my child. I love him. His mother matters, but I'm I wasn't gonna have my time with my son determined by some judge. I'm his father! I'm responsible for guiding him through life. My father was a piece of shit. He beat me, neglected me, never once taught me anything valuable or showed me how to effectively be a man. He didn't care. I care about my son. I never forgot my vow to myself while being bloodied by my father that I was never gonna be like him. Those weren't the footprints I was gonna leave. But I was about to receive help.

I received a call from a man named Neal. He immediately began telling me that he wasn't interested in having sex with me, he wanted to meet me because there was something, he saw in my eyes that intrigued him. Obviously, I was skeptical but curious. Here's a man who has seen me naked, but it wasn't my dick or body he noticed — it was my eyes? I've never played this game before.

We set up our meeting at my apartment with Ritch. When Neal arrived, I peeked out the window to get a glimpse of him. The moment I got my first look of him, I was more intrigued about meeting him than any person I'd ever met. I walked out, stood at the top of the stairs looking down at the kindest face I'd ever seen. His smile was genuine, and it flooded happiness into a neighborhood overwhelmed with the despair of dying men. I bounded down the stairs to greet him.

He took me to The French Quarter in his Toyota 4Runner for dinner. He wanted to know more about me. I worried he wouldn't like my long hair or be turned off because I had a baby boy. But he told me he wasn't. He jokingly said, "I assumed that much because you're quite attractive." I didn't trust his words yet, because my experience since childhood is that men and women will say anything to fuck me. I morphed into the hustler I've always become when I need money. Neal seemed to sense that, and he comforted me. "You don't have to impress me or be something you're not. Just be yourself."

His words felt genuine. I wanted to say the same things to him, but I needed to size him up first. I asked him what he did for a living, and I was stunned when he said he owned 900 numbers (sex lines). He also said he owned the number 976-6969. Owning that phone number at this time in history was akin to discovering oil in the late 1800s. It was a business idea I had in the 1980s that I brought to the attention of John Thompson– I was seeing huge profits, but he turned me down. John also turned me down on buying the photo studio from Kent. I also saw my Beverly Hills clients treating their pets like children, so I came up with the idea of Pet Health Insurance. Not one insurance company was offering it. I took it to my surrogate dad, Joe L., who was an Insurance Broker, and he thought it was a fantastic idea. Nothing ever came of it.

Neal was a listener. I needed that. I opened up to him about my present fears. I was afraid Mindy would take my son Josh away from me because of my actions. I was overwhelmed with guilt, but I knew I had to fight for my son. Neal listened to my fears. He didn't interrupt me. He let me get it out and when I had nothing left, he repeated to me that he understood why I was afraid, but that he could tell I loved my son, and I was over condemning myself. That's all he said during our first meal.

I left him that night with a sense that maybe this was the guy I always dreamed of. But I wasn't even sure what kind of man I "always dreamed of." Is he a father? Is he a boyfriend? Is he a sugar daddy? Is he a psychiatrist? Or is he a man who loves me like I could love a man? I was confused, but very happy. Neal had already begun to win my heart and we hadn't even talked about sex or money.

I still got up at five in the morning every day and drove my old Chevy Nova to Warner Brothers. Though I was making a mint from my ad in the advocate, I would not quit my job. I put all the money "tricks" would give me, into my bank account. I was also still seeing Arthur Travis. I think I had close to $30,000 in my bank account while driving a forklift that paid me $7.92 an hour. I was frugal, which is just a fancy word for cheap. In my head, I believed I was sleeping on the bus benches again, totally unaware of what the future would be. I was starting to write songs again on my piano and guitar. Ritch gave me praise when he would hear one, he loved. He actually came running out of his bedroom into the living room and announced, "You've got to finish that! That's a hit!" I loved it when Ritch gave me praise. He was honest. His job as an A & R guy for Arista Records depended on it. He wouldn't cosign my crappy songs. I needed him for that.

I saw Arthur Travis again when Josh was six months old. They both knew about Josh, because I mailed pictures of him to each of them. I was hurt. While eating lunch together, I told him I couldn't understand why neither of my parents had any interest in their grandchild. He replied to me with words I'll never forget.

"Douglas, they never had any interest in you, why would you expect them to have any interest in Josh?" I'd never thought of that. But I've never forgotten it since he said it.

I was now able to form a band. I put an ad in Music Connection magazine, and I knew I needed a van or truck to haul equipment around. I decided to sell my Chevy Nova and I was able to turn a profit. But I was still cheap and bought a 1969 Volkswagen bus with a 5-speed stick shift. It was so cool to drive around in it with my long hair and musical equipment inside on the way to audition potential band members.

***

One day, I was pushing Josh on a swing at Palisades Park in Santa Monica. It was his first ride on a swing, and you can see the joy he was experiencing in his smile. I heard a female voice say, "Can we push your son with you? We want to have a baby, and he looks so adorable." I turned to look, and it was Julia Roberts sitting with Kiefer Sutherland on a wall right beside us. But they were both smoking cigarettes, and I wasn't gonna let them anywhere near him unless they agreed to put their cigarettes out. I told them, "Sure, but only if you put those cigarettes out and do not light up while pushing him." I was pleasantly surprised to hear both of them say meekly and with understanding, "Of course we will. Thank you so much!" And then Julia admonished Kiefer to stop smoking so they could enjoy pushing Josh in his swing. She was obviously the boss. It was a great day for all of us.

Look at his smile!

Though I was developing bits and pieces of self-esteem, I was still overwhelmed with guilt. I was the reason Mindy, and I were separating, and her anger towards me was justified.

I had not answered any calls from potential "sugar daddies or sugar mommas" because of the developing friendship with Neal. I wasn't into drugs to solve my anxiety. People who noticed suggested valium, but Neal was my valium. For weeks, we'd sit inside my Volkswagen bus, parked outside Ritch's apartment on Laurel Avenue. I'd talk and he'd listen. Sometimes I'd talk for hours about how ashamed of myself I was, and about how scared I was of losing custody of my son. His listening was the start of feelings I never experienced for a man before.

For the first time, while I was speaking to him, I leaned over and kissed him on the mouth. It was sensuous, and I was embarrassed. Neal reassured me that it was a normal reaction. I was confused but decided that he was more important than my self-loathing.

It was after this moment that he offered me a job at his Company: Global Entertainment. The offer included a salary of $4,000 a month plus the use of company credit cards.

It was hard to turn down.

I was still unsure about taking that offer when I had a future at Warner Bros. In addition, I was now writing songs, and had decided to form a band. This had always been my destiny. I was starting to go out to clubs, and I was mesmerized at seeing a video playing on the screen at FM Station, a rock club in North Hollywood, CA. It was like nothing I had seen before, and it jolted every revolutionary musical spark I had within my soul. I was still suspicious of anyone offering me money. To me, that meant they wanted sex.

43

The Early 90's: A Musical Revolution

It was Nine Inch Nails performing "Head like a hole." I couldn't take my eyes off this singer with black dreadlocks screaming angrily into the microphone "Head like a hole, black as your soul, I'd rather die than give you control." FUCK! This was me. I was angry for the same reasons, and for my own personal reasons. I hated the greedy society we lived in; I hated the phony baby boomers who sang about human need only to bow down to corporate greed. I also hated my father for obvious reasons. I hated republicans. I hated phonies, I hated hypocrisy. I sat down later that night and wrote a song incorporating all of these feelings, and I called it Mindfuck:

MINDFUCK

Now that you have mindfucked all of your children tell me how do you sleep
while we're seething with rage
You seem so surprised, as you realize, we see through your lies
And refuse to be slaves
I wonder has it gone so far that no one can be saved

What did you expect when all our feelings you reject
Now there is no compromise
When your life it seems is only filled with broken dreams
You learn the truth is in the eyes

You sang your Woodstock songs, your children came along
When did it go wrong – tell me I'd really like to know
You sang of human need, then of corporate greed, now your children bleed
I guess we reap what we sow
Now someone tell me where the fuck did peace and love go

It has always been my nature to resist control
From anything that I despise
And I will never believe anything I hear from you
Until I see it in your eyes

'Cos all I've ever known are lies - Once I believed in you
Now I know that nothing's true - Now I only cry – please somebody tell me why

"There was a time when you talked about peace and love, but you've been feeding your children violence for so long…what a mindfuck"

Laying it down here for all to see
Lightning striking never bothered me
Living my life has got me feeling like a wounded animal
Somebody come, somebody come save me

Now the time has come, for what must be done, hatred's so much fun
'cos it feels just like a game
Now it's always the same, you deny and blame,everything is alright
maybe we'll all go away – When you know the truth it doesn't matter what you say

You had the chance to change the world like no one ever before
Instead, you filled it full of lies
And now you cannot run 'cos all your children carry guns
And the truth is in their eyes
Doug Probst © 1990 Myamygdala music

I was hearing new bands like Nirvana, Pearl Jam, Alice in Chains along with great new pop artists like Edie Brickel and Sinead 'O Connor who covered a brilliant song by my hero Prince…brilliantly. She also tore up a picture of the pope, and no one seemed to understand why, except me. I was telling everyone how priests had sexually assaulted me, and no one wanted to hear it. This was my time.

Neal was right.

At this same time, my sister Jamie showed up at my house in Venice begging me for a place to stay. I was very unnerved at the thought of a burglar living with me, but I still loved her, and wanted her to know that. She stayed with me for a couple of weeks, and I got her a job at the Salvation Army. Eventually, meth became her best friend again, and I no longer mattered. I had to ask her to leave because I couldn't raise my son with a meth addict in the same house. I loved her very much, and I poured my feelings into a song about her.

I took a lot of time with the music, creating an orchestral section that was commensurate with my willingness to help her become a whole person again. I understood her pain of being sexually abused for all of her childhood and then turning to our mother for help, only to be thrown back into the rapist's den. I decided to call the song "The Truth" because I was no longer gonna hold anything back. I hadn't heard a song about surviving child sexual abuse on the radio before, and I wanted to make it palatable and for radio with the music.

I wanted her to know I would walk her through all the pain to get to the other side. At this time, I still believed there was another side. Later, though my struggles with drugs and becoming a Counselor, going to Alcoholics Anonymous, I realized there is no "other side."

Life's a journey, one day at a time.

THE TRUTH

I know you're trying to break out from that world, believe me I understand
The fears inside of you, remember I lived through it too,
all you've got to do is take hold of my hand
I see that look of desperation in your eyes, you're searching for something pure
It's a struggle every day, it makes you want to run away and reach for familiar
temporary cures

And as I pound upon the wall, I hear screaming down the hall
But there's nothing I can do to make the screaming end
'Cos even though we cry in vain, I know it helps to ease the pain
Daddy's got his fingers inside my sister again

Nobody said this would be easy, but at least you won't be facing this all alone
You're putting the past behind you, and the scars are there to remind you,
Of that fucked up world we used to call our home

You've got my love, please just try and take the time,
I hope it's not too much for you ah to do
When the pain is real, it'll take some work to heal yourself,
and I'll be there to pull you through....

I know you'd rather spend your days in that silent happy haze,
'cos the needle always seems to make daddy go away
And I'm not trying to find the blame, but when I prayed Jesus never came
I guess that he had something better to do that day

And these memories daddy gave, I guess we'll take them to our graves
But if we break the chains, we don't have to live like slaves
Because he may have hurt us then, but daddy's never gonna hurt us again
I promise right now this is where the cycle ends, I'm speaking the truth
I'm speaking the truth
I'm speaking the truth
The cycle's over. you don't have to suffer anymore
Nothing 's ever gonna stop me from speaking the truth

Doug Probst © Copyright 1991 Truthmusic, Inc.

One last event with my mother. Mom had gotten into a fight with two people in a bar
and had been beaten badly. The police were called, and because of her history, they put her
on a 72 hour hold in a strait jacket. Apparently, she wasn't behind bars because Jamie said
mom shredded the straight jacket, ran out of the room, and walked ten blocks from the
Lakewood Sheriff's Station to her house. Later, I heard it was the only time a person ever

freed themselves from a strait jacket and broke out of a police station and made it home free.

When I told Neal about it, he joked that a strait jacket must have felt like too much hugging and love for her, so she had to get it off. "Must break free! Must break free!" I loved Neal's wit.

Because so many of my friends were still dying of AIDS, I went back to volunteering at APLA. I was now a donor too. While I was licking stamps, I noticed an upright piano and started playing. I attracted a small crowd, but one man stood out from the rest. He was Miguel Herrera. He began singing to "Does anybody really know what time it is" – one of my favorite songs to play by the band Chicago.

Miguel and I instantly clicked. I loved his voice, he was kind, and he praised my piano playing. He sang good enough for us to be noticed and many people requested that we play while they worked. Miguel and I also bonded over our troubled childhoods and we both worried that we weren't good enough for anyone to love. I loved Miguel for being open and honest about his childhood wounds that were still unhealed. I loved it when he called me "Dougie."

Miguel sang much better than he thought, and we started playing together as a duo. He and I eventually performed together at clubs and parties. We wanted to bring back many of the same songs we both loved and refused to change our show's song set for anyone. Like brothers, we've had our fights, but nothing has stopped our love for each other. My love for Miguel will never die.

44

Quitting Warner Brothers (Neal Offers Me a Job)

In December 1990, I was in line for the lunch truck outside the WEA Warehouse. When I made it up front and purchased my meal, I inadvertently left my wallet on the lunch truck serving table where the guy takes your money, gives you your change and your burrito, so they serve customers quickly and we can take our food into the lunchroom and eat at the WEA lunch table. But I didn't know it until fifteen minutes later.

I sat down and started eating my burrito. Time passed, and I was immersed in beans and cheese, when I noticed I wasn't sitting on my wallet. I jumped up, searched myself, and it was gone. Immediately I panicked because I had $900 cash in it. My rent was due that day. I rushed back to the truck's serving table and the guy's still there selling food. The line was still extremely long as I was the first in line, in front of 45 other warehouse employees. I asked the server if he noticed my wallet on the table. He said no. Immediately, I exploded in anger.

"You motherfucking piece of shit, you know you stole it, or you know who stole it. I'll beat your ass until I find it on you or in your truck."

All the rage stored inside me for years was consuming me. I now had a justified reason to let it out.

As big as this fat ass taco truck punk was, he was scared to death of me. He kept pleading for me to believe me, while backing away from me in fear. He said one of my fellow employees must have taken it.

"My rent money was in my wallet. I will beat your motherfucking ass if you don't give it back."

I shoved his fat ass into the truck. Just then, someone shouted from behind.

"I think it was one of the guys in line."

I turned to everyone in line and shouted, "Did you hear me motherfuckers? Stand up and give me back my wallet with all $900 dollars inside, or I will break every one of your fucking arms."

They were afraid, but no one stepped up. I then screamed into the lunchroom the same threats and I received no response. Not even a "shut the fuck up." My rage was so palpable, I was scaring the shit out of everyone. But I realized that one of my fellow coworkers had stolen my wallet. And they weren't confessing.

By this time, someone had alerted my warehouse supervisor, Mark Ratlin, to the dilemma transpiring outside. He backed me up and yelled at everyone to give me back my wallet. All of a sudden, some of them started barking back. "I don't steal," and "I'm not gonna stand here and be accused of something I didn't do." A couple of guys I worked closely with every day defended me:

"We love Doug. He's the man! We'd never steal from him. And we don't know who did. If we knew, we'd tell you right now." I knew them and had worked with them every day. I watched them sleep while they were supposed to work. They talked about people behind their backs. They know who stole my wallet and my $900. After hearing them, I was reminded of Ralph Waldo Emerson's words about character: "What you are shouts so loudly in my ears, I cannot hear what you say."

I was done with Warner Brothers.
I had just been offered a job making three times the amount of money I was making here. It was time to listen to the universe.

I told Mark, "I quit. Just mail me my last check." This job and company no longer existed in my world. And for the first time, the voice in my head didn't blame me.

I called Neal and told what happened and I wanted to work with him. I could sense his joy. He even offered to give me the $900 so I could pay my rent. I didn't want to let Ritch down. Of course, I still didn't trust his motives. Even though Neal hadn't made a sexual advance on me in six months, even after he's spent most of our time together listening to my fears about losing Josh, comforting me, and going home without lifting a finger, I didn't trust him. In my head, he was thinking: "You're all mine now baby!"

I'm smart. I know what everyone thinks.

Neal invites me to Egg Entertainment's office on Santa Monica Blvd. I walk in, there's the crew: Zeb, Henry and Albert. In one corner stands Zeb. Zeb was nineteen, and good looking. He barely spoke when I greeted him, but he was gentle and exuded a shyness that was I could tell was hard to get through. I asked him where he was from, and he stammered "Yermo." He couldn't believe I knew where Yermo was. Yermo's not really a city. It's a ghost town (population 790), so hot that all the action stops at ten. in the morning. It's famous for being the location where the first Del Taco fast food place was built. Moving on…
In another corner stands Henry. He was closer to my age, average looking, and very

effeminate. He was nice but seemed peculiar. As he greeted me, he farted. They all laughed, and I felt uncomfortable. I didn't feel threatened though, so it was still good.

And in between everyone's dogs in the far corner sat Jabba The Hut; Albert. But Albert weighed in at 400 pounds, so Neal wasn't giving him a job for being a hot twink with a big dick. I was confused, but since I was an employee now, and Neal and I were together nearly every day – with my son Josh, I knew it was paramount for Josh's safety and my sanity to figure out what the hell this shit was all about.

Immediately, I was rolling in money. Neal was paying me more than $4,000 a month for jobs like doing call counts. Doing call counts encompassed listening to all the customers' messages on our dating lines like 1-800-844-9595. I'd spend a couple of hours listening to our "bulletin board" customers talk about how they wanted to meet people who would tie them up, pee on them, or put a diaper on and fuck them in the ass with their bottle, and this was all before lunch.

The reason we had to listen to their conversations was to look out for child molesters and rapists. We had to turn people over to the police. One guy I'll never forget, left this message:

"I want to meet a woman with a thirteen-year-old daughter who can fuck a forty-year-old man better than her dad."

We had to turn those conversations and messages over to the police. To find these motherfuckers and get them in custody became a personal mission for me. I wanted to take vengeance for all the children who whose cries while being raped by adults they trusted. We were the original "To catch a predator."

It was fun listening to some of these people's fantasies and simultaneously make money off of them. One guy wanted to meet a woman who would dress up like Tina Turner and pee on him while he's sucking on a bottle soiling himself in a diaper. And she's doing this while singing "What's love got to do with it?" You might think that's kinky, but what astounded us is that he received calls. He eventually found his fantasy woman and when I think of them, I wonder if they made a family and watched their children graduate from college dressed in diapers. Just a thought.

45

AIDS Death Tolls Rise As I Become A Father

As the money rolled in, I decided to move out of Hollywood. I wanted to live in Venice, California as it was the coolest spot to live in for musicians, hippies and mental cases who walked up and down that world famous boardwalk. I was already driving a 1969 Volkswagen bus, my hair and Josh's had grown long, and I was writing songs about a peaceful, harmonious world. This was the dawning of the age of Aquarius for me.

I rented a condo on Pacific Avenue right at Windward Place, a block from the beach. Josh and I, Venice 1991 and 1992.

At this time, I was also still in contact with Troy Meyers, more famously known as Jeremy Scott, a huge gay adult film star from the 1980s. We were still very good friends. I was jealous of his cock, but I made up for it by fucking his sister. Anyway, Troy told me in 1990 that he had AIDS and he wanted to see me.

When I saw him, he was gaunt and lethargic. Although it was obvious to both of us, he was gonna die, he still joked with me about our past in the Adult Film Industry, our laughs at the beach together, and me fucking his sister. At least I got to spend time with him before he passed away. When Troy died in 1991, he became the 110th person I knew who had died of the plague. His funeral was the 89th funeral I attended. I cried for him, but I also cried because of the shame I felt about our country. No one cared. There were no medications except AZT, and that only added to and prolonged your suffering, making it harder, instead of easier to die.

But, as you can see, even in his coffin, Troy was still smiling as if he was on his way back to the beach.

I love you, Troy.

Re: 1991, I attended an event fundraiser for AIDS Project Los Angeles at The Universal Amphitheater in Hollywood. Many Hollywood celebrities were there but it was Bette Midler who reached in and grabbed my hear when she performed my favorite Beatle song "In My Life" by my favorite Beatle John Lennon.

I was there. 1991 was the year that hopelessness reigned. By this time, ten years of death along with no lifesaving medications on the horizon had left us more than demoralized. Even my friend Robbin Crosby, guitarist for the rock band Ratt had HIV. Robbin was a great songwriter, a beautiful man, and a compassionate friendbut when I heard the news, I knew he was going to die. Just another day in the world of AIDS. The collective conclusion was that we were all going to die, it was just a matter of time. Friends of mine started committing suicide. It still hurts when I think of friends like James Hajdukiewicz, who died just before the first lifesaving cocktail was made available. This was a heartwarming, yet heartbreaking night. We all felt the gloom. I loved Bette for "not running to the hills" as she said that night. Many stars stayed away from helping us because they didn't want to be associated with "faggots" or AIDS. Bette wasn't one of those people. Thank you, Divine Miss M., You cared when others didn't. I'll always cherish the memory of watching you sing my favorite John Lennon song "In my life" for my friends who were dead or dying. I'm grateful every day for having survived.

***

I loved living in Venice. It was my kind of town. Neal and I agreed to start eating nothing but health food. I remember when I sat down at a health food restaurant called "Juicy's" and ordered organic pesto pasta. I was ready to dig in and start living a healthy life. After all, I was only giving Josh carrot juice in his bottles and he loved it. I dug in and took my first bite and nearly threw up. Neal began laughing because he knew what real organic food tasted like and I obviously didn't. The damn food tasted like shit. This crap would be a great thing to eat of you're used to a steady diet of worms. In a strange way, Neal's laughter was one of our hundreds of bonding experiences. He let me find out for myself what organic food really tasted like. I began to love him more because I was feeling loved.

I also began to love him for his willingness to learn from me. This man had an IQ of 152 and when he was twelve years old, had taken a car engine apart and put it all back together just for the fun of it. He invented a remote by taking a rotisserie chicken knob and somehow wiring it to his little tv in 1969 when he was nine years old. This way, he wouldn't to have to walk to the tv to change channels. I just wondered how many burnt briskets they had for dinner after that.

When we first met, even though he knew I had a baby boy, he admitted he wasn't fond of being around kids. They made him feel uncomfortable because of their energy. When the company crew was together, Henry and Zeb would comment how kids were a pain in the ass, and even though Neal wouldn't go that far, I could tell he empathized with them. I didn't.

Every time my father beat me when I was young, I vowed to never hit my child. I knew how much it hurt and I never wanted to hurt anyone, especially a defenseless child. It was a promise I made to myself that I would never break. When I became an adult, I loved being around kids, and I always wanted to have at least one of my own. But I had no idea how much I would fall in love with my son, Joshua, after he was born.

Neal told me many times how much he was learning from me. He saw how much I loved Joshua. When we went out to dinner, I brought him with us, and asked the restaurant for a highchair. And we ate the best restaurants in town: Chasen's, Morton's, The Warehouse in Marina Del Rey, Orso's, and at all of those, I demanded no fuss from anyone if they were to be at the table with Josh. He was more important than the food. And I couldn't understand people who'd say a baby doesn't belong there. Joshua never ONCE created a scene or made people uncomfortable. He was always a joy to be with anywhere we went. He sits in his highchair and let us talk until it was his turn to be heard. And we listened with love. Neal was learning.

When we finally went to court to see who would win custody of Josh, the judge was influenced by my love for my son. Even though most men settled for weekend visits, I made it clear to the court I would never accept someone else controlling how much time I was able to spend with my son. "This is not about time, this is about raising a child," I said that in open court, and the judge was impressed. Mindy me for loving her baby like a real man should. He granted us joint custody just like Neal predicted he would.

Because Mindy had entered college to start her career (and I respected her for it), I was taking care of Josh nearly full time. Egg Entertainment gave me the financial ability to be with Josh 24/7 and sometimes for two to three weeks straight. Some of my musician friends and men I met from the Advocate ad were astonished.

"You are an amazing father," "You're not with the mother but you're taking care of your son?" "Wow, this is unheard of," "Most men value the pussy over their kid." – These were statements I'd hear all the time. For the first time in my life, I was actually offended. I'm amazing because I take care of my son? That's something I'm supposed to do. It's my responsibility. To me, though, it wasn't a responsibility, it was a joy to be with my son. I didn't feel that my life was over by having a baby. My baby isn't a hardship. My baby isn't a burden. My baby is a human being; dependent upon me to love him unconditionally. I loved him too much to see him any other way. It was as simple as that.

I started having feelings for Neal that I never felt before. Was I falling in love with a man? We were both atheists. To be in love with any gender, that had to be a pre-requisite. We both agreed that believing some cosmic being controls us all from some magical place called heaven is either a sign of mental illness or sheer stupidity. When around people who believed in "God" we both realized it was like being around fish swimming back and forth in an aquarium. There's no reasoning with them. They have a closed system imaginary world of thought. We were out of place. Let's face it. We aren't the sharpest species. We kill each other over arguments about what happens when we die and fail to see the irony in that. We had different but similar reasons for our atheism.

He came to the conclusion there was no god simply because he was a natural born scientist. I came to that conclusion after pulling my cock out of Christian male asses and then watching them get on their knees to pray their gay away. And the only time a religious woman would talk about god was I had her feet in the air and my cock in her vagina. After talking dirty and watching porn with me, never once mentioning Jesus or whoever their "God" was, they were yelling out his/her name ONLY while being fucked. I guess it gave me a god complex. But these hypocrites, along with my own critical thinking skills convinced me there wasn't any god no matter how you made him up. And people always used bible verses to justify their hate. You can safely assume you've created god in your own image when god hates all the same people you do. Being raped by a few priests helped my decision process too. And a demon can't take my soul. We'd have too much in common.

I told him I was a musician and songwriter. I had my piano in Ritch's living room. I looked at him and said I wanted him to hear me play a new song I had just started writing. He cheerfully agreed but his body language and eyes couldn't hide his skepticism. He had grown up in Las Vegas and was the son of a musician and songwriter who had his own orchestra. He thought he knew great music. I expected this from him though. And his eyes betrayed his kindness. I didn't care. I started playing.

Almost immediately, from the moment I touched the keys, his mood shifted. I knew he knew he was wrong. He sat down and watched as my fingers bled my soul onto the keys, and he was impressed. He became entranced and I received from him what was most important to me: He understood I was good. Not only good but fucking phenomenal at my craft. He won my heart right then and there.

So, I thought about it. Neal had listened to me for six months with genuine concern for my feelings. He gave me cogent, compassionate advice without judging my "enemies." He had given me a job that paid me more than $4,000 a month, he was genuinely kind and honest. And now he understood he was with an equal. I was talented and he recognized it. All he could say when I was finished with my song was, "Wow. That was incredible. You play with feeling and that's something you can't teach." Neal was now my superhero. I had never had a real superhero in my life before. I guess not all superheroes wear capes.

One night it just happened. I was at Neal's home in West Hollywood and it felt right. We were on his couch, each sipping from our glasses of red wine when I moved closer to him and gave him a sensuous kiss on his lips. Neal was hesitant, I think, because he worried about me engaging in an emotional sex act I wasn't prepared for. But he returned my kiss. We caressed each other through our clothing. As we wrapped our arms around each other in a loving embrace, we both realized this was more of an emotional experience than a sexual one. Throughout my life, intimacy was the quick removal of clothing. The only person I felt I had made love to instead of just having sex was Mindy. I felt we were making love. Could this be the beginning of making love to a man for me?

Both of us chuckled as we moved from the couch to the shower. Neal and I were both clean freaks. We both valued good hygiene ahead of everything. And I mean everything. We bonded over that. We got naked and turned on the shower water. We were still embracing each other when I noticed his hardened cock. I was surprised at its beauty. The length and girth of his penis was above average, nearly as long as mine. He could have done nude modeling with his dick. While we were soaping our bodies, Neal was very sensual. Although he was sensual, he was also nervous. But as I arched my head, he abruptly stopped. I could tell he was nervous. We both felt awkward.

It wasn't long before our touching made us feel even more nervous. Even though the sex between us was awkward at that moment, the love was real. I was still doubtful that I was gay, I knew I was bisexual, but sex was sex. I didn't know what love was. Emotion hurt. It didn't matter which gender was by my side. I loved Neal but he sensed that I was emotionally detached. Maybe he knew what real love was. To me, I was feeling it for him.

But I was finding out what real love was in another way that for me, was a more life altering and life lesson than any adult could ever teach me. It was the love I was feeling for my son, Joshua.

46

Raising Josh Changes My Life

I had heard the term unconditional love many times in my life. Because I was bulldozing my way through life; one day writing the song of the century, the next day selling my body to the highest bidder, I was unconscious to the meaning of "unconditional love." That is, until I became a full-time father.

Where I come from, babies and toddlers are menaces. I had heard about the "terrible twos" so much, I imagined these parents must be either ignorant or terrible themselves. If you characterize your child as "terrible," there's something wrong with you. It's not the child. It's how we see the child. Those were the words my heart would send to my brain so I could mouth them to everyone. But before I actually had Joshua full time 24/7 for the majority of his first five years, the voice would rear its head and tell me I didn't know shit.

You're the son of a pervert and a child molester. And your father had no patience with babies.

But, through my own achievements, and getting in touch with me, that voice didn't exist anymore.

I was ready and I had legal joint custody. In addition, Mindy and her parents saw how much Josh meant to me, and once the court decision came down, they knew Josh was in good hands with me. Mindy made a good decision to go to college and get her degree, and I'll never forget the day Mindy's father met me at the door of their home when I picked Josh up and apologized to me. It was after eleven months that he told me this, just before Josh's first birthday. He said he misjudged me, and he could see I was a great father to his grandson. We hugged and I cried a bit, because I always loved him, and I wanted his approval. Still, Josh came first. I thanked him and off Josh and I went in my 1969 Volkswagen bus on the long freeway to freeway journey from Alhambra to Venice for the next two weeks.

In this period, the first five years of Josh's life, I discovered things about myself and my childhood. I needed to develop a loving relationship with Josh for him to trust the world.

Intimacy, to most of us means figuring out how to understand and get closer to your life partner. And we already know what it meant to me: nothing – before Josh. Now, I had that aha moment when I learned the true meaning of intimacy. It's "Into me I see." I needed to examine me first, before I could be an effective father. But, at the same time, I needed to do it while I'm with him because prior to Josh's entry into the world, I hardly made serious effort into changing myself into a better person. I bought books, and thought I was progressing, but I was an expert at deluding myself. While watching friends die of AIDS, although I participated in some of the very same acts they did, I mentally distanced myself from them. I was smarter, I had goals and talent. I was better. My life's journey was more important than theirs. I was a narcissist.

Loving Josh changed all of that. I realized my boy's needs came before mine. I became unselfish because he deserved that. Maybe the universe had finally given me my life's purpose, and although music and sex and "all about me" were still important, they took a backseat to Josh. Maybe I wasn't a narcissist. I had to step up. I couldn't be as sick as my secrets. I had a baby who was completely dependent on everything I said, everything I did, and every choice I made. As I said before, he was NEVER a burden. And I had him 24 hours a day. My Venice apartment became a sea of diapers that I was changing 24 hours a day.

The musicians who lived in the building — some very well-known ones in bands like Jane's Addiction and Suicidal Tendencies — couldn't believe that the person they knew was changing from hanging out, playing clubs and fucking every girl within ten feet, into a real full-time father. Josh was my boy, and he was my new life project.

Girls who wanted to fuck me all the time had to take a raincheck. One gorgeous girl who lived down the hall from me knocked at my door all the time just to get in and have sex with me. She didn't understand that I was on a different path now. I knew she smoked, and I couldn't imagine letting someone light up a cigarette around Josh, let alone have sex with anyone while he's in my care.

I had to change his bottles four or five times a day. I loved seeing his backwash in the bottle when he fell asleep with it in his mouth. How the fuck can anyone complain about it? They're babies! That's what they do! I loved helping him learn how important he was. I was making nearly $10,000 a month and I could have bought a house on the ocean and filled it with $50,000 worth of Japanese antique furniture with a Picasso or two, and I chose to buy the shittiest, particle board furniture from thrift stores.

I wanted him to know he was more valuable than furniture.

When Josh turned two years old, I finally broke down and called my mother. We hadn't spoken since April 1st, 1986 when she held my twenty-first birthday party at her house. But according to Jamie's reports, my mother didn't care. She was happy with her booze and without me. But I knew deep inside her, she really wanted to see me again. But she never contacted me. I took the first leap, calling her because I wanted her to get to know her grandson.

Josh was turning two and it was a perfect time have a birthday party date for him. My mom wanted to have Josh's party at her new house in Bellflower. Mindy, Mike Ray, Neal and Ritch came. This was a new Doug with his boy. This time it was a civil party, and everyone had a good time.

All he had when he was with me was carrot juice, milk and meals that I made for him – and healthy restaurant food. But When Josh was three, we passed a McDonald's restaurant and I thought – I'll let him have his first burger and fries.

I remember when he tasted McDonald's French fries for the first time and his eyes lit up and he excitedly told me: "These tastes good!" And I told him: "Yes, but they're not good for you." Josh answered back, "Then why are you letting me eat them?" He knew who was responsible for his health and wellbeing. And he let me know. I felt like I let him down.

I was making between $6K an $10k a month, depending on the amount of calls we received, and allowing me to buy anything I wanted. I could have bought antique Japanese furniture and filled my Venice condo with expensive breakable items if I valued them more than Josh. I chose to buy the cheapest, shittiest furniture so he could explore his surroundings without having to be shamed for "damaging" my expensive toys. He was more important than the furniture.

I'll never forget when Josh was running through my mother's house with a bottle of grape juice in his hand and the top flew off just as he fell into my lap. I was wearing my favorite white pants, and they were now stained forever with grape juice. I immediately picked Josh up from the floor to see if he was ok. I then picked up his bottle and tightened the cap back on. There was grape juice all over my pants and a stain on my mother's carpet. I wished Robert would have been there to bitch about my boy because I was now older, stronger, and I'd have taken him out back, beat his ass, left him armless and in need of paramedics, had he called Josh one pejorative name.

I looked at my mother and asked her what my father would have done to me had I had spilled the juice on him. Without hesitation she replied, "You would have been flying across the room."

47

Paradigm Shift

At that moment, I understood. My parents were the bad people. I kept this question inside me at the time, but I wanted to grab my mother around her neck and scream, "How could you let him do that to me?" I didn't ask her because I didn't want to startle Josh, but I hated her with a passion after hearing more about how my father would have hit me if I had done things Josh was doing.

Who the hell beats their kid so badly that they fly across the room just because they spilled grape juice on them? My father does. Not me. It was MY responsibility to tell him not to run in the house, it was MY responsibility to make sure the cap on the bottle was secure. He's fucking two years old! It's his job to explore his world. He was doing his job; I should have done mine. And what kind of mother allows her two-year-old to be beaten and thrown across the room for being a baby?

I'm not saying I was perfect, what I'm conveying is that I learned through having him on my own, is that there is NEVER a reason to hit a child. There's no such thing as the "terrible twos." If you see your child as terrible for being two years old, what does that say about you? I couldn't imagine making Josh think he's bad and teaching him that I have to use physical force to get him to do what I want. That would turn wonderful experiences into permanent scars. It's not hard. It's only hard if you "have to." It's easy if you want to.

When I put Josh to sleep that night, I was overwhelmed with sadness. It was slowly sinking in that I'd been tortured, and no one cared. I still had a hard time crying. I felt angry, frustrated, sad and helpless at the same time. I was an open wound, with a severed artery, but I had to stop the bleeding. I had to care about that little boy: Me.

I began to cry, but I stopped. I wondered why, and then it hit me — every time my father hit me, and I cried, he hit me again, commanding, "Boys don't cry." The tears were hard to come by. I hated him so much at that moment in my Venice apartment with Josh. All the frustration was welling up in me and I had to counteract the belief that was embedded in my brain: Boys don't cry. I knew I had to write a song about it, and the title came to me:

"Only a man will cry."

I worked on it the next day and the words came easy. I wrote the music to it later.

Only a Man Will Cry

Digging in my mind
Through the pain that I was sure I'd left behind
The truth it can be so unkind

There is no escape
The more I find the more I know I have to face
It's taking me back to that place

Locked inside that cage turned my innocence to rage
Bringing me to realize – Letting go
Is the only way to survive

'Cos fools would rather die
But Only a Man Will Cry
Let me tell you why
Only a Man will……….

Is this anger real?
Who am I if I deny all that I feel?
All I want is a method to heal

The truth is coming clear
Getting through to me means getting through to the tears
If there's nothing left there's nothing to fear

I begin to understand what it means to be a man
I have to reject these lies
And cut through to the pain inside

'Cos fools would rather die
But Only a Man Will Cry
Let me tell you why
Only a Man will……….

I've got to get down to the core if I don't wanna hurt inside anymore
I'm making a promise to my pain: I will defeat you
All the anger all the shame & all the wronging and the blame
Daddy I'm leaving you behind, I've got no room for you in my mind

Now that I believe – for myself I can grieve
I will no longer deny – anything that I feel inside
'Cos fools would rather die
But Only a Man Will Cry

***

I knew I needed to develop a long-term relationship with a psychologist or become one.

I felt I was seeing things in my relationship with my son that the world was missing.

I moved Josh and I into Neal's condominium on Crescent Heights on West Hollywood. He had his own room and Neal, and I could give him the attention he deserved. We bought a brio train set for him and he loved playing with those rail cars, naming each one after his favorite trains on his favorite show: Thomas the Train.

Taking care of Josh changed my life. Although I bought books on healing myself from the abuse I suffered at the hands of my parents, I knew my parents would never agree to any communication about what they had done.

I took my mother to lunch once and asked her how she could have left me in Boys Homes' and allow Jamie to be raped. Her answer spoke volumes to me: "I was afraid of being alone. And I wanted you out of the way because I didn't know how to handle you."

In her mind, that was as good as an apology. What she never understood was that by being honest with me at that lunch, she was revealing how selfish she was. She cared more about herself than her own children. Every time she had the chance to protect us and that we mattered, she chose her needs over us. And she couldn't help herself from driving a knife through her children's hearts one last time. She had become a born-again Christian and now declared that because Jamie was a lesbian and I had sex with men, WE were going to hell.

There would never be a confrontation with my father. He simply didn't care. I wasn't interested in having a relationship with him, and after I beat him up, he wasn't interested in having one with me. In fact, I never heard from him again until I was informed at the last second that he was dying. He was in the hospital to receive a pacemaker for his heart, but he had smoked so many cigarettes all his life that he died during surgery. Such an easy death for an evil man. My family was of no help to me.

Even then, my uncle Lyle broke into his house and stole everything he could get his hands on before I realized it was my responsibility to lock his house. Lyle, also went to the banks to clean out his accounts, but they denied him access because he wasn't the biological heir. I was. When I got to the bank, the branch manager informed me that someone claiming to be my uncle had already been there trying to get all of my father's money. The court made me the executor of his estate which consisted of his bank accounts, his townhome, and a self-storage locker. I dreamed of finding gold bars stashed away in that locker when I opened it up. Unfortunately, when I opened the locker, I found it was stuffed end to end with porn videotapes. Later, when I watched a few, I saw my father sucking big transexual cocks. There was some good porn too. Thank god they were on VHS.

Even at his funeral, I felt victimized. I was denied my dream of ripping his head off in front of everyone and tossing it around like a bowling ball. He didn't have any friends and only ten people showed up to his funeral, and six of us were family members — me, my mother, my sister, his brother, his brother's wife and their son Scott. Only four other people showed up and they looked frightened to be there. They were his co-workers. They shook my hand with sorrow and two of them felt sorry for me, saying to my face, "I'm so sorry you were his son. Kurt was a prick. I hope you're ok."

When the pastor saw everyone's reaction, he looked stunned and was at a loss for words. My mother had no filter as usual and broke the uncomfortable silence by yelling, "He's going to hell anyway, so just get it over with." If my father could have heard her, he wouldn't have cared. He didn't care about anything.

There were times when I admired him for not caring. I wanted to be like that. It's easier to survive in this world if I just don't care about anything, anyone, or my own actions, because that way, I never have to feel guilt, I never have to worry about consequences, and I'd never fear being alone. But I'm not like him. I care.

Sometimes I made reckless decisions without thinking about the consequences, and I believe those decisions were because of the struggle within me to love myself. And I've paid dearly for those decisions. The scars I cannot conceal. They remind me of the price I've paid for losing sight of what's real.

I'm no one to lecture anybody, but I disagree with society's obsession with forgiveness.

All I ever hear is "you need to forgive," and "to heal yourself, you've got to forgive those who've done you wrong" forgive, forgive, forgive. I'm gonna burst that bubble. I don't have to forgive anyone to feel better. Especially my parents. In fact, I used to feel worse when I'd try to forgive, and I couldn't. Now I "can't forgive enough." That's just making me feel more guilty.

I can very easily forgive people who have apologized to me, and I've asked for forgiveness many times from people I've wronged. It's easy to forgive when someone acknowledges what they've done. When they can see the pain, they have caused you and can look at that pain through your eyes. But my parents were incapable of that. I don't know why, and it's a waste of time to try to figure out why. But why should I forgive people who abused me and continue to hurt me by not giving a shit about what they did? In fact, they thought they were good people. I learned a lot by observing this weird trait they both had. You can confront them with their actions and they'd still believe they're "good people" because they can lie to themselves. I see this all the time. People hurt people and still, if they believe they're good people in their own heads, that's all that matters. I've done it myself.

I'm still learning not to judge myself or stay angry. I was very angry for a long time and it didn't serve me at all. A boy who is hateful becomes a man when he's grateful. I'm no guru, sage or angel. I'm a person who's still learning to walk on the road less traveled. Someone once said that knowledge and ignorance will lead us into the same smoldering pile of ash if we don't put humility first. I believe that's true. Like one of my favorite songs tells me: "If I claim to be a wise man, it surely means that I don't know." I'm still learning how to remain humble and grateful.

48

Final Thoughts

I don't know how to categorize my sexuality and I don't think I belong in a category anyway. It's important to recognize that being gay is not a choice. Most everyone I've known who was or is gay, was born that way. In my case, I was attracted to both sexes before I heard about labels. I had sexual feelings as a child, but that didn't give any adult the right to determine when I wanted to have sex for myself. Child sexual abuse is an abomination and destroys lives. Of course, it influenced my life and career choices as an adult; how could it not have? But that doesn't mean all my choices were influenced by my abusers; call me bisexual or trysexual, I don't care. My sexuality is mine to define, no one else has that right. If my son was gay, I'd immediately take him to a gay bar and celebrate with him.

In my opinion, the only reason homosexual, bisexual and transgender people are castigated, berated, shunned, ignored, told they're going to hell from childhood, murdered, tortured and executed still, is because of one reason: It simply looks odd to straight people. Nothing more. It's that simple. That's how stupid and infantile mankind is. Man has made up religion to justify hatred for homosexual and bisexual people just because we look odd to them. They create gods who supposedly say we're going to hell if we live as we were born or as we choose. Fuck them. They base their prejudice on their imaginary "gods" judgments or they just hate us because they're assholes. It's no more complicated than that. Having been a drug addict, I see the same need to control and complicate everyone's lives with religious people. They're addicted to judging people. They're addicted to controlling people. They're addicted to thinking they have rights they don't have.

People judging other people fascinates me. Let's pop the trunk open to everyone's life and see what we find?

I learned through a lot of self-inflicted pain that one of the sources of my pain was my tendency to judge people. AA taught me to meditate and pray every day to please help me change my tendency to prejudge and categorize people and replace it with reverence and a sense of discovery for our differences.

No one is better than anyone. Everyone counts or no one counts. I believe that when we die, the king and the pawn go back into the same box.

When have LGBTQ people ever advocated taking away religious person's rights?
Answer: Never.

When have Christians advocated taking away Gay people's rights?
Answer: Every day in every state there's a Christian proposing a new law attempting to remove a human right for a gay person.

How long have LGBTQ people attempted sane dialogue with religious people over marriage rights, housing rights, domestic partnership benefits, simply having the right to be gay, ending conversion therapy, etc, and have been met with absolutely nothing but hate?
Answer: Forever.

When has an LGBTQ person ever held a sign up in a straight neighborhood telling them they're going to hell for being straight while Christians continually harass gay people in their own neighborhoods damning them to hell in front of their own houses?

Answer: Gay people: NEVER.
Answer Christians: Since the beginning of time and today.

When has any LGBTQ church advocated killing Christians for being Christian?
Answer: Never. When has a Christian church advocated killing LGBTQ people? All the time. Most Christian churches preach to their people that homosexuals deserve the death penalty. I've attended and played music in churches that advocated it to our faces. Which is why we no longer sit through the hate.

When have gay people fought against lifesaving medications for any Christian with any malady or disease?
Answer: Never.

When have Christians fought against AIDS research or for the "right: of emergency medical personnel to refuse to give emergency medical aid to LGBTQ people?
Answer: Every day in every state in this nation.

When have LGBTQ people in any of the 187 countries around the world ever executed men, women and children in the most gruesome ways just because they're Christian, Muslim, Jewish, Catholic, African Methodist, or any other religion they belong to?
Answer: Never.

How many LGBTQ men, women and children are executed daily in the most gruesome ways in other countries around the world, and how often?
Answer: Nearly every single country has executed gay men women and children either by government decree, religious decree, or by some fanatical nutcase.

You can safely assume you've created god in your own image when god hates all the same people you do. So, I'm gonna fuck whoever I want, whenever I want, (with their consent), and so should you.

This chapter of my life ends here when I'm 30 years old. Josh is five now, and I've learned more about life through him being completely dependent on me than in any other situation I've been in.

Although there's another chapter to my life coming, I want to share what I learned from being a father during these early years.

I learned that I was more than words. I had to be an example of good behavior for him to learn what good behavior is.

- I had to be a model, not a critic.
- I had to be a light, not a judge.
- I had to be part of the solution, not part of the problem.

It began with listening to him. Listening to his words, but also listening to his behavior and body language. By doing this, I let him know he was loved. I sought first to understand him, and then he would listen and understand what I had to teach him.

I learned that he wouldn't care what I know unless he knew that I cared.

During this next phase of my life, I wrote more songs, played with more industry stars, and managed singers. I got further into the music industry than I thought I would.

Over the next 25 years I made a lot of mistakes... But I learned from those mistakes. I'm a slow learner, but I learned to look at the weaknesses of others with compassion, not name calling and blaming. I still struggle with anger, but life is a one day at a time journey.

If I'm kind, it's hard to be an asshole at the same time.

Blessings.

236

Made in the USA
Columbia, SC
19 June 2021